W9-BCF-411

Sierra Leone

Sierra Leone:
A CONCISE HISTORY

A. P. KUP

DAVID & CHARLES
NEWTON ABBOT   LONDON   VANCOUVER

0 7153 6805 2

Set in 11 on 13pt Monotype Baskerville and printed in Great Britain by Latimer Trend & Company Ltd Plymouth for David & Charles (Holdings) Limited South Devon House Newton Abbot Devon

Published in Canada by Douglas David & Charles Limited 132 Philip Avenue North Vancouver BC

Contents

	List of Illustrations	7
	Acknowledgements	9
	Introduction	11
1	First Inhabitants: The General Pattern	16
2	The Northern Influence: Fula, Susu, Bunduka and Sofa	41
3	The South: The Mende and the Afro-Europeans	80
4	Creole Origins	114
5	Colonial Expansion	161
6	Modern Political and Constitutional Change	191
	Notes and References	224
	Select Bibliography	267
	Index	270

List of Illustrations

PLATES

Steatite *nomoli*	33
Koranko bowman	34
Rice empoldering in the northern rivers area, 1794	34
Coastal peoples at the end of the eighteenth century	51
Sulima and Koranko musicians	51
Fula slave coffle in the 1790s	52
Maroon ambush on the Dromilly estate, Jamaica, 1795	52
Governor Rowe's map showing chiefdoms round British Sherbro, 1876	69
Chief Kai Lundu, Luawa chiefdom	70
Chiefs Momo Kai-Kai and Momo Jah	70
Diamond digging operations	87
Boats bringing country produce to King Jimmy Market, Freetown	87
Weighing palm kernels at the new oil mills, Wellington	88
Weaver in Kono country using portable Mandingo loom	88

MAPS

1	West African population, rainfall and rivers	17
2	Coastal peoples in the mid-sixteenth century	38
3	Trade routes via Bumban and the north	43
4	Temne and adjacent chiefdoms in the nineteenth century	62
5	Samory's empire with reference to the border of Sierra Leone and trade routes to Falaba	72
6	The area of Ndawa's raids	105

7   Chiefdoms in the south-east in the 1870s   111
8   Sierra Leone in 1900, showing the five administrative
        districts   182
9   Trade patterns   189
10 Sierra Leone constituencies, 1962   213

Acknowledgements

Thanks are due to the following libraries for permission to use manuscript material in their possession: Bodleian; British Museum; Huntington; Public Record Office; John Rylands University of Manchester. The Rt Hon Earl of Crawford and Balcarres, KT, GBE, DLitt, kindly gave his consent for the family muniments in the John Rylands University Library of Manchester to be used.

For permission to use, or adapt, maps and illustrations I am grateful to the following: Longmans for Map 1 from F. J. Pedler, *Economic Geography of West Africa* (1955); the Clarendon Press for Map 2 from W. Rodney, *A History of the Upper Guinea Coast 1545–1800* (1970); the Public Record Office for Maps 3–7; the University of London Press for Map 9 from A. M. Howard, 'Trade Patterns' in *Sierra Leone in Maps*, ed J. Clarke (1966); the University of Toronto Press for Map 10 from J. Cartwright, *Politics in Sierra Leone 1947–67* (1970). Map 8 is by the courtesy of the British Museum from J. J. Crooks, *A History of the Colony of Sierra Leone* (1903).

Note: the Colonial Office maps have been redrawn by the Graphics Department of the Library, Simon Fraser University, to whom thanks are due. They are considerably reduced in size and therefore certain locations had to be omitted. Map 3 is from CO 879/4, No 318, p 75; Map 4 from 879/318a, p 82; Map 5 from 879/24, No 318, p 4; Map 6 from 879/24, No 322, p 35; Map 7 from 267/335, Desp 182, 9 Nov 1878.

I have to thank the following for permission to reproduce plates on the pages indicated: Dr John Atherton, Portland State University, Oregon, p 33; Methuen & Co, p 34, from J. K.

Trotter, *The Niger Sources* (1898); the National Maritime Museum (MS 53/035), pp 34 and 52; the British Museum, p 51, from A. Laing, *Travels in Timmanee, Kooranko and Soolima Countries* (1825), and p 51, from J. Matthews, *A Voyage to the River Sierra Leone* (1785); the Institute of Jamaica, p 52; the Public Record Office (CO 267/329, bound before Desp No 60), p 69; Macmillan & Co, p 70, from T. J. Alldridge, *The Sherbro and its Hinterland* (1901); T. J. Alldridge, p 70, from *A Transformed Colony* (1910); *West Africa Magazine*, pp 87 and 88, Sierra Leone High Commission, London, p 88.

Finally, the research for, and the writing of, this book was facilitated by the generosity of the author's university, Simon Fraser University, British Columbia, which provided several vital sums through the President's Research Grant, and awarded sabbatical leave. Above all, a Leave Fellowship from the Canada Council enabled the work to be completed expeditiously.

Introduction

Unusual difficulties still confront the historian in Africa. Indigenous sources are scarce; written ones, produced by occupying powers, suspect: the work of men concerned with law and order rather than with social and historical change.

Few district commissioners spoke any African language well. Those like Thomas J. Alldridge who used the Royal Geographical Society's system of orthography were rare. Proper names acquired several variants, wide enough at times to be unrecognisable. In Sierra Leone standard usage today, for good historical reasons, favours the Mende form of place-names in the south, though before that hegemony was stabilised in the nineteenth century, Bullom names were current. The river Bagru has thus become the Gbangbar, the Jong the Taia, the Bum the Sewa, and the Kittam the Waanjie.

Today, clan names are found everywhere. Every adult and child amongst the northern peoples (Temne, Susu, Yalunka, Koranko, Limba, Mandinka) has, and uses, one of them. Every Fula uses one of the four 'family' names, Bah, Diallo, So, Bari—though Diallos sometimes call themselves alternatively Fula. Where there is northern ancestry these clan names exist in the south, so that there are, for instance, Mende Kamaras. However, there are other names in the south which the bearers habitually use—for example the Gallinhas princely family of Massaquoi (originally one of the family divisions of the Vai). Finally, there are those Caulkers, Rogers, Tuckers, Domingos, and others, descendants of Europeans reaching back into the seventeenth, even the sixteenth century.

On the other hand the typical southerner has no main name,

differentiating himself when away from home by the name of his village, eg Bokhari Bo, Morlai Moyamba. With given and first names it is usual for the mother to show the child to the father on the seventh day after birth, when the father gives the child a name. If from a Muslim family, it is usually a Mohammedan name and the child bears this throughout its life. Among southerners, and northerners too whose village includes a society such as the Poro (Mende) for men, or Bundu (Bullom) or Sande (Mende) for women, a child will be given a new name when he or she enters the bush at puberty for training. This, and the original given name, will be used indifferently henceforth.

Place-names in Africa (as in Scotland, Wales, or Ireland, where similar confusion arose) are frequently descriptive, not readily understood by foreign administrators. The language of their founders may no longer be spoken there. In Mende country, one finds Bandajuma, a Kono or Vai name, and towns bearing it show the route taken in migrations to the coast. Bumpe, so common in Mende country, is a Gbanta Temne name. Sumbuya is Susu and means 'where different people dwell'. In fact it was a main port for inland traders, the Susu its principal inhabitants, though never its conquerers.

Nine times out of ten neither administrators, traders, nor foreign cartographers were aware of these implications, and used indiscriminately any name offered. It is polite (and informative) to refer to a stranger by the first name as well as the family name, and to accord to rulers their titles. Not to do so is to impugn their ancestry and imply disrespect for their status. It is much regretted that it has often been impossible to do so here for lack of information.

With any proper name over two or three generations old one must do the best with what there is; it is too late to ask now. One must decide upon a spelling which will be recognisable both in the written record and in common speech. The literature with which a district commissioner was perhaps best acquainted was the Bible. It was readily available in the bush, and this no doubt accounts for the Old Testament minor prophet appearance of so many figures from Sierra Leone's past in official records. For example, district commissioners favoured the spelling Jaiah, which must have seemed almost familiar to them, rather than Jahrah, a rendering by one of the Caulkers, highly literate, as well as indigenous, and likely to be more correct.

African history has been written largely by townsmen from a different culture and race which decided several hundred years ago to regard the country-dweller as simple. In fact rural people everywhere are more observant, in a familiar setting, than their *soi-disant* superiors, and live an efficient and productive life. Most people in the developed world today are unwilling to accept this and do not see that all of us depend for our lives on the world's farmers dwelling mainly in the poorer places. Exploitation is not necessarily economic. The chauvinism which permits America, with 6 per cent of the earth's population, to consume 33 per cent of its energy, a hundred years ago viewed Christianity as the only religion for a gentleman, and today accepts sonic booms over the Victoria Falls but not over Virginia Water.

Few Europeans understood African wars and politics, even when witnessed at first hand. Ethnocentrically they saw them as competition for the white man's status and commerce. In reality, though control of the paths did enable one to deny an enemy ammunition whilst providing the salt, rum and tobacco demanded by one's own mercenaries, chiefs and their warriors were concerned only incidentally with Europeans or their commerce.

The seven major reasons Governor Samuel Rowe offered the secretary of state for unrest in the south-east in 1878 were entirely African:

1 The Bullom trader, Tom Kebbi Smith of Kambia (Small Bum), had died after trying unsuccessfully for years to acquire sovereignty of the country between the rivers Jong and Small Bum. Slave-born, however, the chiefs would never elect him, despite his great wealth. None the less, a general struggle was expected over the distribution of his slaves and property.

2 In the Kittam there was ill-feeling, it is true, between

white and Creole traders, but the real concern was the
likelihood of marauding warriors spilling over from the
Bum. There was in addition a war on the south-east
borders of the country which might spread.

3 A local war behind Sulimah could be expected to descend
into Kittam. At the end of the year the chief of Bandajuma
took 14 towns in 3 months from Shaffah Tom, a nephew of
Jahrah of Gallinhas.

4 The great Mende warrior, Chief Gbanyah, at Senehun,
died on 30 July, and the chiefs were to hold a meeting to
elect a successor, and during the palaver a power struggle
was anticipated.

5 Chief Sisay Hannimoh, Bullom chief of Gbendemah, died
on 18 July, and the country fell into lawlessness in the
interregnum.

6 The Tikonko and Bumpe Mende, whom Rowe had
persuaded to meet him, had not held a palaver for a quarter
of a century, except as enemies. There was every chance of
friction.

7 The rival factions of the Caulker family at Bumpe and
Shenge were feuding again, and were likely to call in
Mende mercenaries.[1] Rowe also reported the embarrassing
fact that Chief Cannah Gboh, escaping from prison in
Freetown, had gone home and was raising warriors against
those who had betrayed him. He had perhaps more influence than usual, because King Jay of Bumpe died in
June, leaving the country leaderless. Thus what was known
as the second Cannah Gboh war in Sherbro had begun.
He had taken war down as far as the Bum river and was
threatening British Sherbro.

In addition there was the war between Masimera and Yonni
which, starting in 1874, was not over until 1879, spreading into
Koya, Marampa and Port Loko. Further north, fighting seemed
likely between the 'old' faction, led by Alimami Bokhari, in
Moriah, and the 'new' one, under Alikali Quia Dowdah, over
alleged harsh rule, taxation and excessive capital punishment.
At Gbinti, French merchants were confronting the king of
Samu.

One cannot chronicle every petty war and cabal, but it is shortsighted to write, as one British author did in a standard work: '1878 was a quiet year in Sierra Leone'.[2] Independence, beginning in the 1950s, at last convinced white scholars of what the African intelligentsia had long advocated: the need to stop seeing African history as the expansion of Europe. Moreover, the *Pax Britannica* imposed upon warring petty tyrants in Sierra Leone at the end of the nineteenth century conferred undoubted benefits. To underrate these is to denigrate the brief but not ineffective era of colonial rule. War fences with piles of human skulls at the gate were quickly abolished, Britain being fortunate that her imperial designs occurred when rulers, surfeited with war-chiefs, were glad to play them off against the white man.

There is a tendency today to belittle imperialism, and indeed much of it is unpalatable. However, whatever else may have happened in British territories, at least at the end of the year the books balanced. That is a tradition which has been upheld, after Africanisation, almost everywhere in the civil service.

It would be unimaginative to pass over the courage and sacrifice of many good men working for what their generation saw as right. The adventurous lived under constant strain, as did the more pedestrian administrator. Even as late as the inter-war years, Paul Shuffrey, a liberal-minded and sympathetic district officer, in the 1920s spoke of feeling bereft of the civilisation which meant so much to him; no clubs, no religion, no stimulus save what he could conjure up from within. He felt this drove most people to drink or, rarely, to bury themselves in their work. Others spoke of steeling themselves to expect nothing, and so not being disappointed. George Garrett, trekking intrepidly round the north, visiting Samory's Muslim empire, sleeping fearlessly amidst the warring Sofa, and surrounded by smallpox, speaks when recovering from a dose of malaria of receiving a bounty of four letters from home: 'the excitement rather threw me back, but I was very much pleased'.

CHAPTER 1

First Inhabitants: The General Pattern

Physical Features
West Africa, running from Dakar to Lake Chad, today contains
over 25 per cent of Africa's population, despite the fact that considerable parts of Mauritania, Mali and Niger are desert. Much
of the area is made up of plains and low plateaux under 1,500ft.
On the coast is a zone of sandbars and behind often lie mangrove swamps and lagoons. Inland the coastal plain, rising
gradually to a more or less well-defined escarpment, though the
mountainous peninsula of modern Sierra Leone is one of the
exceptionally high spots on the coast, is otherwise generally low-
lying. The high forest of this area, which looks so fertile, lives in
fact partly on its own decomposed leaves and stumps; with
notable exceptions like the Niger delta, or the rich mangrove
swamps where the soil trapped by the roots lies mostly below
high-tide level, West African soil is both shallow and poor.

Further inland is the West African plateau and beyond that a
huge alluvial low-lying basin, around the Senegal and Upper
Niger rivers. There is reason to believe these two once flowed into
a vast inland sea, before they were captured by the headwaters
of the rivers which flow into the Atlantic; indeed the main rivers
of northern Nigeria, the Challawa and the Hedejia, still flow
inland—into Lake Chad. The first 200 miles of the Black Volta
were captured only recently by the Volta from a tributary of the
Upper Niger, a river which rises in modern Sierra Leone.

The Stone Age Man
The rivers of West Africa, fed by the heavy rains, today dig
deeper and deeper, thus capturing new streams as tributaries,

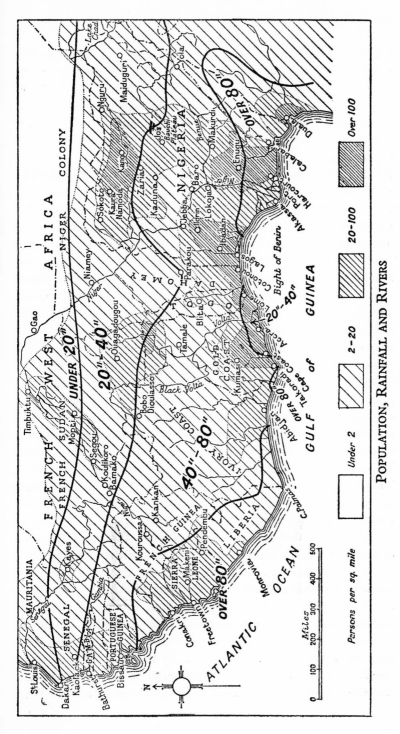

POPULATION, RAINFALL AND RIVERS

Map I

taking the water away from rivers bordering the desert which, silted up with sand, become smaller still. In general, man's penetration into the West African forest, and the clearing of large areas is not older than the Neolithic, and where Paleolithic tools have been found it has been assumed the forest was not there at the time of occupation. The forest would not burn and man could not clear it until he had developed efficient tools to cut timber. In any case, thick forest makes movement difficult, except along rivers or game paths, whilst food and game were often found only high in the tree-tops where primitive man could not go. North of the forest, in the wooded savannah or orchard bush, man found a suitable habitat, however, his food provided by valuable fruit-trees like the shea-butter tree and by tubers such as wild yams. There was plenty of game, though the danger of getting lost in the tall, trackless grass, kept man close to the rivers.[1]

West of the Ivory Coast the existence of pre-Chellean man is very dubious. There was a long interval between the very late pre-Chellean and the late Chellean during which we have no evidence, and probably West Africa was uninhabited. This period covered the Kamasian I pluvial when, under wetter conditions, the forest may have extended far to the north. The late-Chellean people pushed into what is today modern Ghana at the end of this period. They occupied the west flank of the Togoland mountains and then pushed along the Volta river. Then, as today, those mountains were probably forested and the plains open. We do not know whence they came. Later, they spread along the coast to the river Pra.

Next came the Kamasian II pluvial, the forest became denser again and man probably left the forest zone once more. Then came Sangoan man, to be partly driven out by the Gamblian pluvial. But Paleolithic man with his Sangoan culture was really a savannah person and though he seems to have lived a little further south than in Acheulian times, he could not successfully penetrate the forest. However, he now had fire, and thus canoes were feasible. By the time the Gamblian pluvial subsided and man could re-enter the forest, it was the Lupemban culture he brought, and a little later what has been called Guinea Aterian, a Middle Stone Age culture,[2] definitely associated with *Homo sapiens*. From now on, the pace of culture change quickened.

By Neolithic times man, hitherto dependent on hunting and gathering, had learnt to master his environment and his food supply, and there was a population explosion. Agriculture, of course, implies settled habitation, and man gathered the fruits of the oil-palm, kola, baobab and sesame. It is possible that he began to domesticate the guinea-fowl on the edge of the Sahara. A short-horned species of cattle, of unknown origin, was also kept. Agricultural techniques and domestic animals reached Egypt from Asia about 5000 BC. These ideas spread west fairly quickly and carbon 14 dates for the central Sahara give us the fourth millennium BC. Millet and sorghum were the staple crops and in the westerly regions the cultivation of rice (*oryza glaberrima*) diffused especially from the swamps of the Middle Niger and the Gambia rivers. All these grains are of West African origin. The planting of tubers such as yams, a staple further south, which was easier than planting grain, since tubers will sprout unaided from a midden, may well go back further than that of grain, and in any case yams yield a considerably higher tonnage of food per acre than millet. The earliest negroid skeletons recognised today are those from Khartoum, some time later than 8000 BC. Negroid peoples, who had probably developed in the forest margin, where they were so well situated to develop the new skills, now spread into the Sahara oases, and later westwards, bringing Neolithic techniques and ways of living.

We can form a reasonable picture of the Sahara, but know little about its margins, save in a few discrete areas. Nothing is known about the history of Liberia at this time; little about Sierra Leone. It is suggested that a pre-Neolithic phase may be characteristic of West Africa in places where the climate did not permit the basic Neolithic techniques. A few thousand years ago these places were in the orchard bush and forest margins; today they are on the fringe of the desert. In this zone, cultivation is impossible or chancy and population could not agglomerate; scattered groups of man lived upon nomadic animals (either wild or domestic) and the economy was one of hunting and herding, with a dash of brigandage against the cultivators.[3] Many sites, excavated in Ghana, reveal microliths only; no pottery or hoes, for nomads have few possessions. But the desiccation of the Sahara beginning perhaps 10,000 years ago drove these people southwards where they merged with the Ultimate Middle Stone Age culture. They brought with them the stone hoe and presumably the culture of tubers, and also, probably, certain crude, waisted, axes, necessary to deal with heavy vegetation.

Negro peoples of a Neolithic technology lived in the rain forests from about the third millennium BC. Some sites are covered by secondary, even primary, forest and the ability to clear it suggests quite a large labour force.[4]

New types of stone tools and pottery, often associated with the cultivation of indigenous rice, appear quite suddenly in the semi savannah region about 3500 BC, and in the more wooded area about 2500 BC. In Sierra Leone they have been found in, or very near, the savannah woodlands of the highland zone in the north-east. Here, access was easier, the caves and rock shelters giving protection, as at Kamabai, Yagala, Kabala, Kakoya, Yengema and Bunumbu. Carbonised fragments of palm-kernels occur throughout one site, suggesting that the oil-palm has always been an important food, together with locust beans, bush yams, game, fish, honey and small fruits. The Yagala and Kamabai sites in the north are held to represent the woodland type of later Stone-Age culture known as Guinea Neolithic. Its greatest feature is the double-bladed polished celt, used as an adze. These celts are restricted to a fairly small area of adjacent West Africa (mainly Guinea and Guinea-Bissau), and are thought to have been used for carving the intricate and often beautiful wooden objects associated with ancestral figures and society paraphernalia.

Excavations at Yengema, on the western edge of the eastern savannah woodlands, have revealed the presence of an industry, perhaps towards the end of the second millennium BC, with ground stone axes and pottery (two techniques associated with the Neolithic) but no microliths. It has been suggested that people with a Lupemban tradition of working went south at the time of the Saharan desiccation (third millennium BC), adopting pottery techniques and the making of ground stone axes from the Neolithic people who had themselves moved south recently and come into contact with them. The Yagala rock shelter, on the other hand, is microlithic and has been held to derive from quartz assemblages such as that at Iwo Eleru in Nigeria. Some are composite, macro- and microlithic, such as Kamabai.[5] Perhaps not surprisingly, since it has been one of the cross-roads of Africa from early times, certain pottery finds resemble Lake Chad styles.

The Iron Age

These cultures seem to have remained fairly stable until the coming of iron. West Africa had no Bronze Age and almost no Copper Age. Iron appeared in Sierra Leone in the seventh or eighth century AD, being used alongside stone tools. About the seventeenth century, beginning on the coast, iron came gradually to supersede them. There are huge smelting sites in Koranko country in the north-east, for which we have no dates. The Koranko know nothing of their origins. Slag appears in northern sites at roughly the same age as iron. It seems as if iron and the techniques for its extraction and working reached Sierra Leone together. Possibly the skills were introduced by traders from the early states of the western Sudan who exported it to ancient Ghana and her successors.[6] There can be no doubt that iron-working, and its magical associations, provided favourable circumstances for the constant and successful spread of northerners into the forest. Even as late as the 1820s Major Gordon Laing found the Temne had no knowledge of smelting or metal-working.

Forest Cultures

About half the population of West Africa today lives in the rolling savannah—from 10° to 17° north of the equator. This concentration far from the coast was, however, no great handicap to the latter's occupation. The average easy elevation and the lack of scarps make communication over land easier than, say, in East Africa or even in the rest of the west coast of Africa. Disease, of course, was a hindrance, and in modern times at least a chain of thinly populated areas has stretched from Sierra Leone across to the Bauchi plateau in Nigeria. This is the tsetse belt where sleeping sickness kept the population small and scattered; where the weakness of the people and their unsophisticated social organisation invited attack from the northern parts.

No one can say when these marauding conquerors first entered; given the limited means of access into any forest and the tendency to favour known roads, the invasions may have begun earlier, and penetrated further west sooner, than is often supposed. The early kingdoms of the western Sudan are known to have traded silk, cotton, and a little gold for oysters round the northern rivers (ie those rivers—Scarcies, Mellacourie—to the north of Sierra Leone), and Guinea forest pottery has been held to date probably from the early Iron Age. The steatite ancestor figures in Sierra Leone and Liberia, known as *nomoli* or *pomdo*, and the megaliths found from the Gambia to Liberia (neither of which are accounted for in the traditions of contemporary inhabitants) are both probably approximately contemporary with the introduction of iron. The Gambia megaliths have yielded a radio-carbon date of AD 750±150.[7] West African forest kingdoms are probably a very much earlier development than has hitherto been supposed.

The Sahara was a barrier. Only the north of West Africa had contacts with North Africa. With the advantages of a written language and of the camel (introduced by the Romans), ox, and donkey, it alone was insured a better way of life.

Neither linen nor wool was available (the West African sheep is hairy, not woolly) and leather was probably confined to North Africa. Cotton came in with the Arabs; before the coming of Islam, people wore little except on ceremonial occasions when bark cloth, beaten out with stone hammers[8] and scored at the base, was worn. Forest cultures were perhaps more uniform than has been imagined, and it is assumed that the characteristic globular-shaped pottery, with constricted neck and flaring rim, made in the north of Sierra Leone today, may continue a tradition begun in Neolithic times. The Bunumbu rock shelter, between Kabala and Bafodia, supplied sherds characteristic of the northern half of the country today, as well as other artifacts considered to be Neolithic and resembling those from Futa Jallon in Guinea.[9]

It has been said that the whole area between Senegal and the Ivory Coast at the beginning of recorded history 'must have been within the barbarian fringe, beyond the ken of the civilisation of the Middle Niger and beyond the goldfields. Groups of people lost in the Guinea forest must have made pottery, of which we have a few collections, probably smelted a little iron, and indulged in pagan rites of which occasional stone circles and monoliths preserve the memory.'[10] Even so, they were not without some attributes of state formation.

In all Black Africa, land was of prime importance. Priests of the earth gods or spirits of the dead often held their position as descendants of the first settlers. They alone could intercede with the ancestors to avoid calamity. Thus in some ways they were sovereign. Conquerors could not rule without them and where they introduced new gods they were careful to have the old cults celebrated. Today they often exist side by side[11] or, where the former is forgotten, such relics of the old cult which do survive are revered, like the pre-Mende *nomoli* found in south-east Sierra Leone. Over all the Sierra Leone countryside a man, if asked how land is held, will reply that it belongs to him who first brought it under cultivation or, if he is dead, to his descendants. Tribute was of two kinds: symbolic and actual. The former, implying overlordship, as well as acknowledgement of the legitimacy of the giver to subordinate office, was often the more important, though of nominal value only. Several different rights might be exercised simultaneously over the same piece of land; rights to plant crops might belong to one family, rights to pasture goats to another; fruit trees might belong to an individual, but the right to hunt would belong to a wide tribal group. Trade, too, would require some kind of central surveillance.

Population Layers

It has been stated that the western Sudanic states, menaced by nomadic Berbers and Arabs, began to exert pressure which led to population drifts to the coast as early as the third century AD.[12] This continues today and there are, as it were, a series of population layers. Spreading outward from the coast are found first the remnants of the indigenous peoples. In Sierra Leone these are the Bullom, closely associated with the Kissi and the Krim, the languages of all three being related. Place-names indicate that many parts, now occupied by Mende, Kono and Vai, were once Kissi. Along the present Liberian frontier lie the Gola, also of ancient stock, speaking, like the others, one of the southern Mel languages, operating a system of 'noun-classes' similar to that of the Bantu of central and southern Africa. The Limba, too, have a system of 'noun-classes' and are often grouped with the other Mel language speakers in the 'West Atlantic' family. However, though they are indeed of ancient stock, no close relationship has yet been demonstrated between Limba and any other African language.[13] The Bullom have long dominated the coastline virtually from Cape Verga to Cape Mount.

Somewhat later came the Baga and the Temne, close relatives, speaking a northern Mel language, settling a little inland. These Temne, along with the Nalu, Landuma and Cocoli, further north, seem to represent a second, later, layer, and have been called the 'Pre-Mandingas'.[14] The Temne, Kissi, Limba, Baga and Landuma, were thus all early inhabitants of Futa Jallon. Finally displaced about the twelfth century by the Mande-speaking Susu, they tended to move west and south to occupy more fertile land towards the coast. The Susu, taking their place, in turn began a move coastwards as they multiplied. Being defeated in 1233 by Sundiata, of Mali, the fleeing Susu caused other migrations, including those of the Baga who settled in the northern river basins, and of the Temne.

The Sapi (see p 32 below) and the Landuma remained in the hinterland immediately behind the Nalu and the Baga, but the Temne eventually pushed down to the mouth of the river

Sierra Leone, cutting the Bullom in two by the sixteenth century, and becoming one of the most powerful tribes of the Sierra Leone coast. It has been suggested that the Temne and Baga-Landuma were the same people until the Susu drove between them. The Baga-Landuma, now occupying Guinea, are being gradually absorbed by the Susu; the Temne, their counterparts in Sierra Leone, have kept their identity and have themselves absorbed numbers of the coastal Bullom, as well as Loko, Koranko, Fula and even Susu further inland. Several words of Sapi vocabulary collected by Europeans about 1500 are the same as Temne.

Patterns of settlement since then have tended towards greater density as one goes south. On the northern high plateau, settlement has been more uniform with fewer though larger villages than those in the south dominating areas up to thirty or forty square miles, though the average for Sierra Leone today is one village for about every four square miles. Settlement has been much denser in the forest where the high bush was both a defence and a restriction on wide movement or cultivation.[15] None the less, tribal differences and economic and environmental variations have not produced any wide range in choice of village sites, building styles, arrangement of houses, village forms or farming practices, perhaps because Sierra Leone history, though full of small local wars, has always been overlaid with larger, more uniform movements and influences which have penetrated large tracts of country at once.

The Mande Speakers

About the fourteenth century considerable changes occurred in the coastal pattern, and Professor Oliver Davies[16] thinks it likely 'that a whole chapter of West African civilisation remains to be unearthed'. The newcomers, in an arc almost stretching from the estuary of the Gambia to the coast of Cape Mount, brought in a more advanced culture. They were people whose speech belongs to the language family known as Mande—in particular Manding (some of whom were known to Europeans in the sixteenth and early seventeenth centuries as Mani), Susu, Yalunka (closely related to Susu),[17] Koranko, Kono, Vai and

Loko—and they formed a third layer of population, sometimes settling on territory geographically external to the other layers, but frequently, with superior political, technical, economic and military skills, imposing themselves in small groups upon the others. They built—or had their captives build—hilltop forts and forts with entrenchments. A traditional Temne account of the Mani, Bai Farma, says he 'encamped each night in a round trench'. At least one of these, which has not so far been excavated, exists in the south-east of Sierra Leone. Often, however, the newcomers spread peacefully, as traders or hunters. It seems this is how the Koranko entered the country. Famous for their skill with the bow and arrow, they were invited into Loko territory, presumably to live symbiotically. The Loko themselves were recent immigrants—some arriving perhaps as early as the thirteenth century—who had settled in Temne country. The Kono and Vai arrived later, perhaps in the half century before 1500.

In the course of time the Koranko's status improved and the crown in at least one chiefdom soon alternated between Loko and Koranko houses. Other Koranko, from the north-east, drove a wedge between the Limba and the Kissi, following perhaps the same route as the Loko. Koranko territory was larger then; when the Kpa Mende arrived in Taiama in the eighteenth century,[18] it was a Koranko chief in Yonni who became their landlord, though the 'owners' of the land were Gbanta (Temne). Even in 1886, when a famous Temne warrior, Sebankolo Gbandegowa, was preparing to attack the Mende, it was to a Koranko chief he went for 'medicine'. Several of the Kuniki and Bonkorlenken chiefdoms, in the extreme east of Temne country, have an authenticated tradition that their ruling families are of Koranko origin. The Kanu clan hold the crown in at least seven Temne chiefdoms. They are the same family as the royal line of Keita, rulers in ancient Mali. According to E. F. Sayers, a former district commissioner, the house of Massaquoi in the Gallinhas stems from the same line.[19]

Bands of Mande speakers thus entered either as warriors or as traders, the latter known as diyulas (see pp 29, 42 below). The diyulas soon penetrated the coastal lands further south, notably along the trade routes to the gold-producing areas of Begho in modern Ghana. They came in successive groups and even singly, dealing in slaves and kola, besides gold. They followed two main trade routes, shaped like a bow, from the Niger Bend down to the Volta and back again to the headwaters of the Niger, over the area which the tsetse fly had kept relatively underpopulated. One route covered the Niger Bend and led to the gold areas of Asante and, later, Elmina. The other, beginning at Timbuctoo and Mali, ran up the Niger to its source and then westwards to Sierra Leone, whence tributary routes ran east along the forest fringes until they joined the first near Begho. Their presence along the trade routes has been seen as a major factor in converting societies that were possibly 'stateless' ones into states; or, to put it another way, 'stateless' societies today are mostly found away from the great long-distance trade routes.[20]

The second route, as yet sparsely populated, partly because of the tsetse fly and partly because there was still ample room for the much smaller population then living in the West African forest, was quickly settled by Mande speakers (often quite peacefully), and may be traced by the occurrence along it of Mande dialects. Both Vai and Kono are found; they settled between the Limba and the Kissi. Traditionally, the Kono descend from one Fa Kono, who was buried at Sungundu, in Guinea, near his capital of Kono Su. Like many people in Sierra Leone, they tell of a kind of golden age, an age of peace, when families spread over uninhabited land, hunting, and herding a few cows, sheep and goats. New villages were formed, as so often in West Africa, by break-away groups, able to hive off because the small population aroused no land-hunger—a factor which was later one of the greatest causes of war, even of anarchy.[21] The Kono settled on the Melli river at Yawando, Yamba, Kongofie and Senge Senge. They spread slowly from there to Kayima and the river Sewa, as far south almost as Pendembu. The original leader, it seems, was Yara Kafi, and it is he who is specially remembered today.[22]

Traditions in Wenchi and Demisa today support the thesis that the Vai came from that direction and originally the Kono and Vai were one people. The Vai, however, in search of salt, a valuable trade commodity, went on to settle by the sea. It is said there are two divisions amongst the Vai, both descended from a common ancestor, Fandole, who had two sons: Passidi, from whom the Gallinhas or Massaquoi branch descend, and Kajoa, from whom the Kpaka or Rogers branch come.[23]

The Loko probably came in by the same route. The gold and kola trade, involving middlemen and the safeguarding of sources of supply, were complex ones. Though little gold came from Sierra Leone, the Scarcies basin was a well-known source of kola—the Portuguese said it produced the best on the coast. Competition for it was keen and today the Loko, and in many cases the Temne, say the land between the Scarcies and its tributary, the Mabole, now occupied by both Temne and Loko, was once solely Loko territory.[24]

Competition for land, the common enjoyment of it, the owning of allegiance to a common leader/priest, the need for commercial organisation and defence, engendered increasing political integration, and thus a rudimentary concept of sovereignty. It was therefore the black agriculturalists in West Africa themselves who created the states known in tradition and history today. There was no need to wait upon notions of Egyptian divine kingship, or for Caucasoid pastoralists like the Fula to enter as state-forming invaders.[25]

The central feature of these Mande-speakers' rule was the creation of provinces under a *farim* or governor, under whom ruled the petty chiefs, very often the indigenous élite. Over all was the king who, in Mali, was known as mandemansa, a title which has spread amongst Sierra Leone rulers.[26]

The Mani

Sierra Leone's recorded history reveals a quite well-documented Mande invasion between 1540 and 1550. It was a major incursion led by those known as the Mani, who were said at the time to have encountered others with customs like theirs, relics of a similar invasion about a hundred years earlier. These may have been Loko because though one hears of war between the Mani and the Bullom and Temne, and of continual raids on the

Limba for slaves, there is no record of any major Mani–Loko hostilities, even though Bai Farma, a Mani war-chief, became king of the Loko. Weight is lent to this theory by the Loko being thought to descend from the Toma–Gbande branch of the Mani. The latter seem to have brought the Loko almost completely under their influence and today the Limba call the Loko *Gbandi*. Also, one Port Loko tradition says the Kanus (or Gbaras) were the earliest Temne immigrants. It is said the first ruler was the Bai Sebora (Shebora), *Sebora* being a contraction of Gbara Seri. The Seris (an alternative to the clan name Kamara) are held to have been introduced to Port Loko by the Kanus. Thus the Kanus who came to rule the Loko could have been followers of Bai Farma who led Temne allies to settle in the district, or they may have entered sooner, but from the same direction, perhaps leading the original Loko immigrants in the thirteenth or fourteenth century. In 1582 John Hawkins encountered a 'Sherabola', a Mani, allied to another Mani war-chief, Sasina, against Bamfora, king of the Bulloms.[27]

The Mani, entering by the same paths as the Loko, Vai and Kono, carried, like the Mande speakers encountered on the Upper Gambia by the contemporary Portuguese, small bows—useless to the larger bows of their enemies—and, as on the Gambia they used large reed shields, two knives—one tied to the left arm—and two quivers. Their clothes were loose cotton shirts, with wide necks and ample sleeves, reaching down to the knees. They stuck numerous feathers in their shirts and red caps.

They may have lived, but certainly traded, in the hinterland of modern Ghana. Indeed they traded all along the route which ran above the forest zone, from the Gambia to Asante. A contemporary Portuguese, Alvares de Almada, from Santiago, Cape Verde, said some had come 'behind Mina, and by the coast of Malagueta'.[28] A few years later Balthasar Barreira, a Jesuit missionary, said Turé, the leader of the Mani, whom the Jesuit had baptised Don Pedro, told him they had taken ten years on the journey fighting all the way, and that he still re-membered (in 1606) the shots the Portuguese castle of Elmina had fired against them.[29]

Traditionally, their leader was a woman, Maçarico, driven

out by the Mandemansa, with a large following. Forty years after leaving Mali, arriving at Cape Mount, they encountered a group of Vai, Kono and Kru. They joined together and fought a major battle against the Bullom, in which Maçarico's son, running into a Bullom ambush led by Bamfora the Bullom king, was killed; his mother died of grief shortly after. This battle was in 1545.[30] Subjugation of the Temne took three years and altogether fifteen passed before the Sapi were conquered. The Mani moved slowly northwards, incorporating the Temne and Bullom, their defeated enemies, into their ranks. Mande family names became common: Kamara, Bangura, Kanu, Kargbo, Konte, Koromo, Sila, Sise, Ture. The Temne even today are aggressively independent, almost anarchic, by nature; they could not present a united front for any length of time and were conquered without much trouble. They were easily ruled too, because they were easily divided. The Limba and Yalunka, already known to the Portuguese for their fighting qualities and for their rocky fortified villages, were carefully avoided.

At last they faced the Susu who outwitted and outfought them. Pretending to be feasting, the Susu ran away leaving behind poisoned meat which the Mani ate. The Mani barricades, thrown up to meet the Susu attack—on the far side of a river running between the two armies[31]—could not withstand the weight of a charge by seven Fula horsemen, a novelty in forest warfare, and the Mani allies turned and ran.

This battle was long remembered in Sierra Leone, both sides having armies larger than ever before.

They settled down, however, dividing the country between them, roughly along the line of the river Sierra Leone: Susu, Yalunka and Limba on one side and Vai, Kono, Kru, Loko, Temne and Bullom on the other, the latter being ruled by Mani chiefs who, on a clan basis, apportioned the country amongst themselves.

The historical process which laid down these layers of people and at times superimposed a conqueror's language is evident in traditional accounts gathered carefully and scientifically by Dr Thomas Winterbottom, the Sierra Leone Company's medical officer, at the end of the eighteenth century:

The Timmanies possess the south side of the river Sierra Leone, together with its branches of Port Logo and Rokelle . . . Thence they penetrate to a considerable distance inland, where they are subdivided into Timmanies, Logos and Korangos; all of whom it is said speak dialects of the same language.[32] This nation formerly lived at a distance from the seacoast; but forced themselves down the river Sierra Leone, among the Bulloms, who formerly possessed the whole region from the river Kissee to the Sherbro . . . They have in a like manner forced themselves down the river Scarcies . . . To the Northward of the Scarcies the Bulloms occupy the sea coast, as far as the mouth of the river Kissee. They also inhabit . . . the river Sherbro, the Bananas, the Plantains, and some other small islands. This once powerful nation formerly possessed the whole of the river Kissee, from which they were driven by a Nation called the Susoos . . . The Sosoos extend from the river Kissee beyond the Rio Pongos, nearly as far as the Rio Nunez, of which tract they dispossessed a nation called Bagoes, who . . . still retain a few straggling villages . . . among the Soosoes . . . They make earthen vessels of a blue kind of clay[33] which they use for holding water and sell to their neighbours.[34]

There were four Mani kingdoms. That of the Bulloms extended northwards from Tagrin Point and included the Iles de Los. Mitombo, the second, also known as Logos to the Portuguese, was centred on Port Loko. The third, the kingdom of Sierra Leone, or Bouré, ran inland from the Sierra Leone peninsula, which it embraced, to merge with the fourth, the kingdom of Sherbro. Ruling houses cemented their authority with diplomatic marriages. Turé married into the family of Fatima of Bullom, his overlord, and into that of Flambure, king of Sierra Leone and son of Bai Farma I, the first Mani king of the Loko. Their rule was not despotic. They acted with the advice of their counsellors and their titles were not hereditary. The Poro Society titles for the male counsellors in the kingdom of Sierra Leone were: Naimbana, Pa Kapr, Naimsogo. There were also three 'Mamy' queens: Bome Pose, Bome Warah and Bome Rufah. When the ruler died, each surviving counsellor, in order of seniority, had the right to govern the territory as regent. Only when all the counsellors had died was a new ruler,

the Bai Farma, installed, and with him a new group of counsellors. At a lower level, government was in the hands of sub-
chiefs, no doubt the 'owners' of the land.[35]

The newcomers overlaid coastal culture with the attributes
of their own civilisation; in particular, perhaps, a more centralised type of state organisation—but in the process they became
partly assimilated into coastal society themselves. This fusion
Baumann termed West Atlantic, in contrast to the Upper Niger
circle, where the Mande and the Fula speakers lived. He considered them the 'kernel of the West Atlantic circle'.[36] A good
example is the collection of peoples known generically as Sapi
(singular Tyapi), a Fula word used today for the Landuma. In
the sixteenth century it included the Sapi, Yalunka, Susu,
Limba, Bullom, Temne and Baga, but, though it presented
some kind of united front against the Mani, it was joined
together primarily by a social homogeneity, not a political one.
In no way was it comparable to the well-disciplined empires of
the western Sudan of the same date.[37] There seems to be, even
today, a basic linguistic and cultural unity corresponding to
this geographical unit—more or less that of the northern rivers.[38]
The linguistic link has been appropriately illustrated by the
radical *bulom* which, in various derived forms appears amongst
all the coastal population to imply the low-lying lands and
stagnant water there, the process associated with salt extraction,
the agriculture practised on swampy soil, and the settlements
people have made there. Thus the Bullom took their name
directly from their habitat, and all Sierra Leoneans know the
flat coastline north of Freetown as the Bullom Shore. The
cultural unity, too, was largely the result of their common
habitat where the canoe was a vital part of their lives for both
trade and war. Sea-salt, though less prized than the far-off
rock-salt mined in the Sahara and exported in exchange for
gold, was essential to life and cheaper than any other source.
Exported inland, it attracted people from afar and was the
most important product in the inland trade network. The names
and processes associated with salt manufacture often derive
from the term *bulom*. It has been suggested that the wet rice
species of *oryza glaberrima* had a 'secondary cradle', beside the

Page 33 An example of a steatite figure—a *nomoli*

Page 34   (*above*) A Koranko bowman; (*below*) the earliest known illustration of rice empoldering in the northern rivers area (1794)

Middle Niger, and that domestication was also achieved between Sine-Salum and the Casamance.[39] Whether this was an indigenous culture, or whether it had been introduced by the Portuguese—as it was in the creeks round Port Loko—it is now impossible to say, though early in the sixteenth century a Portuguese noted that the people of Sierra Leone ate rice as one of their staples, and in 1794 a ship's captain remarked on the empoldered rice grown by the Temne in the north of Sierra Leone.[40] What is certain is that, far from 'barbarian' in their agricultural skills, these people have unfortunately been called 'primitive' because they have been judged by Europeans who frequently and erroneously equated the feudal type of government with the 'best' kind of government. In fact, that kind, far from being the most sophisticated, is often only the first form of government—as their own history after 1066 might have told the British.

The Kru, Kono and Vai

The Mani kings and their followers representing the vanguard of greater forces remaining behind in what is now Liberia, paid tribute to an overlord at Cape Mount. Traditional stories of these overlords were gathered in the early seventeenth century by Dutch merchants at their factory in Cape Mount.[41] They heard of people known as *Monou* or *Manoe*, whose emperor received tribute from all. The Manoe (the name still exists as that of a small Mende-speaking group in the hinterland of Liberia) though few in number, had imposed themselves on other ethnic groups and led them into battle, in particular, the Quoja, the Karo and the Folgia. The Folgia (?Gio/Dan), apparently also Mande speakers, attacked the Karo (the Kru) in the hinterland of the river Junk when Flansire, the Folgia king, married the sister of Flonikerri, the defeated king of the Kru. Flonikerri agreed to join his forces with the Folgia, and to attack neighbouring peoples. He was a successful general and as a reward was allowed to attempt the conquest of Cape Mount, then inhabited by Vai and Quoja (Kono).[42] After a great contest, the land was overrun at last by Zyllymanque, Flonikerri's brother. After that Flansire advanced against Sierra Leone. The

C

Sierra Leone river mouth was apportioned to Kandaquelle, Sherbro to Selboele (or Sherabola) and the Gallinhas to Syrte— all Kru and Folgia viceroys, each subject to the manimansa (the emperor of Manoe).

Flansire's eldest son, Flamboere, was (according to the European sources, gathered from Father Barreira, collected by Fernão Guerreiro, translated into French by Jarric and re-translated by Dapper) christened Philip by the Jesuits. If that is so, then this Flamboere was Flambure, the son of Bai Farma, the first Mani king of the Loko.[43] This story is important, since it seems to establish the truth of the traditional account of the overlordship of the emperor of Manoe over the territories of Sierra Leone.

Corroboration is found in an anonymous English account written about 1568, probably by a member of John Hawkins's third voyage,[44] telling how their general at a town called Bonga, went to the help of Sheri, the 'Kinge of Serra Lione' to help dislodge from a fortified camp, two other Mani kings, Sasina and Seterama, who had challenged Sheri's authority. Sheri's headquarters was further south, at the river Cess. It has therefore been deduced that by about 1616:

> . . . the authentic Manes who were still to be found were the Queas, Quojas and Cubales. These formed the élite which ruled the province of Sierra Leone and Bouré. They claimed to have fought alongside the father of 'Filamanqua'; and even allowing for the fact that similarity of names can be notoriously misleading, this 'Filamanqua' seems to be the 'Zyllymanque' of Dapper. The Father of Zyllymanque was the Kru King who put up a desperate resistance to the Folgia invasion. He was succeeded by his son Flonikerri, who in turn was succeeded by his brother, Zyllymanque.[45]

The name Shere, or Seri, which occurs frequently at this time, is an alternative for the clan name Kamara, traditionally the oldest clan in the Mande-speaking area of the western Sudan. In their descent from the Niger to the hinterland of Sierra Leone, reaching the Liberian coast and then moving westward, they incorporated into their army such Mande-fou

elements as the Gbande and Toma. In the seventeenth century,
Barbot, copying John Ogilby said: 'The Folgias depend on the
Emperor of Manow . . . The Folgias as well as the Bulom and
Silm [Krim] call the subjects of this emperor Mendi, that is
Lords.' This is the first mention of the name. On linguistic
grounds also this seems correct. Northcote Thomas, the Sierra
Leone government anthropologist, linked the Mende with the
Gbande and Toma, suggesting that the Mende were 'the por-
tion of the Manes who drove out the aborigines or completely
dominated them'.[46]

Traditional Mende beliefs seem to support this view. They
speak of the earliest settlers, distinguishing them from invaders
who came from the north, whose leaders became their chiefs.
This occurred outside the boundaries of modern Sierra Leone,
in present Liberian territory, which the Mende left only in the
eighteenth century, to overrun southern Sierra Leone. The
Mende thus seem to represent the Mani fusion with the Kissi
and Bullom. Certainly the appointment of military viceroys is
more typical of Mende government than that of any other
people then in Sierra Leone. Traditionally the role of the Mende
chief seems to have been that of a military leader, with absolute
powers in secular matters, which were sometimes delegated to
lieutenants in other parts of the chiefdom. On the other hand,
the semi-sacred nature of a Temne chief restricts his authority,
and makes his deposition almost impossible.

Bai Farma's subjects were Temne and Loko; he is remembered still. The word Mani fell quickly into disuse, except
in the Scarcies area where a people with that name, refugees
who fled from the victorious Susu at the time of the great battle,
are found today.

Contemporaries rated the Mani very highly as warriors.
Barreira praised the Sapi for their intelligence and learning
ability, though he thought them weak and effeminate in some
respects. By their salt manufacture they had become rich,
supplying the caravans from the interior, and receiving in
exchange white cloth, cattle and gold from the Fula and
Yalunka. The Susu paid them in iron and dyes. Possibly, after
an earlier history of conquest by land and sea, these trade goods

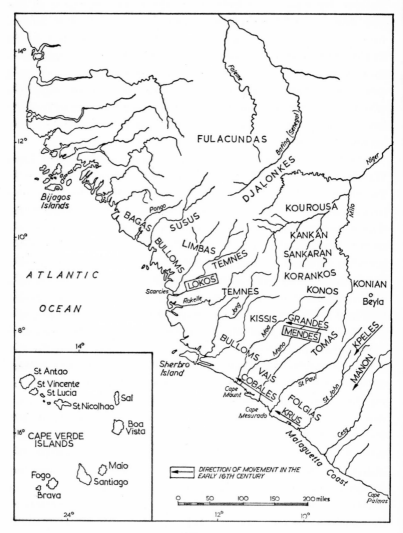

Map 2

and the abundant riches of the forest had made them soft. The Bullom, by now, were held to be the most aggressive of the Sapi and under Mani domination soon learnt to fight in formation, using squadrons of archers armed with the big Mani shields, and fighting behind entrenchments known as *atabanka*— though this was possibly a Temne word.[47] Other people adopted this form of defence and it was necessary to develop measures which would make it ineffective. Hitherto battles seem to have been fought in daylight, but now it was more satisfactory to attack at dawn, a practice which soon became universal.

The Mani viceroys had to put down occasional revolts; John Hawkins was involved in one. Later, in 1572, some Bullom in the Sherbro rebelled and their Mani ruler, Seri Mambea, was unable to quell it without calling on other viceroys for help. This seems to have been a revolt of domestic slaves who were used to turn Sherbro Island into a land of intensive cultivation, growing millet, rice and tubers and producing palm wine for their masters who did not have the skill themselves. The general effect of their rule was the destruction of much that was sensitive and artistic amongst the Sapi. Early in the century, the Sapi had a very high reputation for their skill in raffia work and ivory carving. They were soon producing works of art for the European trade—especially ivory salt cellars and spoons.[48] By the end of that century, after the Mani invasions, these crafts had been entirely forgotten: 'It is the fault of foreign kings that the country is so poor,' wrote Manuel Alvares early in the seventeenth century, 'because they have captured so many potters and . . . have committed so many vexations on the indigenous people that these latter have become less and less concerned and have given up the exercise of their arts.' A pottery complex associated with thin-walled type vessels is thought to have come to an end in the sixteenth century, along with the carving of *nomoli*, with which the pottery is often found associated today.

The Mani bestowed one great blessing. It was a skill which had enabled them to become such fine warriors. Like the armies of ancient Ghana who overran their enemies, they had superb weapons and tools of iron, which they were said to manufacture better than anyone. Though the Sapi had iron weapons too, often they were not properly tempered and were brittle.[49] It is likely, also, that they brought with them the techniques of cotton-weaving. Today the smaller Mende loom, which is portable, is favoured by the Mende, Sherbro, Vai, Krim and some Kono.[50] The heavier, more permanent, Mandingo loom from the north is used by the Limba, Koranko, Upper Kissi and Upper Kono. This division resembles closely the political boundary separating the two major alliances after the Mani conquest.

The European Disruption

About the middle of the seventeenth century the Mani system of viceroys—dondaghs as they were called—began to break down. Indeed western Sudanic practices upon the Upper Guinea coast generally declined. Such kingdoms as existed were no longer part of a centralised empire ruled by the mandemansa. About 1650 the dondagh of the Bulloms was overthrown and fled to the adjacent Banana Islands for safety.[51] In the Gallinhas, officials threw off their allegiance, dividing the territory between themselves. There is evidence that the rulers along the river Sierra Leone also rebelled, and later fought one another. European trade was disrupting the coastal states by now. Rival chiefs fought to control trade routes and to exact tolls, going to war with any withholding their share of customs and 'dashes'.

Soon the southern forest was divided amongst a host of chiefs. War and intrigue flourished. 'Each of these petty kings,' wrote John Barbot, 'has an absolute authority in his own districts, and can make war or peace, without consent or approbation of this, or of any of whom they hold.'[52] Many went in fear of being poisoned.[53]

CHAPTER 2

The Northern Influence:
Fula, Susu, Bunduka and Sofa

Trade Routes
Early trade routes ran from Bullom, Temne, Krim and Vai
territory, up the coastal estuaries, through northern Temne and
Limba country, via Port Loko and Tonko Limba in the west,
or Bafodea and Bumban, thence to Falaba (after 1768) in the
east. Most traders preferred the easterly route because it was
only partially forested.

Caravans came down from Timbuctoo, Bamako, Segu, Kankan, through the gathering points of Seguri and Faranah, by
way of the main inland centres of Timbo, Musaia, Bumban,
Samaia, to barter at the coastal towns. Markets along the Great
Scarcies river, from Kambia to the sea, were already flourishing
when the Portuguese traded there.[1] The rivers Mano, Moa,
Bum, Jong, Bagru, Rokel, Great and Little Scarcies were all
important highways northwards into the interior for the export
of slaves, cloth, palm products, kola and sea-salt.

The Temne were especially favourably placed, and many
routes ran through that country; important markets grew up at
Kambia, Mange, Port Loko and Magbeli. Long before the
Europeans, caravans of Susu and Yalunka travelled annually
to the coast. Mande-speaking ruling families were widely
established in Sierra Leone before 1500, though a sign of Fula
influence and power is that the Susu and Limba sought Fula
help against the Mani. However, though the latter were checked,
the Susu took their trade to the Rio Nunez, fearing reprisals
from the Mani-dominated Sapi federation.

Mandinka and Related Societies

The Muslim theocracy of Futa Jallon which the Fula created in their holy war drew considerably upon indigenous Mande-speaking societies for its institutions and political vocabulary. Descendants of the Fula aristocrats had very mixed origins, having absorbed their early allies—frequently Yalunka and other Mande-speaking peoples.

This society contained an ancient and diversified working class, segregated into castes. Above these were certain professional groups, belonging to no caste, including the extremely individualistic diyula or tradesmen, whose competitive spirit and belief in material values was unusual for West Africa.[2] Above them were the warriors and chiefs.

Today this mode of life is based on the West African forest from the Upper Niger to the Upper Sassandra rivers. It derives from a constructive, symbiotic, relationship worked out between the animist masses and the new commercial minority—the diyula. Before the second half of the nineteenth century, local chiefs still held at least nominal military and political power, their people producing cattle, slaves and kola nuts for the diyula.

Clan Names

Rulers with Mande clan names are common in modern Sierra Leone. They represent an influence of considerable antiquity, still actively working upon the country's political and economic forces. In the 1920s E. F. Sayers, a district commissioner with probably more first-hand, intimate, knowledge of the country than any other, estimated that in Temne country alone Kamaras held twenty-two out of a total of seventy-three crowns.[3] Next came the Banguras with ten, often alternating in chiefdoms with Kamara royal families. After them numerically came the Kontes and Kanus with seven crowns each.

In Port Loko the earliest Mande-speaking chiefs were possibly Kamaras. A King Seri, an alternative to Kamara, was ruling in Sierra Leone near the peninsula in the 1560s. Next came the Kanus, arriving immediately from Bombali, and before that no doubt from Koranko and Limba country.

Kanu chiefs are known today in Port Loko as Baki Foki, though formerly they styled themselves Bai Sebora. Sebora is an alternative to Kamara, and seemingly they married into that family, taking the cognatic name and system when they took

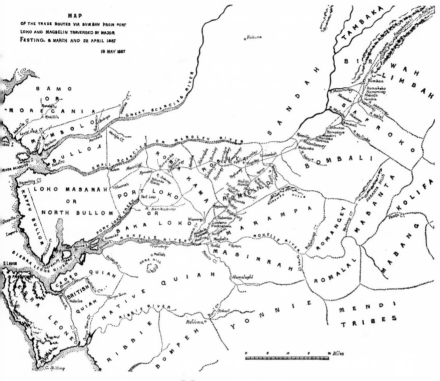

MAP
OF THE TRADE ROUTES VIA BUMBAN FROM PORT
LOKO AND MAGBELIN TRAVERSED BY MAJOR
FESTING. 8 MARCH AND 22 APRIL 1887
19 MAY 1887

Map 3

over the chieftainship, and adopting the royal style of their predecessors.[4]

The ancestors of the Kamaras found in western Temne country were considered by Sayers to have derived from:

Baga of the Mendenyi or Bullom Empire, allied with early Susu adventurers in the country, and partly from Soninke Kamara from Bure, led into the country by a djihading Muslim of Moorish or Torodo descent, named Lahai Salihu . . . who drove numerous Temne and Limba from the west bank of the Kolente river, into more or less the positions they now occupy east of that river. This Lahai Salihu married the daughter of a Baga Bullom chief, and from him are descended the present chiefs of Melikuri on our western frontier.[5]

Lahai Salihu seems to have come from Bambuk in Senegal; and at one time had 15,000 followers; he was killed by his generals in 1793.[6]

Kanu is an alternative clan name for the ruling house of Keita in ancient Mali, as indeed the Vai Massaquoi in the Gallinhas is said to be. Bangura, an alternative for Konte, is most plentiful in the north-west, in Susu country. Fofana, an alternative to Koroma, is another predominant name. They, too, are Susu, like the Banguras, and are an important branch of the diyula.

At the beginning of the eighteenth century certain Yalunka (Susu) Kamara are said to have gone down from east of Futa, on the borders of Sankaran, into Kissi country, mixing with the inhabitants to found today's Kissi ruling houses. Most of these now bear Mande names as a consequence. Kamaras were usually non-Muslim, often actively anti-Muslim, and are thus frequently found in areas outside Muslim influence. Amongst the Koranko all *yelli* (musicians) and *fina* (historians) are of this clan. Sayers called them 'the real rulers of the country', makers of peace and war before the British. Amongst the Mande speakers themselves, since singers and historians require a client, they were looked down on, but in Temne and Kissi country they became chiefs. Many more, though not generally as chiefs, lived in Limba, Yalunka and Koranko country, where they were not without influence.

The Kagbo, a branch of the Keita clan, when they reached Sierra Leone, found the Maras (also a Mande-speaking clan) under one Saramba—from whom all Koranko traditionally descend. They helped them attack the Kuniki (Temne), Loko, Limba and Kono. At one time the Maras ruled most of the eastern and central Koranko chiefdoms, as well as others in nearby Guinea. The Maras and the Kagbos, no doubt for mutually beneficial political reasons, intermarried.

The Fula and Susu Jehad

During the seventeenth century, Muslim Fula from the Upper Niger and Senegal settled in Futa Jallon amongst animist Fula, Susu, Malinka and Yalunka. Muslim traders came to live in small groups, or even singly, amongst the local population, whose life was based upon the extended family system. The Jesuit missionary, Balthasar Barreira, met a Muslim 'bookman' (mori man) at the court of a Bena Susu ruler in the early 1600s.

About 1727 these Muslim Fula began a *jehad* under the Karamoko, Alpha Ibrahim (1726–51); by the end of the century they had constructed a powerful and active Muslim state, with its capital at Timbo and its holy centre at Fugumba. People living in the basins of the northern rivers were gradually overcome by Muslim Mandinka, Fula or Susu—though the latter often rejected Islam. One begins to hear of Koranko towns with names like Mori Kunda, or Mori Fundu which indicate the presence of Muslims. Sulima at that time was occupied by Koranko, but the Yalunka (a branch of the Susu) spread gradually over the country during the eighteenth century, allying with the Koranko chief, Mansa Dansa, of the (Mande) Mara clan.

Susu, with permission of the Sanko family (themselves immigrants from Mellacourie) and of the 'chiefs of the land', soon occupied Kambia on the Great Scarcies, moving on shortly to found Kukuna, Layah and Tasaing. Their chiefs were often called Fodi. According to Sir Samuel Rowe, an energetic and informed governor, this was an infallible sign of Susu origin in the second half of the nineteenth century.

Southwards, at the height of Muslim pressure on the north, groups of bunduka settled along the Sierra Leone river. They have been described by a modern representative as aristocratic Fula, 'reliable sons of chiefs'.[7] Tradition gives them the ritually significant number of seven.

Non-Muslim Fula and others, leaving Futa, infected Koranko and Yalunka, Fula vassals, with thoughts of revolt. About 1756 Sowa, a northern Koranko chief, fearing the continually increasing Fula strength, said he would be a Muslim no longer. Many joined his revolt, and the Fula despatched large armies into Koranko country, sacking the towns and executing rebellious chiefs.

In 1758 an insignificant, though picturesque, Irish slave trader, Nicholas Owen, on the river Jong, heard of a king Musolum, a 'Mandingo' (Europeans called all Muslims Mandingoes since they were the main preachers of Islam) who had 'come down from the inland kingdoms' and 'made 2 or 3 pety kingdoms subject to him'.[8] This was probably Amara, one of Alpha Ibrahim's best scholars (the Karamoko emphasised education with conversion).[9]

About 1760 the Sulima Yalunka, still Fula allies, attacked the Kissi—and again in 1761. The next year Fula and Sulima invaded the Wassalu country of the Koranko, but Konte Birama, aided by unusually early rains, defeated them. This made the Sulima, only lukewarm Muslims, reconsider their position, and they changed sides. In revenge Fula soldiers massacred the Susu elders. The wars continued, the enemies sometimes invading each other simultaneously. It is said that on their way home in 1767, the Sulima made an excursion against the Limba, taking 3,500 prisoners, whom they sold to slave-traders in the Rio Pongo.

Konte Birama was the Fula's great enemy, uniting all Koranko against Islam, and sacking their stronghold of Kankan. He attacked Futa in 1755 and 1766, taking Timbo, its capital. His sister Hauwa is said to have amputated her right breast so as to fight better.

Alpha Ibrahim's war-chief and successor, Ibrahima Suri Pate, defeated the Yalunka at Fugumba in 1767. Two Fula towns were founded: Bankan and Fula Mansa.[10] Losing part of their lands to the Fula, the Yalunka founded Falaba, a new capital, in 1768, at a safer distance from their enemies, and established a line of stockaded villages along the valley of the Mongo river, a main route from the interior to the coast. Besides Falaba they founded at least six other towns: Musaia, Manankong, Sinkunia, Gberia, Ganya and Betaya. These formed a northern march, protecting the trade route and keeping out marauding northern neighbours. This was especially valuable in the late nineteenth century at the time of the Sofa invasions.[11]

In 1776 a large Koranko/Sulima army invaded Fula territory but their respective leaders, Konte Birama and Tahabaeri (the founder of Falaba), being killed, they fell back in disorder. After this the Sulima at least acknowledged Fula suzerainty and that war came to an end.

Tahabaeri's younger brother and successor, Dinka, fell out with the Koranko and attacked these former allies in the very year of his succession. The next year he invaded Limba country and burnt Dangkang. His successor, Assana Yeera, began his reign in 1800 by invading the Limba.

The Tambaca and Kukuna Susu had gained a foothold in Tonko Limba about 1760 and from here they too tried to drive the Limba further south. By the end of the nineteenth century the Susu had taken over most of southern Limba territory.[12]

About 1795 Alpha Sailu, king of Futa, tried unsuccessfully to take Falaba. Ten years later, commanded by a new king, Ba Demba, they marched against Assana Yeera. Despite the help of certain Sulima Yalunka, the Fula were repulsed, and Assana Yeera quickly had his revenge on the traitorous Sulima.

For several years there was peace, both sides sending war parties frequently against the Koranko and Limba for slaves.[13]

In 1796, Adam Afzelius, the Swedish botanist from Freetown, heard the Susu had moved north recently to occupy the Rio Pongo 'driving away the aborigines and Bagas, towards the sea-shore', thus repeating the historical pattern of demographic stratification. The Fula and Susu, he learnt, were keen rivals (as were the Temne and Bullom further south).[14] The Fula made tributaries of the Rio Pongo Susu. In 1822 when the Fula usurper Bokhari, son of Ba Demba, took the throne from Abdulkadir (though the latter regained it), he replaced Abdulkadir's Susu chief in the Rio Pongo with his own nominee, a change they accepted without demur. Puppet chiefs like this had to keep the caravan roads open for their overlords, preserving law and order and refusing entry to other nations. When Fula diplomacy demanded, the paths were 'stopped', as the saying was, reinforcing political with economic arguments.

The powerful Fula caravans made a habit of collecting tribute as well as debts on their way to the coast and unco-operative chiefs, especially if not Muslim, were liable to be added to the slave coffles.

Limba, Kono and Koranko

The less-sophisticated Limba and Koranko, as a defence against the Fula and Susu, built villages on the tops of the highest hills or surrounded them with cotton-tree stockades. Desperate for survival, fighting with poisoned arrows from inaccessible caves and mountain fortresses, they had a ferocious reputation. The Mani avoided them, but during the seventeenth and eighteenth centuries both Limba and Kissi had been harassed by the Sulima Yalunka (Susu) under Geema Fundu (fl 1690) and his grandson Yeena Yella (fl 1730–50) who sold them for transmission to the coast, in exchange for European goods. The Susu Kamaras gained the crown in several Kissi chiefdoms; Fula influence was very strong amongst the Limba at this time. The Koranko were harassed by their eastern neighbours, the Kono, as well as by the Sofas who, in the last years of the nineteenth century, captured Moralli Bokhari, the Koranko ruler.

The Kono remember a great war with the Koranko, when they were saved by a simple man, Tambafassa, who going to Segwia 'where the Korankos were', let out the bees he had captured, as a preliminary to a successful attack. Tambafassa's success made Fakoie, a Kono from Boyia, jealous, but we learn the former turned successfully to a mori man, that is, a Muslim bookman from the north, for help. Another rebellion, by Jafurrie of Jafuyia occurred, under Tambafassa's son Kibunda-foi. Later, Kono and Koranko, led by the Kono war-chiefs, Dahibah and Tembaie, defeated a Mende invasion, but fell out when the Koranko lost the Sanda chiefdom to the Kono and fought each other. The Kono, with Mende allies, then attacked the Kissi and beat them, driving them back over the river Melle.

It is said the Mende kept all prisoners, to which the Kono naturally objected. In revenge they assassinated Yargbakka, the

Mende war-chief, and Sefundi, the Kono leader, drove the Mende southward. The Temne, too, raided for slaves and food, and overcame Borowuri, said to be the last of the big Kono chiefs. After that the country disintegrated into sections, debilitated by continual petty feuding, the curse of so much Sierra Leone history.[15]

Unlike many Sierra Leone people, the Limba have no traditions about their origin. Genealogies and stories of ruling families go back only four or five generations. In fact, they have had contact with the north for many centuries; nearly all important Limba ruling families trace their origins from there. Some are said to be from Futa, some from Sankaran, and all have kept up these connections, sending their sons to be educated there and encouraging trade. In the Wara Wara Limba country (the northern parts of which they lost to Koranko and Yalunka)[16] there are two especially holy places: Masin, and Kakoia, where the guardian spirit of the Limba is said to live. By tradition this chiefdom was the origin of the Limba people. Yet, in Sayers' time all rulers had Mandinka names, not Limba ones. Their politics, too, has been northern dominated; perhaps even their religion also because, though mainly animist, they have a deep regard for Islam, and several of their chiefs have been Muslim. Many place-names are of Futa origin, as well as words referring to titles and religious practices.[17] We learn that Bafodi, 'king' of the Limba, died about 1820, worn out from driving the Fula from Cammanka. Even so his successor, Brima Dansa, was a Fula, appointed as regent in Timbo by the king. Brima Dansa ruled from Warra Warra.[18]

The most important Limba towns and chiefdoms were on trade routes. In earlier times the chief of Bumban is said to have ruled parts of Port Loko in the west and of Koranko country in the east. Instead of the many little chiefdoms of today there were only three main ones: Yagala, Bumban and Bafodea, their power and extent based upon trade and trade routes.

Bumban in the south-east Limba country exploited the northern trade with particular success, being ruled by a succession of famous chiefs throughout the nineteenth century. The best known were Sankelle and his successor, Suluku, who had ruled

for twenty years when he died in 1906. Reputed to have had
300 cattle and 100 wives, his authority was not typical of Limba
chiefs, however, who usually by balancing various forces to
their own advantage seldom gained more than a small and
temporary measure of domination.

Suluku, too, had to consider his relations with others. One
of his main power bases was military. He trained his armies in
the hills, engaging in many wars which are still remembered.
He fought Alimami Suman of Bafodea for control of the hilltop
town of Kakarima. He pushed back the Loko from his territory
and later fought Lankafali, Samory's general, though at one
time, like most Limba, he had been their ally. He entered into
an agreement with the British in 1888 and also with the Temne
Bai Bureh, but his most important alliances were made by
marriages, with ruling Limba houses and with Manding families.
Especially important was the town of Karina, a Manding
settlement with great influence and containing several rich
traders who made repeatedly unsuccessful claims to rule in
Biriwa.

It is a Limba tradition that leading members of powerful
families control outlying villages as their own; thus it was
always open to a member of a ruler's family to assert his power.
Suluku was plagued by the hostility, possibly even rebellion, of
one of his brothers acting in this way. He was, however, spared
one pressure group which chiefs faced further south: the so-
called secret societies. The political and religious influence of
Islam seems to have prevented their gaining power in the
north.

Bai Farma in Temne Tradition
To the south, the northern and western Temne controlled the
important market-towns in the lower, navigable river Scarcies,
Port Loko creek and Rokel river. Formerly the Gbanta Temne
covered the present Moyamba district and all Yonni, and were
linked by trade along the Bagru river to the Sherbro area in
the south. Yonni Temne tradition says, incorrectly, Bai Farma
was of Fula origin and it was he who gave them their first
Fula chief, Masa Kele, who placed present Yonni under two

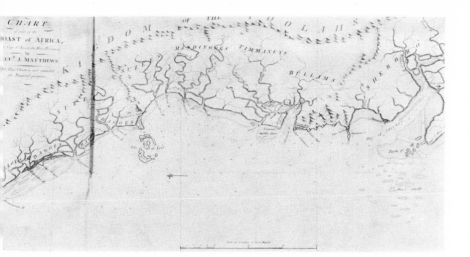

Page 51 (above) Location of coastal peoples at the end of the eighteenth century; (below) Sulima and Koranko musicians

Page 52 (*above*) A Fula slave coffle, 1793; (*below*) Maroons in
ambush on the Dromilly estate, Jamaica, 1795

Fula followers, Araba and Amadu Jello—both Muslim. In the eighteenth century (the Temne say earlier), the Kpa Mende (Taiama) arrived and the Temne appealed to the Fula for help. Correctly assessing the trading possibilities, they were glad to oblige and as a reward the Gbanta formally recognised the Fula Alimami as their own head, calling him Fula mansa (Fula chief). The first two Fula mansa are said to have been Amadu's sons who married into Temne ruling houses. Like other usurpers in West Africa, needing to appear legitimate, they adopted Islamic regalia and administration, and brought in the Poro, a society with strong political motivations. However, the Fula mansa's rule was never absolute and Araba's grandson, Kayito, was deposed for tyranny. No other mansa ruled until the nineteenth century—and only then with British backing when he was encouraged to plunder Koya after it had refused to pay the House Tax.

In the Temne Kunike chiefdom, the earliest remembered chief is a Fula, Pa Kunike, also said to be a follower of Bai Farma and a Muslim. Here the Temne rebelled perhaps early in the eighteenth century. All Fula, it is said, united to teach the Temne and their Koranko allies a lesson. Unrest continued throughout that century.[19]

Nineteenth-century Trade
Temne country links the past very strongly to the north. Port Loko was the greatest Temne centre, attracting trade from innumerable paths and creeks and shipping it from its tidal wharves down to the coast.

The Rokel, navigable for an unusual length, provided outlets for Temne groundnuts, palm-kernels, rice, palm-oil and camwood. From further off came produce from Kono country to the east, Kpa Mende goods from the south-east and Koranko trade from the north-east. The Rokel and Port Loko creeks were worth fighting for; trade wars were numerous. Port Loko had little peace until the early 1840s, and by the time the wars had ended so had its prosperity. Commerce, driven away by the fighting, moved to the Rokel area which, too, became a battle-ground. There was little peace between 1828 and 1884,

D

and by the early 1870s its trade, in turn, had been ruined. Merchants moved to the Bumpe and Ribbi, again followed by ruinous fighting. The colony tried to 'protect' it in 1879, but this did not keep the Yonni Temne out. Traders finally concentrated in the Sherbro. Here, even by the mid 1860s, Sherbro merchants were thought to be drawing out annually trade worth £60,000 from the Bum and Kittam rivers, and £8,000 from the Jong.

The Sanko Family

As trade grew, Muslims were increasingly drawn in, the most influential being the Sanko family, who came from Mellacourie in the 1760s. Allowed to settle by the Temne rulers, they named their town Sendugu after one in Susu country, and were soon joined by refugees from the *jihad*, so that another town, Ro-bat, had to be built. Their Islamic school was attended by the sons of Temne and Loko rulers. The Sanko were good traders, full of Islamic learning, claiming power by witchcraft over the supernatural,[20] and their brutal warriors were feared far and wide. They 'cursed' the Bai Sebora, the traditional chief, saying neither he nor his successors would live long; people soon came to fear crowning or being elected to the Crown. Thus the Sankos superseded the Temne rulers, and Alimami Namina Modu, who had led the family from the Mellacourie, became chief of Port Loko. The 'owners' of the land, descendants of the first remembered occupants who have the right to curse the land and who alone can make sacrifices to the ancestral gods to ensure prosperity, were represented by the Bai Forki and in theory all authority, even that of the Alimami, derived from him. In reality he was now powerless.[21]

Abolition worried the family and Alimami Brima Konkori Sanko planned a coalition with Bullom and Sherbro chiefs to drive the English from Freetown. It never materialised, because the closure of the Sierra Leone river ports to the slave traffic was not as harmful as the chiefs had feared, and anyway they found alternative markets in the north. The Alimami was said to have sent one hundred slaves annually as *douceurs* to his northern relatives and to the Fula chiefs there.[22] In the end his harsh rule led to his overthrow and execution in 1816, by a Temne, Moribu Kindo Bangura, also of Susu origin. Fula traders entering towns in the Port Loko sphere now had to swear at the town *barri* (meeting place) that they did not intend to settle and as proof of sincerity, sacrifice two sheep or one bullock—a heavy tax as they progressed from town to town, and purposely discouraging.[23]

Though the Susu rulers were driven out, their followers, as is usual in African society, were permitted to remain as long as they could accept the will of the majority, which they did.

The Bundukas

About 1810 a Limba warrior, Pa Molai Limba, began to harass the Temne chiefdoms to the north of Port Loko. Loko and Temne, with the help of the bunduka, pushed him back, but in 1828 Moruba Kindo Bangura determined to drive out the Loko, with whom the Temne had for long shared the land. Again he called on the bunduka, Senegalese mori men from St Louis, brought down by the French in the 1770s, who leased Gambia Island in 1772. They had operated by brute force along the Rokel river and the Port Loko creek, as French agents, guarded by armed mercenaries whom their masters recruited from further north. When the French left, they had stayed on, marrying into local ruling houses. They defeated the Loko by 1841. As a reward, they were given six towns in the Sendugu area, and the 'ownership' of the Sanko family there was confirmed.

This Temne–Loko war was the first serious one of the nineteenth century on the Rokel. It lasted intermittently until 1836, disrupting the timber trade and in 1830 holding up 6,000 tons of shipping. The governor patched up a temporary peace in 1831, but war flared up again, when Sebeti, the son of Pa Gumbu Yaron, the Loko leader killed in the previous war, resisted further Temne onslaughts. Loko power there was finally destroyed, but the Alikali of Port Loko, with Fula, Susu and bunduka help, continued to drive them northwards, until he died in July 1840. The bundukas taking up the leadership, under Abdu Rahman Bundu, in 1841 overcame an important

Loko stockade. This long war, though it gave the Temne complete mastery, ushered in Port Loko's decline.

Some of the defeated Loko fled to Masama on the Bullom Shore, where Ali Bundu, a grandson of one of the seven traditional original bundukas, and reputedly the richest, gave them sanctuary, perhaps because his mother was a Loko. Henceforth 'Loko' was added to the name of the chiefdom, now known as Loko-Masama.

The Sanko rulers, driven north, tried for years to incite the Susu to seize control in northern Temne country, especially Kambia. Their leader was Sattan Lahai,[24] a wealthy slave dealer who attacked several Temne towns. Driven out in 1830, he built a town, Layah, near Kukuna. At his death, his son, also Sattan Lahai, built Ro-Wula in the Upper Scarcies, where he soon persuaded the senile Bai Farma of Magbema, in which Kambia lay, to appoint him ruler. Several attempts to regain the Port Loko Crown were made, notably in 1841 and 1852 but, particularly disliking the way they now sided with the British, the Port Loko Temne drove them out. Governor John Hill gave the exiles money to settle on the Bullom Shore with Kala Modu, head of another powerful Muslim family. The Sankos used the gift to buy arms, and choosing a moment when Saidu Kamara, the Temne war-leader, was away helping to drive Sattan Lahai from Kambia, sacked Port Loko, which was undefended, in 1859. Hill was furious, suspecting a widespread Susu plot to destroy the colony's trade; perhaps to attack the settlement.

With arms supplied by the colony, the Temne, assisted by nearby Bullom chiefs, attacked the Kala Modu stronghold at Medina, Bullom Shore, and the governor deposed Kala Modu, recognising instead Fenda Sanusi Modu as head of the family. Thus tribal hostility, not for the last time, was fostered by the British, protecting their neighbours, the Temne and Bullom, whom they hoped to 'civilise' with Christianity, against Sattan Lahai and the Susu. The wars in the Port Loko and Kambia regions had, from the early 1850s, been diverting the caravans from Port Loko, colony trade passing instead through Magbeli on the Rokel, causing a temporary boom there. In 1861 the

British put an end to the fighting for a while by persuading the Susu to give up claims to Kambia, in favour of the Temne, Lamina Barmoi.

By 1800 immigrants from inland controlled the rivers north of the Scarcies. The Moribia chiefs, Bullom in origin, but converted and intermarried with Muslim Mandinka at Fourecariah, claimed the coast. Their rivals, the Sumbia Susu, at Wongapong (originally from Sangara) were also allied, but to a lesser degree, with the Bullom. In 1814 a protracted war broke out, the Sumbia trying to block Moribia trade with the interior, the Moribia to stop the Sumbia buying arms from their ally, Dala Modu.

The Dala Modu Family at Medina

Towards the end of the eighteenth century Mohammed Fenda Modu, head of an influential Susu family at Wongapong, had sent his son, Ala Dala Modu, to settle with fifty followers in Freetown. Ala Dala Modu fought for the colony in the Temne attack of 1801 but, suspected of slave trading, was expelled in 1806, moving to Medina (modern Lungi) amongst the Bullom. The colony generally regarded him as a bloodthirsty monster; even so, his great power made it necessary to gain his goodwill, especially as he had considerable interests in the timber and rice trades, in which Freetown was involved. To secure his friendship, Governor Henry Campbell formally 'recognised' him as regent of Loko Masama—which covered most of the Bullom Shore[25] opposite the colony, across the river. The Colonial Office never ratified that treaty, however, because it bound the colony to return run-away domestic slaves, according to custom.[26] Even so, Ala Dala Modu came to supersede his overlord, the Bai Sherbro, and sent some of his followers to settle in Loko Masama, to maintain his influence there. The new Bai Mauro of Loko Masama, and Bai Sherbro of Kaffu Bullom, complained of the harsh rule of Amara Modu, his successor,[27] and Freetown championed them against the Susu incomers. The Bullom even asked Britain to take over their country and protect them; this was refused but, to keep out the French, a quarter-mile-wide strip round the Bullom Shore was accepted. Amara's successor, Kala Modu, implicated in the 1859 attack on Port Loko, was driven away, a British treaty of 1860 reaffirming the Bullom chiefs' rights there. The great days of the family were over.

The Family of Mori Bundu of Foredugu

Another influential Muslim family was that of Mori Bundu, who had settled in Temne country at Foredugu in Koya, probably about 1770.[28] He was a renowned mori man and had been invited by Gumbu Smart, chief of the Loko settlement on the river Rokel, to make *shebe* (grigri) for him. He had stayed at Foredugu and married a daughter of the Naimbana who had become regent of Koya about 1775 and the subsequent 'landlord' of the Sierra Leone Company. As legitimate commerce grew in the nineteenth century, Mori Bundu grew even richer, enforcing a peace necessary for successful trade, and making a most valuable contribution to the country, since Koya was almost leaderless under the Temne who, for reasons discussed later,[29] were unwilling to appoint a new principal chief (Bai Farma was his title) in Koya. In 1837 Mohammedu Bundu of Foredugu, helped the Temne push back the Kpa Mende (Taiama) from eastern Koya, lending his war-chief Maligi Bundu. Both Mohammedu, a Muslim, and the Temne owners of the land, detested the troublesome, western-educated liberated African immigrants of Mende origin who had settled in Koya and whom the Kpa Mende encouraged in sabotage. When the Temne captured some, Mohammedu's sister, Musa Bundu, sold them into slavery. Later Maligi Bundu turned against him, as war-chiefs often did, and Mohammedu turned to the Loko. Hostilities raged from 1843–6, disrupting the Rokel trade once more.

The timber in the Rokel was running out and merchants were looking for alternative supplies. Both the Mohammedu Bundu family and the Caulkers now claimed those on the banks of the river Ribi. The Mabanta Temne supported the Caulkers.

The colony, intervening in these troubles, in the person of T. G. Lawson, government interpreter, sided with Foreh Bundu, Mohammedu's younger brother, against the Temne.

Peace was restored, but the Rosolo creek timber, some of the last there, was returned to a Koya man.

In 1859 the family had another setback, when the leading Koya dignitaries, significantly excluding Bokhari Sila, Mohammedu's successor, sent to Freetown saying they were at last prepared to install a new principal chief for Koya—an office vacant since 1807.[30]

In 1861 the British navy burnt Foredugu along with the other towns on the Koya stretch of the Sierra Leone river, during the troubles following the cession of British Koya.

Family fortunes improved a little under Alimami Lahai Bundu of Foredugu who was regent of Koya in the 1870s, but without a proper ruler Koya (now retroceded) was constantly disturbed and the family's position insecure. Their predominance and their pro-British stand, roused the Temne, led by Gbana Seri and Sengbe, two sons of the previous Naimbana.[31] With the help of other Temne, Foredugu was attacked in 1879. Fighting spread, the Bundu family supported by the Yonni Temne (long keen to get a foothold on the Rokel), so that for a while civil war raged. Governor Samuel Rowe intervened, routing certain Temne from their strongholds.

In the 1898 rising Senu Bundu, then ruling Foredugu, sided with Bai Bureh,[32] jealous of Sierra Leonean commercial rivalry and of British encroachment.

Bai Simera Kamal, Masimera

When the Kpa Mende arrived in Taiama in the eighteenth century it was a Koranko chief of Yonni who became their landlord, though the owners of the land were in fact Gbanta. They attacked the Mende once or twice, and were defeated. The Yonni, jealous of this growing power, began to raid Taiama and other Kpa Mende settlements. Taiama retaliated by stopping the Yonni from going through to trade in the Bumpe and Ribbi, confining them to the Rokel.

Perhaps the most remarkable figure in Temne politics at this time was Bai Simera Kamal, of Masimera. A great warrior, a member of the Bangura clan, Koranko by origin, he had been invited to lead Masimera against Yonni Temne invaders of the

1850s and 1860s, who had a grudge against Masimera for not
allowing them access to Magbeli and other trading centres on
the Rokel. In 1856 chief Sori Mattot of Yonni sent his war-men
to raid Masimera. In May 1859 Yonni attacked (Temne)
Magbeli. These raids marked the beginning of a long period of
plundering on the Rokel, crippling its trade. Bai Simera's
headquarters were on the river Kapet, a tributary of the Rokel.
Tradition remembers him by his warrior's name, Yirandigi, as
a great sorcerer. Ambitiously he tried to appropriate Marampa
and Yonni chiefdoms to the north and south respectively. In this
he was unsuccessful. He then, in 1872, tried to raise all Temne
Rokel against the colony, but again failed. A charismatic figure,
he led the debates in palavers with the colony, notably that of
1873 which failed to secure peace because the Masimera Temne
chiefs determined to settle their quarrel with the Yonni first. A
further attempt in 1876 failed, because the Yonni wanted to
attack Masimera, which they did the following year, routing
Bai Simera's army.

There were Loko in Koya, some led by Negbana Bureh
from Songo Town; others, led by Sori Kesebi, had settled in
Rotifunk in the early 1840s when expelled by the Temne. They
had originally gone to fight for the Caulkers in Bumpe (see
Chapter 3), but, allowed to stay, had invited two hundred Fula
traders to live amongst them. Naturally the Caulkers could not
control all these strangers properly, and both the Temne and
Mende felt they were dangerous rivals.

Koya had been pacified temporarily in 1880, through the
mediation of Alimami Sanusi Modu of Bullom (though
Foredugu was destroyed by the Yonni in 1881), but in 1880 the
Yonni, turning from Rokel, attacked Bumpe and Ribbi for the
first time. Rotifunk lay on the Bumpe, and neither the Yonni
nor the Mende liked the Loko and their Fula followers blocking the trade paths. In March 1883 Yonni and Mende both
raided Sori Kesebi's country. In 1884 Yonni plundered factories on the Ribbi.

Governor Arthur Havelock engaged Bai Simera to restore
peace, but he openly favoured the Yonni. All Temne disliked
colony influence in Temne country, as well as Loko and bun-

duka settlers in Rokel, Lahai Bundu, and Britain's growing
friendship with the Mende.

The Yonni Temne defeated

In March 1885 the Yonni again gathered to attack; in April
the Mende of Taiama sacked Yonnibana, and the Yonni retaliated. Defeated, they withdrew, concentrating on the Bumpe–
Ribbi front in July. In November they overran Upper Koya,
attacking the Loko there and invading British Koya and Lahai
Bundu's towns, where they were encouraged by Bai Simera
Kamal.

Richard ba Caulker, falling out with the Loko under Sori
Kesebe, planned to hire the Yonni to drive them out. By
March 1887 there were rumours that Yonni warriors were
moving towards the colony frontier. In September a combined
force of Yonni, Masimera, Marampa, Ro-Mende and Koya
attacked and severely defeated the Kpa Mende who were
blocking their trade route via Senehun. They fled to British
Koya for protection, but soon began to collect forces for revenge.
The British expedition against Yonni ended all final resistance
by December 1887, and Treaty No 106 of 1889 at last established peace. The expedition marked a new era in British relations with what was soon to become the protectorate. British/
Mende friendship was cemented and Yonni country was now
considered British by conquest, though no legal alteration was
made in its status until the protectorate was proclaimed in 1896.

Muslim influence in Freetown

In 1788, Lieutenant John Matthews, of the Liverpool Company,
testifying before a committee of the privy council enquiring into
trade on the coast, said the Mandingoes were so well informed
that they had news of the defeat of the Spaniards at Gibraltar
only forty days afterward, before any European knew of it.[33]
He wrote later that he never visited any town in the vicinity of
the peninsula 'where I did not find a Mandinka man as prime
minister, by the name of bookman, without whose advice nothing
was transacted'.[34] On the Banana Islands in 1795, Adam Afzelius,
meticulously collecting material for a proposed flora of Sierra

Leone, was actually given a Mandinka name for a specimen, and he met there four Mandingoes, traders who made regular, if short visits, attracted no doubt by the busy slaving and ships'

Map 4

victualling depot, Bailly's Port. A few weeks later, he heard that the Susu ruler of Wongapong had sent his son to Freetown to settle as a trader. The Fula king sent embassies from Timbo to Freetown; Dr Winterbottom treated one plenipotentiary for elephantiasis.[35] Soon Fula caravans began coming down to Freetown, a few Mandinka and Fula staying as brokers for their countrymen. Others settled as contractors supplying meat or as craftsmen—blacksmiths and leatherworkers. Even today Mandinka and Fula can be found in these occupations. They lived together on the rising ground known now as Fula Town.[36]

Edward Blyden (1832–1912), the West Indian who identified himself passionately with the whole negro race and spoke as an African, wished to ensure the survival of traditional culture, rejecting suggestions that Africans should assimilate to the institutions and values of western Christian civilisation. He rightly saw 'the great Mandingo and Foulah tribes who are Mohammedans' as 'the principal rulers of central Africa, extending their influence nearly across the continent. They have schools and mosques in all their towns, and administer their government according to written law.' He looked on them as developing a 'national and social order . . . growing up gradually and normally to take their place in the great family of nations.'[37]

In the wider context he was right. Many white people, including Lugard a few years later, shared Blyden's fascination for an administration easily understood by Europeans and similar to the ecclesiastically dominated courts of medieval Europe. But if Blyden had stopped to look at the Freetown mosques, he would have been appalled at their pettiness, seemingly generated by the alien society in which they unfortunately existed. 'The mosques,' writes a modern scholar,[38] 'which might have been established as symbols of Islamic Unity, have in practice become tribal strongholds . . . The mosques then coexist in the city with tribal institutions such as the office of Headman.' Indeed, soon after the Fula Town mosque was established in the 1830s the Yoruba recaptive (or *Aku*) Muslims gained control of the district and have kept it until modern times.[39] The longstanding dispute between the Tamba and the Jamaat factions persists still.

In the nineteenth century Christian missionaries tended to see everything un-Christian as 'uncivilised', and when it came to Islam they were not above the sin of professional jealousy too. In June 1839 the Church Missionary Society petitioned the government to stop Muslim missionaries working amongst the recaptives. Devout Christians were repelled by the mori men's use of magic. The governor, Colonel Richard Doherty, strongly prejudiced against Muslims, seems to have connived in the destruction of the Fula mosque 'through a mistake of some officers of the police', as it was reported. One result of this persecution was that many of the emigrants from Freetown to Nigeria in the 1840s were Muslim.

Happily, future governors exercised greater tolerance, though visible results of this liberalism are not very evident until towards the end of the century. Descendants of Muslim recaptives, however, called themselves Muslim Creoles, being held equivalent in all ways to Christian ones. People changed their religion easily, Christian and Muslim Creole families frequently intermarrying. In 1848 there were some 2,000 Muslims in Freetown: Mandinka, Susu, Fula and Aku (ie Yoruba); many were only recent converts, perhaps second generation, the result of *jihads* in northern Nigeria or Futa Jallon. From 1840 to 1870 Muslim Creoles applied themselves to perfecting their understanding of Islam. A typical Muslim Creole was the government interpreter, Mohammed Sanusi. An Aku, educated in Futa Jallon he was also a collector of West African Islamic manuscripts. Literate in both Arabic and English, Muslim Creoles sought the same benefits as Christian ones. Christian and Muslim unity was hastened by a greater immigration of the neighbouring animist population; by an increasing government preference for the latter, and a growing antipathy to Creoles in general. In 1883 Christians contributed to the building costs of the Mountain Cut mosque, Fula Town.[40] By 1890 there were twenty small Koranic schools in Freetown, and little sign of hostility between Creole Muslims and Christians. In 1889 a huge joint meeting of Christians and Muslims was held at the Methodist high school; attended by several thousand and addressed by leaders of both religious denominations, it discussed their joint interests. Unity was strengthened and given corporate existence when the government revived the Freetown municipality and Creoles could stand for office. In 1891, Governor Sir James Hay handed over Pratt's Farm and buildings at Fourah Bay for the education of Muslim youth, with a grant to pay the teachers. Under Acting Governor Matthew Nathan's auspices, the Fula Town Muslims, in 1899, opened an elementary school where English and Arabic was taught.

Sir Charles King Harman, who became governor in 1900, established a permanent department of Mohammedan education, to bring Muslims under western influence without affecting their religion, in order to avoid the error committed by Indian Muslims who, boycotting government schools, had deprived themselves of the education which alone was acceptable for government employment. By 1911 five Muslim schools received government support.[41]

None the less, Muslim disabilities were many. In 1903 they petitioned to have their marriage, and thus their inheritance laws, recognised. Abdallah Quilliam, a Turkish Muslim plenipotentiary, visiting Freetown, wrote in 1903:

> At the present time within the Colony of Sierra Leone there are three distinct classes of individuals: 1. Pagan races. 2. Muslims. 3. Professing Christians. As the law now stands the law courts of the Colony practically bastardise and disinherit the first two classes, who form more than 95 per cent of the total population of the area . . .[42]

Yet Islam has proved the more attractive of the alien religions; the 1911 census gave 3,154 less Christians than in 1901. That tendency continued; today 75 per cent of Sierra Leone are Muslim, or nominally so.

Northern Slavers in the South

Groups of Susu had settled south of Port Loko, at Rokel and Magbeli, towns founded on the Rokel by Temne from Marampa. By 1821, as Lieutenant Laing noticed, they and the Bai Koblo of Marampa were controlled by 'two clever Mandingoes, named Tiakade Nodoo and Fatima Brima'. These were Susu,[43] representatives of the Alikali of Port Loko, maintaining their rule with bands of armed relatives.

In the eighteenth century the trading networks of the rivers Bumbe and Ribbi (south of the Freetown peninsula) were under Fula control. One hears of chiefs called 'Mandingo Mori', 'Salifu' and 'Mori Califa'. The latter came from Matacong, and lived for thirty years or more in Sherbro, sending slaves to his relatives in the north as, no doubt, did the others. He was chief of Baiama, under Charles Tucker. Lahai Senufu (Salifu) was chief of Mongeri.

The chief of Wongapong in the northern rivers area regularly bought slaves in Sherbro. When Consul Augustus Hansen seized a hundred on their way to the sea, the chief protested to the governor, asking permission to collect them and to have the path kept open for seven more years to allow him to acquire a sufficient number of slaves from Sherbro and Gallinhas to work his plantations properly. He was adjusting to the abolition of the trade but he needed time. He pointed out particularly that he was no longer buying slaves for resale to transatlantic dealers.[44] He was being scrupulously frank. Dr Winterbottom estimated that more than three-quarters of Futa Jallon's population were slaves. They often rebelled, and Winterbottom himself saw Susu and Fula armies besieging former slaves in Yangueakorie, in Bena Susu territory.

The Fula sometimes took Temne and Bullom girls as wives. Ambitious men found, like the Gola at this time in Liberia, that if they married 'Mandingo' women their wives acted as entrepreneurs to the nations in the north. Soon half Temne and Bullom Muslims were fomenting wars. Unrest enabled them to intervene and gain political power with their hired mercenaries. War was also good for slave-trading. They intervened in the Caulker wars, siding in the 1830s with Canre Ba Caulker in Sherbro, perhaps the main slave centre at the time. Thomas Stephen Caulker, the rival, was driven out, hated by all slavers because he had promised Freetown to outlaw the trade.[45]

They had, of course, already formed marriage alliances with branches of the Caulkers, as William George Caulker's own pedigree shows:

> I William Thomas George Caulker of Mambo in this Country, son of Tom Kogbah, the son of Adama, daughter of Ibrahim Kunsangfang, son of Foday Kirim Bath, the son of Nang Yombo, daughter of Abdullie the conqueror of Foyndoo, of the seed royal of Falabar who through conquest and intermarriage obtained that portion of the country above Tyama known by the name of Foyndoo, from whence my progenitors of that faith came to the Coast and courted the friendship of the Caulker family, by giving them in marriage my grandmother and several of her relatives to them . . .[46]

Caulker had had a mori man 'cook the war' for Shenge; that is, he had made 'medicine' for the attack—which incidentally failed, but not, it was ingeniously argued, because it had been defeated in Shenge town, which it had ravaged successfully, but because it had been beaten off from the blockaded mission buildings, for which the 'medicine' had not been made.[47]

What was known as the Bum and Kittam War, which disturbed Sherbro so terribly in the 1860s originated in Charles Tucker's wish, as landlord, to drive out Mori Califa who 'took war', as the saying was, down in search of slaves. Also Califa claimed the town of Kaw Mendi, though in fact it lay in the territory of Harry Tucker, chief of Shebar (Seabar, Sebar).

At Mamando in the rich Bum country, a Fula, Ibraima, alias Mori Wye, dealing in charms, had become very influential. His war-parties plundered Mamiaiah in 1876, looking for slaves.

During the 1880s Susu and Fula tried unsuccessfully to establish a monopoly in the canoe traffic (which transported the slaves amidst scenes of horror) on the river Sherbro. It was reported that at Mattru-Jong Lahsarihu, the Fula chief, was so powerful and his charms so respected that all chiefs looked to him for guidance and help. He called a Poro Society meeting, encouraging them to boycott Creole traders. The acting commandant at Bonthe, Melville Laborde, went up to investigate, handled things clumsily and a riot broke out, engineered, it was said, by Lahsarihu on purpose to test British reactions and strength. Governor Arthur Havelock with thirty armed police went down in a naval ship and captured Lahsarihu, in 1882, and put him in Freetown gaol.

In 1889 Governor Sir James Hay told the Colonial Office that he had freed eighty-three men, women and children, all with heavy chains round their necks, from a place called Fula Town, one and a half hours' trek from Rotifunk, 'inhabited by Mohammedans, the chief of the place being Alpha Abdulai'.[48]

Slaves were often sent from Senehun, across the river Bumpe, behind the colony—that is, through Koya, to the Bullom Shore, where they were shipped north, supervised all the way by Fula and Susu traders. Many travelled by way of Bashia, a Susu town in Temne country, and on to Futa. It was said in 1879 that in the months of August and September alone, 2,000 slaves had been sold openly in the market at Lungi, Bullom Shore. A dozen slave dealers could be found there at almost any time, the threatened war in the Port Loko area apparently causing chiefs to sell them slaves for safe-keeping.[49] Wherever business or politics provided an opportunity, the mori men were there. Even a young Creole trader sent up from Bonthe to open a factory in the adjacent rivers to the east, feeling too inexperienced, hired a mori man surreptitiously, to help him, for a fee of £50.[50]

Chiefs favour Mandingoes

Mandingoes had an important influence on the Sierra Leone ruling classes who if they did not change with the times were in danger of being replaced by these 'strangers'. Winterbottom wrote: 'Those who have been taught in their schools are succeeding to wealth and power in the neighbouring countries and carry with them a considerable porportion of their religion and laws.'[51] No wonder a Bullom chief in 1769 decided to send one of his sons to be educated in England and the other in Futa Jallon.[52]

Chiefs sought alliances with Futa Jallon, fascinated by its political and military power but, like the Susu and Koranko in the late eighteenth century, they sometimes rebelled, afraid of annihilation. All chiefs wanted trade, even that unscrupulously engendered by the Fula slavers. It has been suggested that 'the *Jihad* of Fula Djalon went even further than the invasion of the Manes towards creating throughout Sierra Leone and other sections of Upper Guinea a ruling class which was unified in interests and ideology'.[53] It does seem, too, that the extension of the holy war outside Fula Jallon coincided with what the English Royal African Company reported as a 'prodigious' trade in slaves.[54] There was no substitute the Fula could find which, from the seventeenth to the nineteenth centuries, would earn them the equivalent amount of European goods, or provide labour for their plantations, and they would not give it up. The religious aspect of the crusade had to be

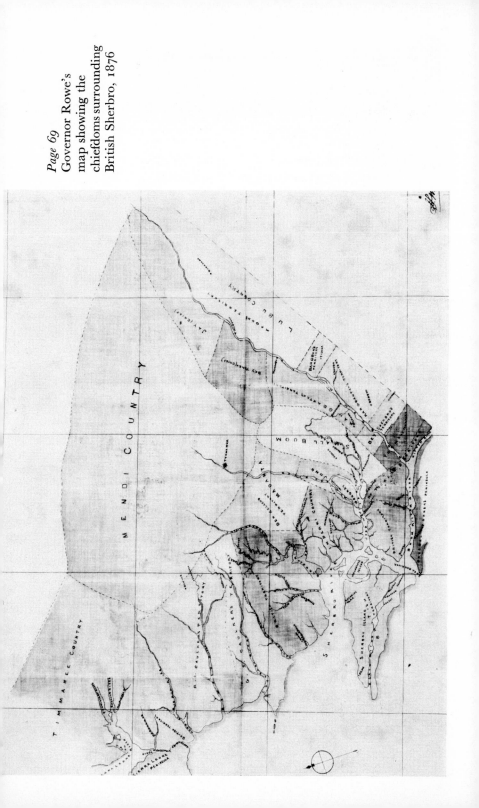

Page 69
Governor Rowe's
map showing the
chiefdoms surrounding
British Sherbro, 1876

Page 70
(*left*) Chief Kai Lundu of the Luawa chiefdom, Upper Mende;
(*below*) Chiefs Momo Jah and Momo Kai Kai of Pujehun and Bandajuma, Kittam

more or less abandoned in the context of the Atlantic slave trade and, later, in that of the political and economic struggle accompanying the establishment of legitimate commerce and the rise of new leaders. Bundukas and other northerners grew powerful. In 1808, when the abolition of the slave trade closed the colony peninsula, the Susu quickly organised alternative routes along the Upper Bargu and Rokel rivers and the Bullom Shore. Fula, settled in Freetown itself, acted as middlemen. Several were brought to trial there in 1853, on the evidence of an Arabic writer, Mamadou Yelli, a Fula who turned informer. The Fula chiefs tried desperately to lay their hands on him, even threatening to 'stop the paths' for seven years unless the government surrendered him, their rage a clue to the size of their profits.[55]

Changing role of the Diyula; the Sofa
After 1850 the passive role of the diyula in the north changed. Their towns were becoming populous, their firearms sophisticated and plentiful. Unwilling to be ruled by animist landlords, they sought the political control obtained earlier in a smaller way in southern chiefdoms of the forest. The best documented example is that of Samory Turé, but though he subjugated the Koranko, extended his powers steadily in Kissi, Kono and Limba countries, took Falaba and filled Port Loko with alarming rumours, his conquests were mostly outside what is Sierra Leone's frontier today. Even so, amidst terrible scenes of plunder and starvation in the 1880s, when professional warriors laid waste large areas of the Gallinhas, Bum, Kittam and Krim people, Chief Nyagbwah of Panguma, a Mende, sent for some of Samory's warriors. In May 1889 the Sofa captured his great enemy Makaia of Largo who, with another notorious warchief, Ndawa, held over 3,000 starving captives at Wende, their capital.[56]

Further north, in 1884, Alimami Bokhari, a Susu, whose rule was very harsh, asked Samory for help in making peace with his subjects, notably his nephew, the Alikali Quiah Fode Dowdah, who sought the Crown. (During the fighting warriors from Mouricariah overran most of the country between the

E

Scarcies and Mellacouri rivers.) Samory heard that these Tambacca Susu had been plundering his traders on their way to the coast and he determined to kill two birds with one stone, sending Alpha Allieu on a double mission, the objectives of which were probably incompatible: as a peacemaker, and as a chastiser of the caravan marauders. In mid 1885 he set up

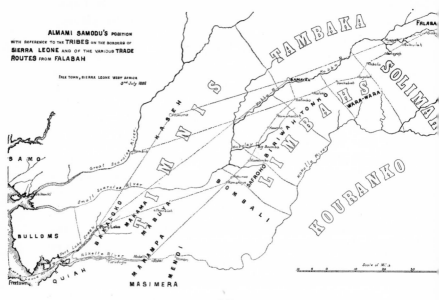

Map 5

headquarters in Samaia, the Tambacca capital on the Upper Small Scarcies. As he approached, the chief fled with most of the inhabitants and the Alpha had thus achieved one of his objectives.

Samory's forces ostensibly were engaged in keeping the road open to Falaba, via Samaia, to Kambia and Port Loko. Soon after their arrival at Samaia, all Limba country, save the double chiefdom of Safroko-Limba and that of Safroko-Bombali, joined them. Later in 1885 the Sofa gutted Falaba, at that time a big city covering 600 acres. Partly rebuilt, it was sacked again in 1889.[57]

As Sofa rule relaxed in the late 1880s, whilst Samory's attention was directed inland, his Limba subjects revolted, attacking

Fourecariah, a town where Alimami Dauda, a Sofa ally, had been left in charge. Dauda got help from the new Susu chief of Samaia, Karimu, who hoped to fill the vacuum left by the departing Sofa, at the expense of Dauda's Limba enemies and their Loko allies. In 1890 the Limba brought in Bai Bureh, the famous Temne war-chief, but in 1891 the British persuaded Loko and Limba to make peace, and the remnants of Karimu's forces were driven off by a small detachment of British police.[58]

When George Garrett, one of Freetown's two travelling commissioners, saw Falaba in 1890, bleached skeletons lay scattered far and wide, and amongst them, putrid corpses. He reported there was 'not a soul' left in Tambacca Susu country. Jusu Seri, the Limba chief of Musaia, told him of the fearful havoc committed by the Sofa in destroying every town in Sulima, save Kalieri, and in ravaging all northern Koranko territory as well as Sangara. He expected them daily, on their way to destroy Limba and Temne countries. Garrett found few Limba willing to venture beyond the village cultivated lands. In fact Samory's messenger soon came, demanding the surrender of Limba country. The commissioner met Kemo Billali, the leader, a man with 'an unfeeling, brutish look', who told him Samory had sent him to eat up Limba and Temne country and open a road to Port Loko.[59] It seems this was in revenge for attacks on Sofa traders going to Freetown, made after misleading news of their defeat by the French in April 1890, when Samory was mistakenly believed killed. All northern peoples had then set upon them, plundering, killing and selling them into slavery.

Other Sofa went south to the Upper Moa river, to help Kafura, a Kissi, in his war with Kai Lundu, founder of the Lundu chiefdom (Kailahun) on the Liberian frontier. These were dispersed by a British attack in 1899. Sofa, under Pokere, also tried to open a road to Freetown through Koranko and Kunike Temne country. Seeking plunder as usual, they joined Fore, a Kono chief, in his war against Vonjo, a Kunike Temne. Asked by the British to leave their sphere, Pokere occupied Tekuyema, a town on the Kono–Mende border, claimed by Nyagbweh of Panguma, the Mende war-chief.[60]

In 1892 the Sofa attacked Falaba again, defended by Manga

Sewa with headquarters in a house with walls eighteen inches thick, built by another Falaba hero, Konte Birama, over a hundred years before. Besieged and starving, Manga Sewa blew himself up rather than surrender, and Falaba fell once more to the Sofa. Refugees are said to have founded the Koinadugu chiefdom.[61]

Many in Freetown, including at times the governor, saw Samory as a potential ally against French expansion in the hinterland. Traders sold him munitions. Some people, like Edward Blyden, welcomed the spread of Islam, wanting it to advance under British protection. Samory, too, would have liked an alliance, but in 1893, fleeing from the French advance, some Sofa laid waste part of the British sphere, and were turned back by a British force at Bagbwema.

Three years later Lieutenant-Colonel James Trotter, surveying the Anglo-French boundary according to a delimitation agreed in Paris in 1895, found the Limba towns being rebuilt. The sole Koranko town reputed to have withstood the Sofa was Kurubundu; the huts having been built on a steep hill amongst huge granite boulders and surrounded by a warfence. Elsewhere the invaders had pillaged everything, carrying off livestock and enslaving every available person. As a consequence he found the Koranko down-trodden and timid, the more so since, when the Sofa left, the Kono, Sofa allies, had fallen on them. To a Koranko or Susu, Trotter said, 'the war' meant the Sofa and Kono invasions. Even so, no towns, save Kiridugu, Kurubundu and Baili had turned Muslim.[62] Today the population is still less dense in Koranko country than amongst its neighbours.

Islam and Colonial Diplomacy

Frequently better acquainted than other Africans with the white men, whom nevertheless they often despised as illiterat,e unhealthy and drunken, Muslims were quicker to make alliances. Both were traders and colonisers, and their interests coincided, first as slavers and then in legitimate trade. The Freetown settlement, engendering no internal trade of its own, increasingly depended on trade with the interior. Inland disturbances affected the Creoles as much as the 'Mandingo' traders. Freetown made continual efforts to found a regular trade with the Islamic states to the north. A factory called Freeport was set up in the Rio Pongo in 1795, in order to tap the hides, ivory, gum and other trade from Futa Jallon. In 1796 Governor Zachary Macaulay, returning from leave, brought recruits for a mission to convert the Fula, though they never got any further than Freetown. In that year Adam Afzelius, went up to Timbo with Thomas Winterbottom. At Wongapong they found a Freetown man, Tom London, already acting as factor to other Sierra Leone Company black traders with business there. The Fula, cut off from Cunia by Susu under Bubakr Sanko raiding their caravans (though they had secured a route giving them an outlet to the Rio Nunez), wanted the company to build a factory where they could trade at Kocundy, Rio Pongo, Kissy (Mellacourie) or Port Loko.

Miss Betsy Herd, as the settlement knew her, a Mulatto and partly Susu, chief of Bereira, was especially friendly with Freetown, visiting it regularly. This, however, did not prevent her calling on the slave factory at Bunce Island. The settlement owed her a debt of gratitude when in 1802 she helped Governor William Dawes persuade the Mandinka and Susu chiefs to stop supporting the settlement's neighbour, King Tom, who had unsuccessfully attacked Freetown the year before. Defeated, he had fled north[63] to Mori Kanu, Bullom chief of Morebaiah. A few years later, Dala Modu, not yet in disgrace with the settlement for his slave-trading, drove Mori Kanu out. Commerce governed politics; Temne and Muslim Fula and Susu rulers would no more surrender the Freetown market to interlopers than King Tom would forfeit his customary tolls without a fight.

In 1816 a British expedition struggled through to Segu. As an indirect result Alimami Abdullah of Futa Jallon approached the governor in Freetown to settle the quarrel between Alimami Amaru of Timbo and others whose wars were closing the trade routes to Sierra Leone. The wars in the north continued, however, and another expedition, under Lieutenant Gordon Laing was despatched in 1822, via Port Loko and Timbo. Laing was astounded to see such quantities of gold. Soon the Sulima Susu and the Fula began to bring it down to Freetown. In 1843, William C. Thompson, the CMS translator and linguist, was hired by Freetown merchants to represent them in Timbo. He was cordially received, living there almost a year.

In 1826 a British treaty with the Sumbuya Susu ended a twelve-year war with the 'Mandingoes'. In 1845 a network of treaties with chiefs ruling the land around the Scarcies were concluded, in the hopes of establishing peace for trading. In 1847 others were signed at Fourecariah and Dubreka. Between 1850 and 1852 a series of treaties finally secured the northern rivers area as a British sphere.

Winwood Reade stayed a month in Falaba in 1869, to be followed in 1872 by Edward Blyden sent to open up the country to commerce. The following year Blyden visited Timbo. According to Blyden, the greatest pagan chief and the greatest Muslim on this side of the Niger were brought to friendship at last, both receiving government stipends, though payments lapsed almost at once. Government hopes of trade, however, were distorted by optimistic assessments of the population of West Africa, as Dr Valesius Gouldesbury, administrator of the Gambia, pointed out after his visit to Timbo in 1881.

Port Loko was the centre of the trading network fed by its innumerable creeks, and the British quickly concentrated their political influence there, acquiring nominal sovereignty in 1825. Soon the Alikali was drawing a stipend of 600 bars, bigger than any other chief (a stipend being calculated at 5 per cent of anticipated trade from, or through the chiefdom). Disturbances there, apart from their proximity, were a worry, since they closed a vital route to the hinterland. In 1825 Alimami Dala Modu was sent as the colony's plenipotentiary to settle the disputed Port Loko chiefly election, when Fatma Brimah Kamara was installed.

The British thought they understood these literate, sophisticated Muslim traders better than the indigenous farmer and warrior. If possible they used them as agents of British policy. In 1836 Dala Modu was formally recognised by the governor as regent of Loko Masama which, conveniently for the colony, covered most of the flat and fertile Bullom Shore across the river from Freetown.[64] The following year he was nominated by Governor Campbell to look after the interests of the Loko on the Rokel but was soundly beaten and scattered by the Temne.[65] In the 1850s Kala Modu, of Kaffu Bullom and head of that family, was discovered by the British to be permitting the slave trade in his territories. Governor Kennedy merely summoned him to Freetown for a severe lecture, writing home that he was 'refactory'.[66] Non-Muslims committing the same offence, and Muslims of lesser influence, could expect harsher treatment. British infatuation with power persisted; Governor Kortright a quarter of a century or so later, wrote home ecstatically: 'The chiefs of the Northern Rivers are more intelligent, more powerful, and wealthier than those of Sherbro, and much wealthier than the Timnanee chiefs.'[67]

In the 1830s, Mohammedu Bundu of Foredugu had been as anxious as the British to keep the warlike Kpa Mende out of Koya. In 1841 the colony sent representatives of the Mohammedu Bundu and the Ala Dala Modu families to discuss the cession of parts of Koya. Mohammedu Bundu was entrusted, too, with the task of keeping the colony's trade routes open between Foredugu and Waterloo, on the eastern edge of the colony. From the 1840s to the 1870s Alimami Sanusi Modu, Dala Modu's nephew, was used by the Freetown government as a peacemaker.

In the troubled Koya of the 1860s and 1870s, the region with the most effective government was Foredugu, under its ruler Lahai Bundu. Since Foredugu was situated on the British frontier, the British relied heavily on Lahai Bundu keeping the peace there. As we have seen, it was the growing influence of this family that led to the Temne attack in 1879, and to a military expedition from Freetown to insure his security. When Bai Kanta of Koya died soon after part of it had been retroceded to the Temne in 1872, no successor was appointed. The two queens of Koyah, Bome Rufa, and Bome Warrah were unable to keep order. In particular Gbana Seri of Magbeni, one of their sub-chiefs, did as he liked until Governor Rowe chased him back north, having, as usual, relied on Lahai

Bundu's assistance. Now that he was strong again, Lahai turned against British interests. Taking advantage of the fact that he had already a war-party in Koyah, he sent it under his brother, Suri Bundu, and nephew, Momoh Bundu, to inspect certain cassada farms whence Governor Rowe had driven Gbana Seri in the recent troubles. Saying it was his land, Lahai Bundu pretended to believe those found harvesting the cassada were Gbana Seri's people and he enslaved them. Bokhari Bombali, a sub-chief and later chief of Koya (and notoriously independent) naturally objected, but Lahai Bundu ordered his warriors to chastise Bokhari Bombali, Gbana Seri and all his friends. The war spilled over into British Koya and, whilst no towns were burnt, several, including Mashenk, were plundered. Police had to be sent into the area before order was restored. None the less, in 1884 Governor Havelock used Lahai Bundu to warn the Yonni Temne of the likely consequences of their raiding the Bumpe and Ribbi regions—whence the centre of trade, thanks to the prolonged unrest along the Rokel, had shifted, and with it, British interests.[68]

That year, Temne resentment at bunduka power on those two rivers led Bai Simera, chief of Masimera, to accuse them of being the cause of war there in the hopes of discrediting them in Freetown. He was unsuccessful, the governor replying he did not believe it.[69]

Creole traders knew the hinterland well, many were hosts to chiefs visiting Freetown. They did not approve of using 'Mandingoes' as government messengers, knowing that chiefs were often surprised at the governor being represented by men others regarded with suspicion, often as people with 'no distinct country', of inferior status and not above buying slaves even when representing the governor—and thus Queen Victoria. Often their use as messengers was considered by the chief concerned as an insult.[70]

By now the rulers of the tidal waterways, rich from tolls and rents, their people short of land as more and more up-country immigrants arrived, fought almost incessantly. Wars raged along the Mellacourie and Scarcies rivers in the north, the Port Loko creek, the Rokel, Ribi, Bumpe, Jong and Bum, and in the Gallinhas.

Political instability made chiefs look for some permanent body of men for protection. The bundukas had prospered and raided in earlier days with hired professional warriors, strangers to the district and therefore more brutal. Chiefs on the estuaries, the Mende seeking access to these termini, and traders with political ambitions, all began to hire warriors. Once the concern of every fit male, war was relegated to professionals trained to use modern weapons. Often they were utterly lawless and the chiefs were powerless to control them. Being professional fighters, they were not interested in peace. War had become almost an end in itself. Sofa and Mende war-chiefs plundered mercilessly.

The colony wanted a stake in the expanding trade. They set up paper protectorates over some of the biggest centres, paying stipends to nearby chiefs to keep trade open. Then, in 1882, the French and British came to an arrangement over the division of the Mellacourie region (though it was not theirs). In 1886 the Anglo-Liberian agreement for that frontier was signed. Four years later George Garrett told Samory the road between Falaba and Port Loko 'belonged' to the British. He even hoisted the Union Jack at Farana and Falaba, taking formal possession of Sangara and Sulima country. Though the Foreign Office disowned the Farana ceremony, it was not out of scruples for African rights of sovereignty, but through unwillingness to seem to countenance Samory's repudiation of a French treaty, in case of setting a precedent which France could turn against Britain just as easily in the scramble. In 1896 the Anglo-French agreement settled further spheres of influence. This left Britain with an implied hinterland which she soon proceeded to 'pacify'. Warriors and Muslim traders alike were eclipsed.

The South: The Mende and the Afro-Europeans

The Mende Wars

The only people at present inhabiting Sierra Leone, of whom no mention is heard before about 1800, are the Mende, yet today they are one of the largest groups in the country.

Related to, if not the overlords of, the Mani who had stopped behind in Manow to the north of Liberia, the nuclear area of the Mende seems to have been east of the river Jong. Northcote Thomas, the first government anthropologist, believed the Mende were descended from those Mani who had completely driven out the original inhabitants, or had at least completely dominated them, whereas the Loko and Temne, he rightly felt, had been only partially subjugated. He suggested the Mende were of Toma or Gbande origin.[1]

This duality is frequently stressed. A Mende-speaking missionary before World War II remarked on the two tonal groups of nouns in the language, and on the mixture of very short and of medium-statured people found in their country. He noticed that as one moved westward, the language changed, as indeed did the Mende, a fact they recognised themselves, calling those living in the west Kpa Mende. *Kpa* meaning 'the different country'.[2]

A modern Mende[3] has pointed out that the genealogy of ruling houses cannot be traced back more than three or four generations before the Europeans came into the protectorate. This suggests that Mende state formation did not begin until the late eighteenth century, hastened by northern invasions of

Mande-speaking ruling stock,[4] the slave trade which bred war, population increases, and the need for political and military alliances.

The usual way settlements develop in West Africa is by villages breaking away from the original site, and gradually extending the agricultural area. The Mende were no exception, and in this way clans—ie heads of sections—settled an increasingly large area. Such was the Macavore clan in Tikonko, or the Kailundu family of chiefs in Kailahun, Lauwa chiefdom.

Normally, as settlement increased, the new foundations created rivalry for land. This could be dealt with either by abandoning the system of fragmentation and developing instead settlements much larger than normal, or by taking land forcibly from unwelcome neighbours thus acquiring satellite villages and farms by conquest. Both would lead to inter-village warfare, since the first would mean increasing land hunger and therefore strife, and the second implied war anyway; war of a more demanding nature and requiring larger political and military units. Conquered villages would be enslaved and the population used to garrison their own villages against other attackers. The need to defend and to feed these slaves would make the village even larger and the land-hunger worse still.

Like the Zulu and Yoruba chiefs, Mende rulers soon found that outstanding warriors had become paramount. There is, however, a Koroma family of chiefs of the Peje district. This name is one of four under which the Mande-speaking traders are known,[5] and they came from Koranko country, but have a common tradition of an earlier home south-west of Kayes on the river Senegal. Although less frequently acceptable, there was, therefore, an alternative to the chieftaincy other than the military one. Many local stories refer to ancestors coming from *Koh*; that is: up country, ie from the north.

It has been said that the extensive tracts of worn-out soil found in Sierra Leone today—often bearing *Lophira elata* and little else—are not due, as agricultural officers in protectorate days liked to say, to mismanagement, but to pressure when the overpopulated village settlements were kept up only by slave labour made to farm the dangerous periphery. Later, in the very disturbed days from the mid-nineteenth century onwards, anarchy itself, once it became part of the soil pattern, was self-perpetuating even without these economic factors.[6]

In the later part of the nineteenth century British and French expansion was an additional and abrasive element in politics. In the north professional marauders, uprooted by European military action, were employed by ambitious rulers. Some had their headquarters at Tambi, on the headwaters of the Small Scarcies, where they were hired by the Susu Karimu of Moria against the Limba. When the British took Tambi in 1892 they fled south-west to Yanya, situated north-west of Bumban. Here they attacked Katimbana, a town belonging to the brother of Chief Suluku of Bumban. The following year, from Kadansu, joined by Temne and Mende mercenaries, they harassed the Port Loko chiefdoms and, allied to Chief Sukuyumbu of Bonkabo Limba, made sorties against Alimami Suma of Bafodia and the Koranko. Large numbers of Sofa, driven across the Niger by the French, conquered Sulima and Koranko countries by 1884. Two years later they took part of Biriwa Limba. Subsequently, often accompanied by Kono and southern Koranko, they ravaged the Liberian frontier, correctly opining that they were beyond reach of British or French reprisal. They also went as far south as Kuniki Temne country, filling the area with Susu slave dealers. Established in four stockaded towns, Robiss, Rosarl, Matassia and Mafori Benni, hiring themselves out as mercenaries in a war arising from a quarrel amongst allies after the British expedition to Yonni, they set upon Chief Vonjo, a Kuniki Temne, and upon his relative by marriage, Nyagwa of Banguma. They failed to penetrate Mende country in any strength at that time, partly because the Kuniki declined to join them, and partly because Mende chiefs, officially 'protected' by British treaties but despairing of assistance, decided to make allies of the Sofa. Moreover, Chief Nyagwa sent war-parties into Kono and Koranko towns where the French were believed to encourage his sorties against the Sofa. In 1892 Sofa were hired by the Gola chiefs in their Mende war. By now the Mende held the British in very low esteem, feeling that all they wanted was their money. It was well known that an agent of the Sierra Leone Coaling Company had crossed the Niger, bringing Samory 400 rifles. Sofa were to be seen buying muskets in Freetown, yet in 1891 Governor Hay had ordered all Mende stockades to be destroyed. The Mende were demoralised and petty wars flourished among them. In places none dared work their farms for fear of Sofa attacks; a principal reason for the British expedition against the Sofa in 1893 was to restore a waning prestige.

War towns had become the dominant feature of the landscape, Mende villages being especially well stockaded, with eight or nine fences, called *goleisia*, while the Temne relied for protection largely on the high bush left standing round the village. Alliances for defence may have helped the process of state formation but, at least until almost the end of the nineteenth century, it would be wrong to think of the Mende as a state or a 'people' acting as a unit.

Mende country lay at the head of the rivers Bagru, Bumpe, Jong and Bum. A line of towns, Taiama, Bumpe, Tikonko, Largo, Wende, Bandajuma and Badasuma, marked their limits, although in about 1860 the frontier began to be pushed southwards. By 1870, when the Sierra Leone government intervened in the Caulker succession, it was evident the Mende, under Chief Gbanya (who settled in Senehun), and other warrior chiefs, were unquestionably stronger than their nominal landlords.

Disturbances in Mende country upset trade and politics on the coast. They were pleased to trade with Europeans—no doubt as land-hunger increased they were glad to acquire machetes, salt, tobacco and powder for their wars.

In their first clashes with the Bullom and Temne, Mende traders are said to have been the injured party, several having been kidnapped while on their way to the coast.[7] In 1825 there were disturbances where a group of Mende stockaded themselves in Peypurra, an island in the river Jong. The Sherbro chiefs led by the Caulkers, carefully mustered forces for a counter-attack, knowing the enemy had fortified it with a view to making a stand during the rains, instead of returning home, as was usual at that season.

The Bullom forces, apparently over-confident, failed to take the stockades, and the town in their rear, on whom they depended, turned on them. Several hundred were killed or enslaved by the Mende who also seized most of the Gallinhas paths and extended them far into the interior. That war, too, was said to have arisen when Mende traders frequenting the Gallinhas markets had been molested.

Mende leaders wanted outlets at the waterside where they could buy salt, tobacco and rum, items so important in the payment of mercenaries. Trade itself was not as vital as the ability to obtain the sinews of war and to prevent them reaching one's enemy. Temne and Bullom resisted the Mende invaders, the Caulker chiefs in Sherbro[8] entering into a treaty with Governor Turner, hoping for British assistance in stemming the perpetual raids on Tasso. Nevertheless, Mende warriors seized parts of Sherbro,[9] and various Caulker factions continued to hire them to do their fighting. The trouble was, they often refused to leave afterwards.

Northern Muslims had become very influential on the Jong, where they controlled Mongeri and Baiama in the Bagru, and the banks along the Bum at Waiima, Momando, Kaw Mende and Lavannah. Some came as warriors, like Brima Fula, ancestor of the Kai Kai family in Pujehun. They dominated the Jong/Small Bum area from the 1840s. In 1852 a war was instigated by Ibibu Salifu, styling himself chief of the Jong river, and Mori Calipha, chief of Baiama on the Small Bum, who took war down into the Bum Kittam country, even claiming the town of Kaw Mende on the Jong, which in fact belonged to Harry Tucker, chief of Sebar, whose territory ran from Mattru on the Kittam to Sebar.[10] Mori Calipha was thus only the Tuckers' 'stranger', though he had lived there thirty-one years, shipping slaves north to his relatives in Matacong. He also traded directly with Freetown, and the British now sent him back to Matacong, though the considerable slave trade from Mende country to the Scarcies continued.

The rise of Tom Kebbi Smith at Gambia threatened this northern monopoly. Originally a Bullom labourer employed by missionaries at Kaw Mende, he had begun to trade along the Bum; prospering, he fortified his town and became a chief. In the 1870s his conflicts with Lahai Goray of Bairama, and Lahai Serifu of Mongeri upset the whole countryside. Tom Kebbi had help from Chief Cannah Gboh of Talliah (see p 95 below), and from the Imperri chiefs who disliked the way the Muslims were encroaching. Mongeri drew in a Mende warrior, Chief Gberri of Gbongeh, who wanted a route to the waterside himself.

Following a temporary lull after Freetown's mediation in 1879 and 1880, fighting continued for most of the decade. The main antagonists were Chief Gberri and a fellow Mende, Chief Seppeh of Yengema (Bumpe). Their towns were only ten miles apart, and land competition exacerbated relations. Chief Gberri brought in the Lower Bum rulers, and Tikonko. Chief Seppeh allied with the Bumpe chiefs, those of Imperri, and with Chief Gboh of Talliah, near the Small Bum, the most powerful chief since the death of Tom Kebbi Smith in 1878.

Other Mende fought to control the paths between Rokon in Temne country, and Mende territory. In the 1820s, when Gumbu Smart, a Loko chief in Rokon, fought with his Temne overlord, Bai Simera, over timber profits, Mende came to help him. Freetown negotiated a peace in 1831, though it did not last long. In the 1830s Mende warriors, helped by T. S. Caulker of the Plantains and Shenge, invaded Temne country on several occasions.

En Kerri, Temne chief of Foindu in Yonni, who had expelled the rightful ruler, Fenda Modu of Yonni, for opposing his schemes, was one of the earliest professional warriors, a calling becoming increasingly attractive to young men with the right talents, as warfare spread. Momodu Bundu, raising a Temne force, drove him into exile in Mende territory, where offering his professional services, he was killed in 1838 in the war between the Mende and Bai Kurr of Mabang.

In 1840 Momodu Bundu, the principal chief on the Rokel, beat off Mende attacks further away in the south-east.

Many disturbances were only petty wars—known as 'ambush wars' at the time—but, being almost perpetual, they were aggravating. Thus, in 1860, a party of Koya (Temne) chiefs going to mediate in the timber disputes, suffered an insult, so they said, at Magbele. Incited by those chiefs, a party of Yonni and Mabanta Temne, with Mende allies, raided Magbele. In 1861 the Mende helped the British against the Temne when the latter attacked the town of Chief Songo, alias Kegbana Bure, a Loko living in Koya—territory ceded that year to the British. In retaliation Temne and Bullom forces raided the Mende lying behind the river Ribbi. In return, the Taiama Mende swept into British Koya and, since Mende were British allies, the governor did nothing; thus Colonel Stephen Hill's annexation of British Koya, intended to secure the colony's frontier, involved it instead in further wars. In 1872 the country was retroceded to the Temne and fell into anarchy, the Yonni Temne raiding it almost annually from 1875. In 1886, led by the warrior chiefs Kondo, Kallowa and Kango, they invaded Bumpe and destroyed Senehum, on the river Bumpe, seat of the great Mende ruler, Gbanya (originally from Taiama), from whom the British usually hired their mercenaries. This attack brought about the 1887 expedition, under Colonel Sir Francis de Winton, against the Yonni Temne.[11]

These Mende were now the Temne's almost traditional enemy, but in 1889 Madam Yoko, Gbanya's widow, persuaded eight leading Kpa Mende to sign a peace with twenty-seven Temne chiefs at Romess.[12] For many years Madam Yoko headed a powerful Kpa Mende confederacy which had developed under her husband in defence against the Temne and others. She consolidated her inheritance and the British, fearing it could become a centre of Mende nationalism, took care to break it up after her death.

In 1880, Kittim country, said to be the only district so far not threatened by Mende, was plundered by Ndawa who was noted for his cruelty. Hired by Krim chiefs to help them fend off threats from the interior, he had stayed on plundering caravans, his excuse being that the Kittim chiefs had not paid his warriors.[13]

Bumpe and Tikonko Mende were the greatest rivals, frequently at war with one another until about 1890. Both

Page 87 (*above*) Digging for diamonds; (*below*) boats bringing
country produce to King Jimmy Market, Freetown

fomented wars in the lower reaches of the river, joining either
side indiscriminately for plunder.

Mende tactics began to change. They seldom raided southward now on their own; only when called in by the local chief.[14]
The Bullom still kept them away from the coast, and so the
Taiama Mende traded at Senehun and the Tikonko at Mafwe,
the highest navigable point on the Bum. Governor Samuel
Rowe drew parallels between the relationship of the Mende and
Bullom, and that of the Marabouts and Soninke in the Gambia,
the Fante and Asante in the Gold Coast, and the Lagos villages
and the Egba in Nigeria.[15]

It would be wrong, however, to see these wars simply in
terms of trade or access to the coast and European goods. In
fact Mende often moved peacefully into Bullom villages,
gradually coming to outnumber the chief's own subjects, elect-
ing their own headman and turning them into Mende villages.
The commandant at Bonthe was swamped by Mende asking for
work; by the second half of the century their language had
ousted Sherbro there. John Harris, a Jewish tailor from Chatham
who established himself about 1850 near York Island, said
Mende migration to the coast had occurred largely since he had
arrived. By 1861 immigrants from the interior looking for work
had reduced the labourers' daily wage from tenpence to sixpence.[16]

Effects of 'Legitimate' Trade

Chiefs complained that British traders undermined what influence they still had over their subjects.[17] Rulers once had a
monopoly of European or American goods; now they were so
cheap they were within reach of all, especially as wages could
be earned in Bonthe or Freetown by labourers, or as allies of
the British in war time. Formerly, the salt trade had been paramount and by it chiefs had got slaves and mercenaries very
cheaply. Now foreign traders imported salt, selling it cheaply
and directly to the interior where chiefs were no longer willing
to part with slaves to get it. Slaves cost three times as much as
a few years before.

Legitimate trade thus took both power and profit from the

F

chiefs' hands. If one wanted slaves to exchange for European goods, one had to catch them oneself. To prevent arms reaching one's enemies, it was necessary to control the trade routes so as to be able to blockade them. Chiefs did not like the way Creole traders sold supplies to their enemies. Though trade was largely a political matter, it did, however, offer older men an outlet for employing wealth gained in earlier warfare, an additional reason for opposing Creole merchants.

Dislike of Sierra Leone traders (and this included Creole ones) led chiefs to put a Poro (ie an interdict commanded by the Poro society) on their factories and rouse their people against them, saying the traders had sold their country to the British. The Bai Sherbro visiting Freetown from Mambolo in May 1892, wrote to a newspaper, complaining of the 'many mischievous Creoles from Sierra Leone who are disgracing themselves in my territory by their mode of life and by mixing in native customs and manners and in conniving in shady dealings'.[18]

A combination of poor harvests and cheap gin (part of a world trade recession) selling at five shillings a case could have fatal consequences if chiefs seized their people's rice to exchange for the firewater. In the late 1880s, to avoid starvation, oppressed villagers raided their neighbours.[19]

About 1860 there may have been a population increase; or perhaps several population shifts, as refugees fled the wars; at any rate in the late seventies more and more Africans flocked to Freetown seeking food and work; farmers in the colony villages could not manage without their accustomed labour. Temne, Limba and Loko began to replace recaptives in menial jobs, causing resentment in Freetown where the newcomers overcrowded the labour market. In Wellington they were driven out and their houses demolished. Doubtless retaliation was taken against Sierra Leone traders up country. Looking for work, Mende crowded into Bonthe. Chiefs complained that many immigrants given sanctuary by the British were their slaves, whose freedom was thus sanctioned at their expense. Others, they said, were even their wives, seeking shelter from a legal union.[20]

Ineffectual Colony Policy

Government vacillations, frequent changes of governors, and even astounding ignorance, must take its share of the blame for the increasing unrest. Imperri, the fertile land between the Mano and the Jong districts, ceded in 1825, was left untended until 1890. Governor Samuel Rowe had to remind the secretary of state in 1879 that the treaty had never been wholly enforced —though it had never been publicly repudiated either.[21]

By custom, neutral local chiefs, powerful enough for their Poro to be respected by all, were called in to settle wars. An example is Mendegrah who was requested to help pacify the Gallinhas hinterland after Freetown had removed chiefs Makaia and Bokhari Gomna in 1889. Chiefs began to look to the colony to do the same, some keeping Creole secretaries to interpret correspondence, and sending customary presents of leopard skins and ivory.

The colony, however, did not always behave scrupulously, sometimes using its prestige for its own ends. Adjudicating chiefs, too, enlisted help against rivals or rebels.

A landlord's standing could be enhanced by the presence of important 'strangers' on his land. Several chiefs had permitted mission stations with this in view.

Besides success in trade and war, there was now a third method of achieving eminence: that of friendly relations with Freetown. Betsy Gay owed her crown as queen of the Jong in the 1880s to colony influence rather than hereditary right. It was probably only colony support, intervening in 1875 and 1878, which kept George Stephen Caulker in Shenge, and in 1887, Neale Caulker in authority. Queen Nyaro of Bandasuma, on the Moa, was given Rowe's special protection under the 1885 pacification at Lavannah, her town being declared neutral territory. Madam Yata, sister of Prince Mannah, was granted official recognition in 1890, as being in charge of the Massaquoi dominions. Madam Yoko emerged supremely powerful from the 1887 Yonni expedition after the British deported Chief Kamanda of Bauya, her rival. Nancy Tucker, a trader from Kittam, was installed by a sergeant of the Frontier Force in 1897 as a successor to Rowe's deceased ally, Humper Rango, in Sembehun; Rango having helped drive off John Caulker's Mende allies when they were attacking George Stephen in 1875. Madam Tucker had no connection, bar trade, with the Bagru, but the government recognised her and indeed enlarged her chiefdom as a reward for loyalty in the 1898 rising.

Traditional chiefs complained that Freetown and the Creole traders respected only warrior chiefs, often strangers, who, by their fighting, 'spoiled the country'. In the late 1870s and early 1880s, Chief Gberi of Gbongeh was in conflict with Bumpe, and especially with Chief Sekeh Seppeh of Yengema. Gberi was willing to have Freetown arbitrate, and this impressed the government who thereafter tended to take his side. In 1882, when Seppeh's ally, Cannah Gboh of Talliah, attacked a government launch carrying police pay, the government retaliated by using Gberi's warriors to do most of the fighting. This permitted him to prosecute his old feud.

Thus, though formal rule was foresworn, Freetown came increasingly to use force, not mediation—particularly from the time of Governor Samuel Rowe's appointment in the mid 1870s, and especially in the Sherbro where commercial fortunes were being made. Rowe called it 'prompt interference', considering it a virtue.

At times the colony developed quite close relationships, especially with the Kpa Mende rulers at Senehun (Chief Gbanya and later his widow, Madam Yoko), with Macavore at Tikonko, and Momo Kai Kai and Momo Ja at Pujehun. In 1861 Freetown recruited Gbanya's warriors to fight the Koya Temnes and in 1873 to join the Asante expedition. Madam Yoko, in return, was supported against the Temne in 1887 and 1889, and Kpa Mende encroachments on Caulker territory to the south were not looked on with disfavour.

The warrior, Chief Macavore, was believed to have influence with Chiefs Ndawa and Makaia (both originally from Tikonko; Macavore's father, Momo, coming in as a stranger, had usurped authority from Chief Chabbah, the rightful ruler, in the 1850s). The colony therefore cultivated him, and he in turn helped restrain the warfare in the Gallinhas hinterland. As a result

Britain tended to accept his version of events there, and so soon became involved in hostility to Bumpe, his main enemy.

By 1885 Momo Kai Kai and Momo Ja were the most powerful rulers along the coastal districts between Kittam and Gallinhas, where they had engaged successfully in war and then employed their riches in trading. They seemed to offer, in the chaos succeeding Prince Mannah Massaquoi's death in 1872, one hope of strong, central authority with whom the British could deal. Their co-operation did not, perhaps even could not, stop them participating in local politics. This conflicted at times with Freetown's interests; supporting Britain, their real objective was to control the Upper Kittam. They succeeded in this, but only after the British were drawn in and attacked their enemy Makaia at Bahama and Wende in 1888 and 1889. In the 1890s, and after the 1898 rising they took over a good part of Makaia's former territory, and in this they were not discouraged by Freetown.

Alliances with ambitious chiefs aroused enmity in others. Friendly rulers were offended when hostile ones received presents, even annual stipends, in an unimaginative policy of expediency. Particular disgust was felt when the war-chief, Cannah Gboh, was loaded with presents and loyal chiefs ignored. Cannah Gboh was soon boasting of being rewarded for killing British subjects; friendly chiefs began to think seriously of joining the Bumpe Mende raiders, thus qualifying, it seemed, for both plunder and reward.

The Bumpe Mende found it hilarious when Freetown sent constables under Lamina Gbap, the Muslim trader in the Bum, to settle their dispute with Tikonko, because they knew Lamina Gbap as a notorious 'freebooter' himself, even a thief.

In 1887 and 1888 Sherbro and the neighbourhood was expecting Colonel Sir Francis de Winton, once he had dealt with the Yonni Temne, to come and settle affairs in the Sherbro. Makaia himself thought so; when de Winton did not come he began to prepare revenge on all the chiefs who had refused to join him (because they too had expected the colonel) on the grounds that they were in treaty with the British.[22] A clearer

and earlier intimation of intent by Britain would have saved
traders and friendly chiefs alike.

Few merchants had any great faith in treaties. In their experience wars always broke out again soon afterwards, either
because one chief insulted another, or because of jealousy, or
when a ruler displayed more wealth than another, or enticed
away another's wives, or when a war-chief, left unpaid,
plundered in revenge.

Rulers were often puppets under their war-chiefs, and even
if given a present by the colonial government would go to war
again when it was exhausted, in the hopes of getting another.
Since there were no British agents in the interior, it was impossible to know whether the terms of a treaty had been
honourably carried out or not. Fore Bundu, one of Freetown's
intermediaries, was said to take money from chiefs to conceal
events from government. Stipends were often used to buy slaves,
even arms for another war.[23]

War-chiefs

War soon created a Mende aristocracy and, in the end, some
kind of national feeling; the office of chief being strictly secular,
successful warriors could carve a chiefdom for themselves, success attracting followers. They were more democratic than some
neighbouring rulers. British officials observed that Mende
leaders spoke and negotiated, not in their own name, like other
chiefs, but for their people, like a republic.[24]

The history of the Luawa ruling family shows how Mende
ruling houses came into being.[25] The Luawa chiefdom is a
border one, where Kissi, Kono, Gbande and Gola elements
are found, the chiefdom once being much larger than today,
having been split between Britain and Liberia in 1911.

The family of the founder, Kailundu, came from Kailahu,
across the Moa in Guinea. He was born in 1845 in what is now
the Luawa chiefdom, though there was none then because that
area was still an autonomous section, with perhaps some
allegiance to an overlord, though in the nineteenth-century wars
towns usually acted as separate units.[26] Dowe Kome, Kailundu's
father, was not of a chiefly family, and the boy was named after

a Gbande chief (akin to the Mende and now found in Liberia) against whom the father had fought on behalf of some Kissi chief. Kailundu was taught skill in warfare by Pawu Bundu of Grema, who was the local war-chief.

About 1880 Ndawa, a warrior chief of Wunde, in central Mende country,[27] began a war known as the *Kpove*—the Dung-pot war—and swept east towards Liberia, burning Manowa and other smaller towns. Kailundu, already known to Ndawa as an intelligent and outstanding warrior (his warrior name being Gendeme), had been asked by the latter to remain neutral, but he refused, drew twenty sections into a coalition and defeated Ndawa, driving him back westward. As a reward Kailundu was made principal chief of all in the coalition—in fact of the Luawa chiefdom, which now came into being, and which included the present one, together with three Kissi chiefdoms in Sierra Leone, the Kissi Tengea chiefdom in Liberia, and the Wunde, Mofessor and Kama chiefdoms in Guinea. Kailundu built his new capital at Kailahun, later fighting the Gaura, Kono, Gbande, Kissi, and Sofas. In 1890 he made contact with the British, and died in 1895. Thomas Alldridge, travelling commissioner in Upper Mende country, said he was the finest chief he had ever met.

Kailundu's influence was strong enough to secure the succession of Fabunde, his Speaker, who may have been one of the indigenous 'owners of the land'. When he died in 1912, his son was elected, against the claims of Momo Gbanya, Kailundu's son. Since a Mende chief's office was very much a personal affair, going to almost anyone who could command a following, sub-sections had begun to split away even in Fabunde's time. It was probably only British over-rule which prevented further fission.

Another renowned war-chief was Canna Gboh. Originally exiled from the interior, he took refuge with Sesay Hannimoh, in Lubu and was soon involved in the struggle between the Bullom- and Mende-populated areas of Lubu for control of that country. From here he plundered the Sierra Leone traders in the Sherbro in 1872. In 1874 Governor Berkeley sent an expedition against him under Alimami Senessi, and the following year the chiefs gave him up, wearied by his fighting which had destroyed fifty towns. After years of plunder, the Small Bum, Jong and Kittam were now reportedly ruined. With Cannah Gboh's capture the regime collapsed wearily into a state of exhausted tranquillity, Cannah Gboh's captors hoping the British would execute him, as they had been known to execute other refractory leaders—even though they were not British subjects. But the warrior escaped from Freetown gaol in 1876; returned to Bumpe and spent eighteen months raising a force to revenge himself on the Bum river chiefs who had given him up to the British.

Assisted by Chief Sekeh Seppeh, he set up a stronghold at Talliah in the Small Bum and threatened British Sherbro. Thanks to the Tikonko Mende, who naturally joined any alliance against their Bumpe rivals, he was driven back. All through 1879, from nearby Bumpe he sallied out to raid the Bum factories, even planning to attack Chief Gberi at Gbongeh whose territory was a buffer between Bum and Bumpe. But Sekeh Seppeh now turning to trade, refused to allow his warriors to cross his territory.

These events were known in Bonthe as the first and second Cannah Gboh's war.

In desperation the Sierra Leone traders in Bonthe petitioned Governor Samuel Rowe for help, pointing out that in their own experience almost every raid upon the south for the past twenty years had come primarily from the Bumpe and Tikonko countries—rival Mende chiefdoms; the Bumpe and Tikonko traders traded at Mafwe, the highest navigable point on the river Bum; Taiama (Kpa) Mende merchants using Senehun. Rowe came and made the Treaty of Lemehjemah, 26 December 1879, the first time chiefs at war had met to discuss arrangements for peace.[28]

Sebore and Bargboh, the principal chiefs of Bum, now thought of transferring their country to Britain, in self-defence, and to prove to Seppeh and Cannah Gboh they were not 'fools'.

All through the 1880s, Sherbro, from one end to the other, was full of war, usually begun by the Mende living up the Big Bum river, and especially by Chiefs Gberi of Bongeh, and

Sekeh Seppeh of Yengema (Bumpe). Gberi, who had at one time been an apprentice in Freetown, was very successful, having formed useful contacts with unscrupulous traders who now supplied him with arms.[29] From 1880 Freetown made ineffectual attempts at establishing peace.

George Garrett, one of Freetown's two travelling commissioners when the government, by treaties of 'peace and friendship', was preparing the way for a declaration of a protectorate, who knew the hinterland well in the 1880s, said the Mende:

> . . . supply the fighting men in all the wars in the surrounding country, hiring themselves out for a little cloth, tobacco or rum, and relying for recompense on plunder. They would appear to fight for the love of fighting and will, when hired, as readily attack their own people as any of the adjoining tribes . . . They are faithful, quickly attach themselves and will stand readily by you in time of danger.[30]

He discovered the strongholds of the war-chiefs Ndawa and Macavore comprised 13 towns, each with 3–5 fences and 3,000–4,000 captives who were gradually being sold off into slavery. Five miles further on, on the left bank of the Kittam, was Gorpende: 2 large fenced towns, both surrounded by an outer fence. The road onwards, evidence of military planning and unlike the normal bush path—a narrow tunnel amongst the trees—was 40ft wide, the streams being meticulously bridged. Bumpe, which in Mende means slippery or low-lying, consisted of 8 towns, 3 of them stockaded (in 1877 it had been reported to hold a population of 9,000). Tikonko had 4 towns, 2 being strongly fenced, the largest with 805 houses. Twenty-five miles south-east lay Largo, with 9 towns, of which 4 were fenced, the main one being Gupaybu with 340 houses and 5 fences. This was Macavore's headquarters. Ndawa, Mendegrah of Juru in the Gaura country (an ally of the Massaquois), and Macavore supplied most of the mercenaries for the fighting in the lowlands at this time and had recently taken Goorahung, a stronghold of 8 towns in Upper Kittam.[31] Ndawa was ambushed and killed attacking Mendegrah, whose riches he coveted, but not before he had devastated and pillaged most of the Upper Mende regions as far south as Pendembu.

Whilst Ndawa pillaged the right bank of the river Sewa, Macavore overran most of the Gallinhas and Kittam countries, attacking Sulima in British Sherbro in 1887. Between them they carried off thousands of Gallinhas, Bum and Krim people.

Macavore had a war-chief, Makaia, who, like Ndawa, had been originally acquired as a slave. He soon became renowned

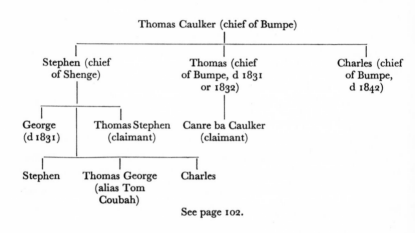

See page 102.

as a warrior, and obtained his freedom, the Mende rallying to his leadership, as they did to any successful warrior. Ruling from Sulima, it was said his authority extended over 700 square miles, though his raiding parties ranged over an area six times that size.

Governor Rowe did his best to bring peace, getting many of the chiefs together at Lavannah, British Sherbro, 11 May 1885. But though all the low-country chiefs signed the treaty, Ndawa, Makaia and Mendegrah, the three autocratic war-chiefs who from 1883 on had supplied the warriors for the fighting, did not. Thus the lowland chiefs had promised more than they could perform, and consequently peace was short-lived. Macavore, making peace with Nyagbwah of Mano, told him that Ndawa had got beyond his control, which sounds as though the former had had enough of war. However, Ndawa was ambushed by Mendegrah and killed in 1888.

The Frontier Police dislodged Makaia's warriors from Jehoma, on the left bank of the Kittam, the head town of Momo Kai Kai, driving Makaia back to the headquarters at Fanima and rescuing 500 captives. Pushing on, the Frontiers took Bahama, occupied by warriors of Bokhari Gomna's brother, Gombo Saidu, and by Lahai Vannah, both Makaia's satellites, who fled.[32] The police burnt the town and pushed on to Makaia's stronghold of Largo. Meanwhile the governor, leaving Freetown with another force, had taken Fanima, driving Makaia back to Largo. This was stormed and taken the next day, 3 January 1889. Makaia fled to Mano, Chief Nyagbwah's head town, where his host surrendered him to the British in April. He hoped by that act to stop Mende plundering his country, as they went through to trade at the Bum factories.[33]

Mendegrah himself (who died in 1891) had probably never been averse to peace, but it would be feasible only when Makaia, the last of the 'freebooters', as the British called them, was taken. Makaia, having overrun Gallinhas and Kittam, Mendegrah, at Juru, successfully called in the Poro for that purpose.

A line of Frontier Police was stationed from Dia on the river Mano to Mattru on the Jong, a distance of about two hundred miles, along which weekly patrols moved from station to station.[34]

Even so, peace could not have been established if the older chiefs had not wanted it. There were signs that they were now tired of war; they complained that war-chiefs, only young men, upset the country at will,[35] and they were beginning to turn against them, even surrendering them to the British.

Sir Samuel Rowe who knew Sherbro better than any governor before or since, had said in 1885 that he thought it would take the country twenty years to recover from its years of rapine. Speaking to the chiefs at Lavannah, in May 1885, he expressed his revulsion at the scenes he had witnessed:

I have seen things which should make every King and chief ashamed to sit here. Peaceful villages I knew are now only marked by the mango and orange trees and a few burnt sticks. I have seen a few living skeletons hiding and fearing to leave their places. I have seen hundreds of little children who have run away from parents, villages, etc, and are now hidden in strange lands through fear of returning. I have seen a pile of skulls, higher than you are . . . I say that you sitting here, who have been eating rice every day, have much to answer for.[36]

Four years later, Governor Hay, visiting the country found it 'one solitary desert'.[37]

But, in fact, the recovery was remarkable, and towns were quickly rebuilt as soon as peace was achieved in 1889. In October 1890 a correspondent at Sherbro informed the editor of *The Sierra Leone Weekly News* that Sherbro trade was 'all a reasonable and contented man requires'.[38]

None the less, the area experienced some of the worst excesses of the 1898 rising.

Afro-Europeans

After the sixteenth-century Mani invasions, no signs are found, from the river Sierra Leone southward to Cape Mount, either of prolonged, serious warfare, or of significant immigration, until the late eighteenth century. An era of relative tranquillity seems to have set in, reflected by the small number of slaves exported; the Royal African Company seeing the wisdom of concentrating instead on gold, ivory, redwood and beeswax. King Tom, the chief on the Sierra Leone peninsula, drew his revenue in the 1760s and 1770s merely from tolls for wooding and watering, though by that time the Bunce Island factory, situated where several rivers met, and gathering its trade mainly from the north, was exporting slaves in larger quantities again.[39]

Although the Portuguese had left Sierra Leone by the end of the seventeenth century, Bunce Island and its trade had fallen to the Afro-Portuguese—descendants of mixed marriages. They dominated especially the Temne towns of Rotumba and Port

Loko. Further south, around the Bananas, the Plantains and
Sherbro Island, Afro-British traders held a monopoly, having
become chiefs.[40]

John Newton, a reformed slaver who knew Jose Lopez, the
Afro-Portuguese leader of an insurrection on Bunce Island in
1728, which had driven the Royal African Company from
Sierra Leone for good, referred to him twenty-four years later
as 'the undoubted King-maker of Sierra Leone'.[41]

Afro-Portuguese political power did not last long, however,
though a kind of false Lusitanian gentility lingered until the
early years of the last century. The known cruelty of such people,
their racial prejudice and unscrupulousness, attested by Adam
Afzelius, a reliable witness, undermined aspirations of permanent authority or of founding a dynasty.[42] Governor Zachary
Macaulay noticed that Signor Domingo, a Koya Temne sub-
chief who could read Portuguese fluently, though he had much
to say at palavers could decide nothing, being regarded as a
'stranger'. He rated him last but one of the nine Temne sub-
chiefs in the neighbourhood of the settlement.[43]

The great weakness of these Afro-Portuguese was that they
were only middle-men. The Portuguese had practised miscege-
nation from earliest times, not with any liberal intent but simply,
as James Duffy has said, as an erotic expediency. A Frenchman
in 1784 estimated that there were 15,000 Afro-Portuguese in
Upper Guinea alone.[44] Thus they did not have, as perhaps the
Afro-British had, the advantage of novelty. Nor did they have
behind them, as the Afro-British had, a European trading company and its armed ships. Moreover, they neither farmed nor
hunted, the chiefs being particularly careful not to grant them
land for agriculture. Thus, ultimately, they were in the hands
of the Africans. They were looked down on by metropolitan
Portuguese, and disliked by all other European traders because
they charged higher prices than the African traders.

Scarcely any Afro-Portuguese were found in the Sherbro,
because lançados[45] had never settled there. Their place was filled
by English traders and pirates, and their offspring.

In particular, there were the families of Caulkers, Clevelands,
Cumberbuss, Rogers and Tuckers. These had the foresight to

marry into local ruling families, using the goods stolen from their employers, the Royal African Company, to acquire plantations, even using company slaves to work them. Within two generations they became rich and powerful rulers, building their own towns and keeping armies of *grumettos* to chastise chiefs slow in repaying their debts, for most petty chiefs got advances of European goods from these slave traders. Debt was the most common pretext for shipping someone off as a slave and chiefs soon came to fear being seized and sent across the Atlantic by these people.

The growing nationalism of the Mende, the commercial and political rivalries of the Afro-Europeans, and the Muslim diyula were shaping new political units in the south at the same time as the Fula, Susu and others were realigning the north.

The Caulker, Cleveland, Rogers and Tucker Families

Zachary Rogers and John Tucker were Englishmen in the service of the Gambia Adventures in 1665. Thomas Caulker was sent to Sierra Leone by the Royal African Company in 1684. He married into the Ya Cumba family, rulers in Yawry Bay. His descendants extended the chiefdom to include the Plantain and Banana Islands.

Zachary Rogers married a daughter of the Sherbro ruling house, and his children, Samuel and Zachary, strengthened the family by taking as wives daughters of King Siaka, chief at Gbendimah, Cape Mount. The latter became known in the nineteenth century as the Massaquois.[46] The Rogers and Massaquoi families soon monopolised the Cape Mount trade, notably round the Moa and Mano estuaries, important slaving centres. Using hired Mende warriors, they became some of the most notorious and successful slave dealers in Africa.[47] James Rogers of Jidaro dined off silver plate in the 1840s.

Little is known of the original John Tucker, but by the end of the seventeenth century the family were influentially established in the Sherbro, some as Royal African Company servants, others as interlopers. Especially powerful in the mid-eighteenth century was Henry Tucker who had travelled widely in Europe, had several wives, numerous offspring, and a large slave-town wherein lay his strength. Most chiefs were in his debt and he was rich enough to use silver at his table.

Tradition says of these families that about 1740 a Caulker stopped at Shenge, a Tucker at Baholl, and a Rogers at Mina Town on the Kife river. This is incorrect, as we have seen, but it indicates their centres of power.[48]

Another agent of the Royal African Company in Sherbro was Cumberbuss, whose son, Zachary, was chief of Jamaica Town in 1726. His Christian name suggests a connection with the Rogers.

So far as the author is aware, no descendants are found today of the Cumberbuss family.[49]

The Cleveland family, on the Banana Islands, were descended from a Devonian, William Cleveland, who, in the middle of the eighteenth century, left a slave ship to marry the daughter of a Caulker, already established on the islands as chief. Their son John did not long survive his father, who died in 1758.

William Cleveland had sent his two sons to Liverpool, England, for education, where no doubt they were looked after by the slaving firm of Robert Bostock, his business agents. After his brother's death, James continued his father's trade in slaves, ivory, gums, gold and turtle shell. He also looked after John's children, the elder, William, helping his uncle; the other son died in 1786, the year after James, turning against his Caulker relatives, attacked Charles Caulker of the Plantain Islands and had Bemba, one of his slaves, cut off Charles's head.

When he died in 1791, though he left a young son born in 1789, James was succeeded in the Bullom way by his brother's son, the easy-going William.[50] He soon had a fleet of ships and factors working for him as far afield as Cape Mesurado. He also grew rice on the mainland for the Sierra Leone Company settlement at Freetown.[51]

William and Stephen Thomas Caulker in Sherbro were too preoccupied with the family quarrels (which bedevilled the family, all through the nineteenth century) to avenge their elder brother's execution. But William died in 1797. Stephen, allying with King Tom on the Sierra Leone peninsula, and the

Bai Farma of Koya, now attacked Bemba who, for his part in the Plantains campaign, had been rewarded with land at Cape Shilling, on the mainland opposite the Bananas.[52] Stephen Caulker and his allies drove Bemba out in 1798. In that year Stephen is said to have died, succeeded by his son, George Stephen Caulker.[53]

Cleveland fled from the Banana Islands in 1799, and the Caulkers took possession, carrying off James Cleveland's tombstone, which Messrs Bostock had presented to the family, to use as a doorstep. In 1805 Governor Thomas Ludlam, the last Sierra Leone Company governor, arranged a truce between the two families.[54]

When Stephen Caulker died in 1810, by custom Thomas, his brother, was heir, but Stephen's son George, educated in England, put forward a claim. Thomas agreed upon a division, rather than going to war. Thomas therefore took the mainland and the Bananas while George took the Plantains.

Trade Rivalry

The Clevelands had moved to the mainland, when they left the Bananas, ruling lands along the river Jong, where they called in Mende warriors to help them continue their Caulker feud. Mende overran the lands of Chief Ya Comba, the Caulkers' relative, and Caulker territory was constantly raided for slaves. George Caulker asked Governor Charles Turner to arrange a peace, and was glad to agree to surrender part of the peninsula which bears the governor's name today.[55]

Thomas Caulker of Bumpe (the mainland) died in 1832, his brother Charles succeeding him. He opened up the country to the timber trade which was becoming the main source of profit at that time. He died in 1842 and by custom Thomas Stephen Caulker of the Shenge–Plantain line, eldest surviving son of Stephen, the deceased Charles's eldest brother, should have got the crown, but Canre ba Caulker,[56] another nephew of the dead chief, disputed this, saying Charles, before his death, had expressed a wish to see him succeed.[57] Almost immediately they went to war, Canre ba with his headquarters on the Cockboro river, Yawry Bay, Thomas Stephen's at Bendu. The real prize

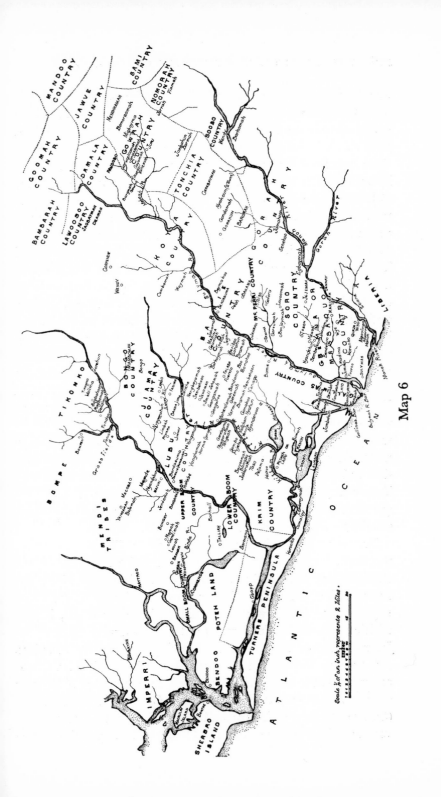

Map 6

Scale ½ of an inch represents 8 Miles.

was the timber trade on the mainland, which was replacing the slave trade as the most profitable enterprise. Thomas Stephen began to find the Plantain Islands of little commercial value. Both called in Mende mercenaries. This occurred just after the slave barracoons at the Gallinhas had been destroyed by the Royal Navy in 1840, and it was important to see the Sherbro did not become an alternative resort for slave traders. The Fula traders further up river had been doing their best, it was said, to fan the war and 'acquire influence and ultimately sovereignty over the country'. Siding with Canre ba Caulker, they reduced Thomas Stephen on the Plantains almost to ruin. Sisay Wuru, a warrior first hired by these Jong chiefs, quarrelled with his overlords, establishing himself at Gbambaiah, Imperri, with an outlet near the coast. Now, supported by Canre ba during the late 1840s and e ly 1850s, he carried war against all Muslim strangers on the Jong, assisted by the Mende. Thomas Caulker fled to Bendu where his mother came from, and persuaded the Jong and Bagru Bullom chiefs to fight for him (notably Mori Ibibu, chief of Mongeri) but after eight years of warfare, he now asked for British help, which he was given. The subsequent treaty did not restore Thomas to all his country, it being recognised that something was due to the rights of conquest. Thomas thus gained the land as far as Bago creek, which flows into Yawry Bay. Canre ba was allowed to keep what he had conquered to the north. On their death it was arranged the whole should go to the sons of the eldest brother, George.

Bumpe and Tikonko were constant rivals. Chiefs lower down the Bum, such as Karmuku of Hahun and Ba Kolong on the opposite side of the Bum, envied Bumpe's power along the river, and disliked the Muslim strangers living there. From 1852 to 1854 the Lower Bum chiefs, with Sisay Wuru, Momo of Tikonko and the Tuckers, fought bitterly against Bumpe, the Jong chiefs, the Gbanta of the Upper Jong, and the Muslims.

Governor Turner had destroyed James Tucker's slave barracoons in 1825, and had threatened to hang him if he ever caught him.[58] It was Governor Neil Campbell's opinion that the Bai Sherbro of Yonni had given Turner commercial advantages there because, like the Caulkers, he hoped for protection against his enemies—in his case the Tuckers. The Shebar area was dangerous, even impassable, to sailing ships for many months of the year, but the Tuckers being nearer the Gallinhas had a choice of ports: in Shebar or Sherbro Island. They were the prime slave dealers, more successful than either the Caulkers or the Bai Sherbro. Their situation, too, was practically impregnable. In Campbell's opinion, one could not sensibly expect Tuckers to give up those advantages. Moreover, the governor did not believe in military operations 'which irritate and give our opponents proof of their superiority, of which they were not before aware'. Harry Tucker, of Kaw Mende, had just seized a sloop trading from Freetown and now defied all that Freetown could do against him.[59] Even so, the administration in 1853 believed the Tuckers had given up the slave trade and, in that year, the Tucker chiefs in the Bum-Kittam were given stipends. In fact the trade was not so profitable now and, like everyone else, the Tuckers had turned to alternative sources of income. However, they, and least of all their people, had not abandoned it.

What the Tuckers wanted was British protection for a while, because Mori Calipha and Lahai Salifu, taking war down to the Bum and Kittam, were claiming Kaw Mende, a town belonging to Harry Tucker, chief of Shebar.[60] Charles Tucker was engaged in a dispute with the chief of Mongeri, whilst William Tucker, chief of Bullom and Gbapp, and David Tucker of Kittam, were soon fighting with Prince Mannah of the Gallinhas, their great rival to the east, holder of the Massaquoi title.

The Tuckers had no love for the British, and as soon as these wars were patched up, Charles Tucker of Kaw Mende in 1864 gave his attention to attacking British Sherbro, seeking the help of Musa of Bumpe.[61] They also began to look round for ways of circumventing the British customs posts, arranging in 1879 to have John Harris, of Sulima, build a factory at Mano on the Bum-Kittam (or Bullom) river. He was to bring his spirits from Sulima via Kasse, and then into the Kittam country, evading duty. The trouble was, from the British point of view, that ships could enter the river Sherbro via Shebar and avoid

British waters. Governor Rowe consequently felt Harris's[62] action would cost the colony £10,000 in revenue in the following year. This shows what a very astute move the Tuckers had made, and also, how profitable their new legitimate trade might have been—the Bum-Kittam trade accounted alone for 80 per cent of British Sherbro's revenue.[63] But the British unscrupulously reactivated Turner's 1825 agreement—even though Lord Bathurst, the secretary of state at the time, had ordered the deletion of the cession clauses. This, however, had never been publicly done and so, they decided, the treaty still stood.

The guiding hand in this successful policy was William Tucker's. When he died in the late 1880s, he left a vacuum on the Bum-Kittam which led to disturbances for several years. Pujehun at the head of the Kittam was a natural market-place. Here Momo Kai Kai and Momo Jah, said to be brothers, gave up fighting and built themselves up as go-betweens, dealing with European and Sierra Leonean firms on the coast and powerful chiefs, especially Nyagbwah, in the interior.

William E. Tucker ruled the country from Shebar Strait to the river Kittam. From here Queen Messeh ruled at least nominally, but Tucker did everything in her name. Then came Chief Zorocong of Messmah and finally, at Gbendemah, Prince Jahrah of the Gallinhas, a Muslim and blind for eighteen years.[64]

The Massaquoi

The Massaquoi was an arbitrator rather than a ruler, and the chief of Gbandemah as such had no claim to the title. The fighting which brought in Mende war-chiefs was not, therefore, so much about trade or even about territory, as about who was to be the next Massaquoi.

There had been trouble in the Gallinhas ever since Prince Mannah, said to be the founder, but probably the reviver of the title 'Massaquoi', died in 1872. He had been one of the most successful and notorious slave-dealing chiefs in West Africa, owing his power to bands of hired warriors. On his death-bed he left his chiefdom to his son Bai Gbassay.[65] The person of the 'Massaquoi' was sacred (firing on him, for instance, merited death) and he told his son, after he had chosen him as heir, he was not to look on his face again until he died. But Bokhari Gomna, a part-Mende son of a slave of the late King Tharka, Prince Mannah's father, by a daughter of King Tharka, also had designs on the chieftaincy. By a trick he got Bai Gbassay to look on his father's face again whilst he still lived.

Tradition says that, believing his son would soon die as a result, Prince Mannah appointed Bokhari Gomna, the war-chief of Sembehun, instead. Being a slave's son, the chiefs re-fused to accept him, and had elected Lahai Jahrah,[66] Prince Mannah's brother, even though no one liked him.

Lahai Jahrah, old, blind and ineffective, was unable to keep in check the ambitious rival warriors Fahwundu of Manoh on Lake Cassie in Krim country, and Bokhari Gomna, and he ended his drunken days with his throat cut. His friends vowed revenge. Chiefs Fahwundu and Bokhari Gomna were the main contenders now. The former allied with such Gallinhas chiefs who opposed Bokhari. The latter enlisted Ndawa and Makaia. All Sulima was full of war. Makaia's and Ndawa's Mende[67] warriors overran most of Gallinhas and Kittam in 1884 (in-cluding British factories) and again in 1889, carrying away thousands and fighting Momo Kai Kai on the left bank of the Kittam, who for years barred their way to the south.

The Muslim chiefs Momo Kai Kai and Momo Ja had once been mercenaries under Prince Mannah, and then under Chief Fahwundu of Mano in the Kittam, when Bumpe had invaded Mano. They became independent warrior chiefs during these wars, controlling Gumbu, formerly a Krim town, later known as Pujehun. As Massaquoi influence dwindled theirs extended. Chief Mendegrah filled the vacuum further east. Now Bumpe fought Tikonko, Taiama attacked Bumpe. Mendegrah opposed anyone with influence in the Upper Kittam. Makaia, though closely connected with Tikonko, quarrelled with Macavore in the 1880s, and fought him too. Generally, in these wars, Bumpe allied with Imperri and Chief Gbongeh; Taiama with Bagru; Tikonko with the Lower Bum chiefs; Mendegrah with the Gallinhas and Gbemmah ones. With the intercession of Gover-nor Rowe a treaty was made in May 1885 at Lavannah, and the

war fences were pulled down. Fahwundu, however, determined
to destroy Bokhari utterly, persuaded Makaia, now trading in
Liberia, to return to fighting. Invading the Gallinhas, he
attacked Bokhari's allies who were defenceless, having kept
their promise to Rowe at Lavannah to destroy all stockades.
In 1888, Makaia, having quarrelled with Momo Kai Kai,
joined Bokhari instead, building a war fence at Largo, north of
Pujehun, whilst Bokhari fortified Bahama. Bokhari, summoned
to Freetown, was now deported to the Gambia, whilst Momo
Kai Kai helped British forces hunt down Makaia. Only the
latter's capture in 1889 put an end to this warfare.

Renewed Caulker Wars

The Sherbro was disturbed again when John Caulker, a cousin
of the Bumpe and Shenge Caulkers, in 1875, bought war (as
the saying was) from the Mende warrior Gbanya, husband of
Madam Yoko. Returning home full of plunder the Mende were
set on by Gbana Banda, chief of Kagboro and by Humpa
Rango of Dodo, Upper Bagru. Kinigbo, the Mende war-chief,
gathered more warriors and returned south in revenge. John
Caulker joined him, and they plundered far and wide. John
was captured, tried in Freetown and hanged. Unable to pay a
fine imposed, the British made the Caulkers grant them permission to levy customs instead at Bumpe and Ribbi.[68]

William Caulker had been trading in Massaquoi territory
but, anticipating trouble after the Massaquoi's death, had returned home in 1876, laying claim to Shenge and writing accordingly to his cousins Richard Canre ba Caulker of Bumpe
and Ribbi, and George Stephen Caulker of Shenge. The former
gave him a portion of his land, the latter tried to kill him.

George Stephen of Shenge died in 1881 and William, an old
enemy now, decided to eliminate Thomas Neale Caulker, his
cousin, whom Governor Havelock had appointed under the
terms of the 1849 treaty, even though many of the Caulkers
would have preferred the former chief's son, George Stephen
Caulker, as successor. William, buying war from the Mende in
1887, suddenly invaded Shenge in British Sherbro, which had
to be evacuated. Colony forces were brought in and a detach-

ment of police taken up the Yaltucker river and stationed along
the frontier of British Sherbro. William was captured by the
British, tried in Freetown, and hanged at Shenge.

About the same time Richard Canre ba Caulker was removed
by the British, who considered him a weak ruler, and Chief
Gbana Will appointed to Bumpe instead.[69]

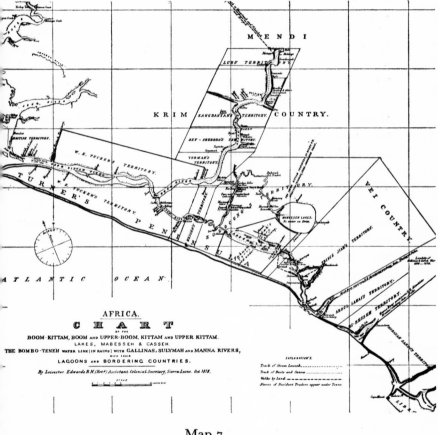

Map 7

British Treaties
Afro-European chiefs, usually English speaking, often educated
in England (or, like William Caulker, at the government school

in Freetown), with trading connections in Freetown and Britain, became progressively more dependent on British protection against the Mende, whom at first they had gladly hired. They thus betrayed their people twice over, by laying them open to plunder and worse by the war-chiefs, and by opening the way for British overrule when making treaties with them.

British and African concepts of treaty-making were different, and the British one prevailed. Administrators never really understood how what appeared at one time to be groups of autonomous political units could become at others a single larger entity.[70] Relatively small lineage groups would be mutually competitive until some outside threat united them. Thus the focus of allegiance was largely relevant to context. This fact made many wars meaningless to white traders, though the latter were generally much better informed than the administration.

Few British understood that in West Africa alliances were seldom permanent. Governors saw treaties 'broken' and thus distrusted African rulers. They spoke bitterly of treaty-making being 'not promising', saying no one thought treaties important, holding them in the Sherbro as *rah tanten deh*, or worthless paper.[71] They did not seem to know that in many cases it was usual to give back towns occupied in wartime, when peace was arranged, that even where sovereignty was granted, the actual 'possession' of the land was not, chiefs exercising ownership as usual, receiving rents and dealing with the land as landlords.[72] Lord Carnarvon, secretary of state, once asked: 'Cannot we secure the object in view [to keep out the French in the northern river territory] by obtaining a right to control the customs duties and so get the fiscal administration of the coast into our hands without undertaking the direct sovereignty of it?'[73]

Lines were drawn on maps in London with no regard for the actual geography. It was the British not the Africans who were ignorant of the precise boundaries between British Sherbro and African chiefdoms.[74] In 1848 when Governor Macdonald asked the Colonial Office to state definitively what was the southern boundary of the colony, the secretary of state replied tartly that no practical difficulty having arisen, it was unwise to raise the question. Even so, it was admitted that the Act was 'irreconcilable with actual geography'.[75] The boundaries between Bagru and Imperri were most imprecise. Some believed Imperri had been ceded in 1861—though Britain denied responsibility there. In 1879 the Sherbro commandant was asked to inform the governor precisely where British jurisdiction did lie. Only in the 1880s, when an outbreak of ritual murders occurred and they were obliged to act, did Britain accept responsibility in Imperri. In 1882 when the Jong chiefs offered to cede their territory, they were informed that Turner's treaty of 1825 had done so.

The Sherbro traders often complained that it was difficult to see what British jurisdiction, supposedly acquired by treaty, actually meant. Most of the time it meant nothing, invoked only when something went seriously wrong, and then usually too late. Troops would then be despatched and governors held palavers where old treaties were produced from the secretariat archives, and sermons preached against those disregarding them. Chiefs had usually lost their copy, or if they had not, sometimes kept it in a tin box, not for what it said, that now being irrelevant to the new political context, but in the hope that conceivably it might turn out to be strong medicine. New treaties were signed and presents exchanged, and everyone went away again, leaving behind a temporary calm buttressed by temporary allies.

However, Her Majesty's Government were beginning to think that by creating a strong frontier police force in Sierra Leone, it might, as in the Gold Coast, be possible to make 'jurisdiction' conterminous with 'protection'.[76] It was time they faced up to their obligations not only to the chiefs but to the Creoles as well as to their responsibilities as an international and colonial power in West Africa. It was far too late to abandon Freetown now; they had governed there for about a century.

CHAPTER 4

Creole Origins

The Meaning of 'Creole'
A modern Creole has written:

> . . . the curious and distinctive flavour of Freetown which makes
> it different from other cities and towns in tropical Africa derives
> mainly from one source, from Creoledom.
>
> The term Creole is used to refer to the descendants of Settlers
> and Liberated Africans in Sierra Leone and to others who had
> cultivated their habits and had come to accept their way of
> living.[1]

Settler was a term soon applied to the survivors of Granville
Sharp's Province of Freedom, to the Nova Scotians and to the
Maroons, who arrived respectively in 1787, 1792 and 1800.
The liberated Africans, often called recaptives, were different;
they had not come voluntarily, were not English speaking and
had never seen the New World nor white men before.

Britain declared the slave trade illegal in 1807—though she
was not the first European power to do so—and Freetown then
became a base for enforcing the laws against it, the Royal
Navy patrolling the coast and intercepting ships for adjudication in the Vice-Admiralty Court and, after 1819, in the Court
of Mixed Commission. The freed slaves, who had been liberated,
or re-captured, by 1812 outnumbered the Settlers. By 1870 they
had merged in large enough numbers with the older, westernised
Settler élite to form the Creole group.

Each group, as well as adjacent inhabitants and the traders
from further off, settled in the town as agents for their country-

men, brought their own culture and responses to the westernised environment and European administration. For the Settlers there were memories of earlier betrayals by white masters and administrations in North America and Jamaica. Even recaptives were at first suspicious, afraid the white missionaries would sell them back into slavery when opportunity occurred.

Sharp's Settlers
In the 1780s many people of African descent were living in England, mostly in London and in the main seaport towns. In general they were slaves brought as household servants by their transatlantic masters, but after Lord Mansfield's celebrated judgement in the case of James Somerset in 1772, which declared that it was illegal for a master to forcibly remove his slave from England to sell him in the New World, all were free. The American Revolution increased their numbers, since former Loyalist slaves had been promised their freedom if they served against the rebellious colonists. Many had found their way to England. All were more or less destitute.

In 1786 in London, a committee composed chiefly of business-men published an appeal to relieve these 'Black Poor'. Its impetus was Granville Sharp, a radical champion of the oppressed who had sponsored James Somerset's case. The number of people receiving charity soon increased beyond the committee's expectations and they decided to approach the government. Sharp obtained a grant from the Treasury enabling him in 1787 to send over four hundred settlers, black and white, to a new colony in Sierra Leone which he called the Province of Freedom. True to Sharp's principles, the new colony was to be entirely self-governing, a settlement of sturdy yeomen. The black Settlers were mostly Afro-American. Active and adventurous, as they had proved, willing to try their hand at pioneering in West Africa, they showed again their inde-pendent spirit and their innate suspicion of whites by demanding documentary proof, before they left England, that they were indeed free. Some suspected the government might be going to ship them to Botany Bay or to abandon them in Africa to the slave traders, and thus, though nearly seven hundred signed the agreement to go, only two hundred and fifty showed up when the time came to embark.

To allay their fear, parchment certificates were issued, bearing the royal arms, granting them the status of free citizens of 'the Colony of Sierra Leone or the Land of Freedom'. These were not real passports and in fact conferred nothing, being signed only by the clerk of the acts of the navy; nor was the 'Land of Freedom' a British colony and, though they swore allegiance to His Majesty, once settled they became independent of higher authority—a feature they came to regret bitterly both in the province and later under the autonomous Sierra Leone Company, though the latter governed from London. A confidence trick had been played by white men upon black.

To fill the transport ships, the City of London authorities rounded up any blacks found begging in the streets. Thus some were not even volunteers. In the end four hundred and eleven sailed, some having died and others run away before leaving England.

However, little expense was spared in fitting them out. Sir Charles Middleton, comptroller of the navy (later Lord Barham), was actively hostile to the slave trade, and the Treasury having given the navy board a free hand, over £15,000 was spent, two-thirds of it on stores and provisions. Middleton appointed Gustavus Vassa, alias Olaudah Equiano, an Ibo ex-slave who wanted to become a missionary in Africa, as the expedition's commissary. At Plymouth, where the little fleet put in for repairs, Vassa accused the navy board and Captain T. Boulden Thompson, RN, in charge, of cheating in ordering stores, and of ill-treating the Settlers. The Treasury dismissed him.

Arriving on 10 May 1787, they were soon told by Thompson of a treaty made on their behalf with the Temne, whereby the latter were supposed to have surrendered sovereignty of a stretch of 400 square miles of land, based on the shore from the watering place near King Tom to Gambia Island. But Britain misapprehended African land law so that once more the Settlers were deceived—though not intentionally this time. Also, put ashore at the worst possible time for health, at the beginning of the rains, and with unsuitable seeds sent out from England, a number were doomed from the start. Some soon wandered away, often into the slave factories where their literacy in English made them valuable clerks.

Sharp sent out others to replenish their numbers; several white settlers were among them, some of whom, including the doctor, also went into the slave trade. Slaving captains resented the Settlers' claims to be an independent community and incited the Temne to attack, which they did, on 6 December 1789, burning Granville Town, their little settlement near the watering place, to the ground. Survivors fled to the protection of Bunce Island and the fortified slave factory there, to Pa Bosun, a nearby Temne chief, or to Namina Modu, of the Sanko family and ruler of Port Loko.

Some made their way back to England, where John William Ramsay, one of their headmen, wrote to Sharp saying self-government had been a failure; they must have someone to govern them.

The Sierra Leone Company

Meanwhile, the evangelical left wing of the Church of England were discussing how best to 'civilise' the known parts of Africa and India with European culture and Christianity. They usually met at Conservative MP and banker Henry Thornton's house on Clapham Common. Among them was William Wilberforce, long dedicated to ending the slave trade. These Clapham evangelicals or 'saints' made the Sierra Leone venture the symbol of Abolition when they founded a second company, the Sierra Leone Company, to run a settlement there.

The new company passed over Sharp to elect Henry Thornton chairman. Thomas Clarkson, a humanitarian who dedicated health and fortune to Abolition, was another board member. Unlike most abolitionists, Clarkson was not a Conservative, and unlike Wilberforce, also on the board, he possessed neither charm nor guile. With Sharp, he did not entirely approve of the new company's policy which, contrary to that determining the government of the Province of Freedom, required the new settlement to be run from London, expecting it to yield a return for its shareholders through trade and taxes on the land.

A surprising aspect of the Sierra Leone Company was the rashness, haste, and ignorance of its directors, who were otherwise cautious and successful businessmen accustomed to public affairs. Ironically, they might have listened to their colleague Sharp who, perhaps the least practical of them all, was yet unexpectedly well informed about conditions and customs in Sierra Leone.[2] At least he restrained the more ardent from retaking the territory from the local Temne by force, correctly arguing that the Temne attack had been inspired by offences committed against them by white slavers in the first instance. Alexander Falconbridge, formerly a surgeon in the slave trade, was sent out to re-negotiate the land settlement amicably.[3]

Sharp was very much one of the 'saints' and his views were sometimes in conflict with his fellow directors. He was bitterly disappointed that the Settlers were no longer to be self-governing, no longer able to grant land by a free vote of their common council.[4] He wrote to a friend that such restraints 'could not accord with your ideas of liberty and justice. But I could not prevent this humiliating change: the settlement must have remained desolate if I had not thus far submitted to the opinions of the associated subscribers.'[5]

The main obstacle was the British Ministry which, after 1783, was in no mood to speculate on new forms of colonial government. Seldom was an age so barren of political measures; statesmen, concentrating on the expansion of trade and on maintaining maritime supremacy, gave no financial help, no monopoly, to the Sierra Leone Company which was left as independent and unsupported as was compatible with its creation by an act of Parliament. Philanthropy had to give way to commerce, and consequently Sharp misconstrued the intention of the new board of governors over the question of land allotments. In 1791 he wrote to the surviving Settlers that the British government intended to 'invest the general property of the King's lands in the care of the St. George's Bay[6] Company ... and the Company will grant free lots of land to all the settlers who will agree to support the British government according to the former Regulations'.[7] In fact, the board did not intend to grant land free and in their declaration of October 1791 they stated that land revenue was to be one of their three main sources of intended income, 'derived partly from quit-rents, partly from a gradually increasing tax upon the district'.[8] About the same time John Clarkson, sent over to supervise the removal from Nova Scotia of any Loyalist ex-slaves who wished to go to Sierra Leone, was telling the prospective Settlers that 'no-one should have a lot without paying a reasonable price for it' and that the money so collected would be used for public purposes such as churches and hospitals.[9] Yet the company's printed promise given to the Nova Scotians in Halifax by Clarkson spoke of land 'free of expense'—whatever that meant. It certainly did not mean no payment at all, since Clarkson had told them they must pay taxes to support their poor and to gradually reimburse the company's expenses in establishing the settlement, and they had agreed.

This muddle nearly ruined them, since land was the one issue capable of rallying supporters to any group of dissidents. No wonder Clarkson admitted in 1793 to Cato Perkins and Isaac Anderson, Nova Scotians sent over from Sierra Leone with a petition containing various grievances to the directors: 'You may have misunderstood me in one or two instances.'[10]

In their haste the board misjudged the intentions of the British government, appointed unsuitable personnel, set up the 'colony' without proper legal sanction, sent Clarkson to Nova Scotia without proper diplomatic clearance,[11] brought the Settlers from Nova Scotia to Freetown before they had really defined the kind of settlement it was to be or the sort of constitution they intended it to be governed by, sent out unsuitable equipment, and loaded Clarkson with a burden of duty which soon became insupportable and often contradictory. As a result, a sensitive humanitarian anxious to ameliorate, perhaps even to atone for, the injustices suffered by black men in England[12] was changed into an overworked, slightly neurotic governor who had to be forcibly retired. Looking back on the company's failure in the autumn of 1792, Henry Thornton blamed the climate, the character of some of the Nova Scotians, the

difficulty of recruiting suitable personnel, and the hazards of
'reconciling men of different rank, education and colours to
their new situation in society'.[13]

Resettlement
About fifty Sharp Settlers sadly reassembled, some so naked
and dirty that Falconbridge's wife was amazed to find they
were white women.[14] Falconbridge settled them in a second
Granville Town east of Cline Bay, but he soon left them,
putting them in charge of his Greek servant, Theodore Kalin-
gee, who abused his position by selling their gunpowder to the
Temne, by laziness and gluttony, and by giving them all such
a bad name that the company in 1791 sent out white settlers
only, to the number of 119, as colonists and (mainly) administrators and other officials. Most of them died. Clarkson, arriving in 1792, to supersede Falconbridge, decided to keep people
with such an evil reputation away from his Nova Scotians, lest
they corrupt them. When Signor Domingo, a chief round the
point, at Royema, complained about them, Clarkson replied
Domingo could do what he liked with them, they were not his
subjects.

But the company were not so certain. Thornton felt they
might have a better claim than any on the settlement's land,
since the English treaty stated it had been granted to George III
for their use. Clarkson, too, was inconsistent. He had once said
to them he would flog any entering his settlement, and he had
denied any responsibility for them. Yet he was determined to
punish any engaging in the slave trade, even though they lived
outside his settlement where neither African nor British law as
yet forbade it. In the end, and typically, he took them in,
offering them the same chance as his Nova Scotians: 'determined to forget everything that has passed, and consider you
and our people as one'.[15]

The Nova Scotians
In 1783 and 1784 alone, it was calculated that 30,000 Loyalist
refugees had arrived in Nova Scotia, mostly destitute. This was
a great strain on a community of fishermen and small farmers.

As disbanded soldiers, black as well as white Loyalists were entitled to a land grant, but there were thousands of whites, and these received the best allotments. Half starved, working for white masters in share-cropping schemes indistinguishable from slavery, averse to agriculture, preferring urban occupations like carpentering, building, boot-making, the black refugees sent Thomas Peters, a former millwright, still awaiting his allotment after six years, to London in 1791 to seek help. Peters was introduced through Sharp to the Sierra Leone Company, which offered the Nova Scotians refuge, and to the secretary of state. Glad to solve an embarrassing problem on the cheap—as he thought—the latter instructed the governors of Nova Scotia and New Brunswick to give land to those wishing to stay, and to allow the rest the choice of enlisting once more (a solution HMG produced monotonously for several decades when asked to solve the problem of employing free blacks), or of going to Sierra Leone. The travel expenses of intending Settlers were to be paid by Britain.

Originally the Sierra Leone Company directors had contemplated sending out more white settlers, but the high mortality of the first batch, and the simultaneous possibility of an alternative source of supply of free black men, altered their plans. They did not, of course, feel strongly about black men, any more than any of their contemporaries. Even Sharp said he had no 'particular esteem' for them; though he explained that since he felt 'obliged' to consider them as men, he was thus obliged to use his best endeavours 'to prevent their being treated as *beasts* by our unchristian countrymen'.[16] Wilberforce echoed this in his speech in the Commons on the East India Bill, 1813: 'in truth we find the morals and manners of the natives of India just such as we might have been led to expect from a knowledge of the dark and degrading superstitions . . . under which they have been so long bowed down.' Thus, even amongst the Humanitarians they were held to be different from, and less 'civilised' than western man, and when the Nova Scotians later sent petitioners over on their behalf, complaining about the white administration, it is not surprising they were listened to with only half an ear, if at all.

H

However, Thomas Peter's mission bore fruit, and the directors despatched John Clarkson to Nova Scotia to supervise their removal. Arriving in October 1791, it had not taken him long to discover that black Loyalists had been taken advantage of in the land allotments there, and that with regards to their coming emigration to Sierra Leone the British Government was playing a double game in the face of the West India lobby's opposition.

Knowing Clarkson's mercurial temperament and his impatience with obstacles to his humanitarian goals, Wilberforce advised him to use caution in Nova Scotia, anticipating he might be thought to be spreading dissent amongst the black people, that white employers of cheap black labour would dislike it if he encouraged emigration. The governors in Nova Scotia might feel that too ready acceptance of an emigration scheme would underline their own failure to tackle the black problem. It was said that black men were idle, without aim in life, and therefore would be in debt, and their creditors would obstruct their departure. This was a calumny, scarcely any were in debt, and Clarkson told Thornton most of them were a better type than the usual English labourer.[17]

Clarkson soon discovered that Sir Evan Nepean, the permanent under secretary to the Home Office under which colonial affairs came, had written confidentially on 8 August to Governor John Parr of Nova Scotia, asking him to delay Clarkson's affairs.[18] At a large dinner party Colonel Parr held forth on the anticipated difficulties in Sierra Leone. Clarkson, never able to dissimulate, interrupted him, and relations between them became very strained. Fortunately the governor fell ill and died soon after.

Clarkson bustled on enthusiastically rather than wisely, promising that in Africa neither rent nor taxes would be demanded. This was incorrect, and indeed contradicted some of his other public statements, as we have seen. The directors, too, misled: speaking of a charter, of land purchases, of large grants from the Treasury, as though these were facts rather than aspirations. Perhaps worst of all they promised larger land allotments than they could survey, clear, or even protect in Sierra Leone.[19]

The Temne

The Temne had always been suspicious of the settlement. They did not see any difference, at least at first, between an abolitionist and a slave trader; both were white and therefore rogues.[20] They certainly did not understand that they had 'sold' their land, and Naimbana rightly told Falconbridge that 'he had been hastily drawn in to dispose of land to Captain Thompson',[21] an act for which he must have the consent of all his headmen.[22] Clarkson soon realised that although the settlement thought it had bought the land, the chiefs 'had not the least idea we would want to make use of the whole and therefore they are not prepared to part with their plots of ground hastily'.[23] At a palaver held on 27 September 1792 Clarkson agreed that the surveyor should work around rather than through any cultivated land, 'for I consider,' he said in his reasonable, sympathetic way, 'that the people when they sold the land had not the most distant idea that they would ever be disturbed'. Of course, the Temne had no conception of selling as defined by British law. Settlers allotted Temne land previously under cultivation were, and still are, considered to be under the protection of a landlord. Though their right to occupy it grows progressively with time, they are none the less dependent upon their landlord's goodwill, and at first, at any rate, a formal arrangement, even submission, is periodically required.[24]

Other Neighbours

The slave traders, black and white, were naturally hostile, enmity exacerbated by the fact that a runaway slave was by coastal custom the property of the chief with whom he took refuge. The settlement thus became a potential asylum, not only for black escapees but also for white seamen who deserted from slave ships. When Captain Thomas Thompson brought out the first Settlers, he had been unable to persuade a deserter, who swam across the shark-infested bay, to return, and so had

had to enlist him into the navy—itself not a happy life, but a desirable alternative to a slave ship. As long as Thompson, and indeed Clarkson, were aboard ship, they held statutory authority as naval officers. The moment Clarkson stepped ashore as a civilian superintendent, however, he lost it, and could only advise ships' captains to anchor elsewhere, 'as . . . seamen will certainly desert . . . and plague me; some take the hint and thank me for it, others do not and they are sure to lose their seamen, give me an immensity of trouble, unsettle the minds of the Nova Scotians, and mix their morals. We begin already to feel the bad effects of so many changes of different characters among us.'[25] It was absolutely essential, he felt, to have a man-of-war stationed in the harbour to deal with the numerous shipping complaints, 'and other business requiring legal authority to settle which I feel I do not possess'.[26]

He referred not only to slaves but to the 153 nearly destitute white survivors of Dalrymple's ill-fated Bulama expedition, which arrived at the settlement on 7 August 1792.[27] They swarmed ashore offering the settlers inflated prices for goods the company had especially imported for the settlers' welfare. Clarkson was forced to shut the store—the only source of supply since the company held a monopoly—and he wrote in despair that he felt the progress of the settlement was put back at least a week for every day they remained.[28]

There was also the problem of the survivors of Sharp's settlement. Captain Thompson had castigated them as 'a worthless, lawless, vicious, drunken set of people . . . a few only of them (who possessed some industry which they used in cultivating the land), if they were supported and encouraged, I think had a prospect of doing well'.[29] This group was probably no better or worse than the white 'decayed gentlemen and dissolute adventurers' sent to Bulama, but they were well organised and moral enough to apprehend and surrender five of their number to the hated slave traders at Bunce Island when the latter complained of thieving. They had twice punished white slave captains with fines and even imprisonment, both times on just grounds.[30] Of course they had no legal right to do so, and Sharp well knew that the anti-abolition lobby would label

them 'mere robbers and banditti'.[31] This enmity was naturally
extended to the adjacent Sierra Leone Company. Moreover,
since they lived outside the settlement, their legal position was
unclear. Were they subject to the company's laws? If any of
them engaged in the slave trade, were they subject to penalty?
That trade, illegal in the settlement, was still quite legal for
other British subjects, and for Africans. Clarkson decided
offenders would have to be punished, if only 'to convince His
Majesty and the British Parliament that we felt the value of
the clause they had inserted in the Act'.[32] In other words, for
political reasons.

Company Government
Abolition was still some years off, the political climate not very
favourable to a company founded on those principles. The
government was accordingly cautious, their dilatoriness a
source of considerable confusion. Although the directors received parliamentary sanction by the Act 31 George III, c 55
of June 1791, they had been unable to expedite either the grant
which would hand over the land supposedly ceded to the Crown
by treaty, or the much-needed charter which would legalise
their jurisdiction and indemnify the board against any company losses. Thornton busied himself trying to bestir the
solicitor general and the attorney general. In August 1791 all
seemed to be going well, but within a few days both officials
were asking for the 'concurrent sanction of His Majesty's
Government' before proceeding. Faced with the anti-abolition
lobby, they were stalling. Thornton was desperate because in
a very unbusinesslike way the company was already committed, their plans implemented at no small expense. As he
wrote desperately to Henry Dundas, the secretary of state, 'we
have already the sanction of Parliament to our undertaking,
have involved ourselves in much trouble and expense and have
invited people to settle at Sierra Leone whom it seems now
doubtful whether there will be any means of governing when
they get there'.[33] The company did not in fact receive the charter
until 1799; until then they had no legitimate authority, but
there was no alternative, given the *fait accompli* of a settlement,

to acting as though jurisdiction was real. The 1791 directors' report speaks of the land in Sierra Leone as 'actually purchased and given up by the native chiefs . . . so that it is not only an English settlement, but an English territory, where all the free customs and rights of the English common law immediately take place'.[34]

Despite the presence of Wilberforce and other MPs on the board, the directors underestimated, not for the first time, the strength of the anti-abolition lobby. Although the slave trade was still legal by British law, they naively hoped to get a special Act forbidding it immediately in Sierra Leone. After an audience with William Pitt, Thornton wrote confidentially but mistakenly to Clarkson in 1792 that it was evident His Majesty's Government wished to abolish the Company of Merchants Trading to Africa. This company, whose slaving operations centred on the Gold Coast, had strongly opposed the formation of the Sierra Leone Company. Thornton now inexplicably thought that not only were all the forts on the coast to be put under the Sierra Leone Company control, but that the £13,000 Parliamentary grant annually given to the Company of Merchants, plus a little extra, would now be diverted to them: 'The Purse of Government is to be opened,' he wrote. 'New establishments are to be formed . . . You are considered as placed in a more exalted and enviable position than any Governor whatever.'[35]

In fact Clarkson, now in Sierra Leone, was already desperate. He wrote of his all-white council: 'nothing but pride, arrogance, self-sufficiency, meanness, drunkenness, atheism and idleness were daily practised by those who were sent out to assist me . . . Besides they were men who had been in mean situations and the title Councillor had turned their brain.' Within a month of arriving, he sourly informed the directors that his council might suit the settlement in three or four years' time, after it had been established, but at present it brought only disorder 'and the future if not prevented by a speedy alternation will be ruin! Eight gentlemen all invested with equal power, each of them acting for himself and none of them accountable to the other, form to be sure a system of government as pregnant with contradiction and uncertainties as can well be imagined.'[36] Every dispatch, he said, was discussed as openly as a newspaper, and it was difficult to get these inexperienced men to distinguish between their corporate authority as a council, when they could take cognisance only of official business, and their individual magisterial jurisdiction,[37] where they did have authority, in so far as they had no charter, to act 'agreeably to the laws of England in all affairs that may be brought before them'.[38] Clarkson asked for more authority, and pledged himself to redeem the settlement if it did not come too late. Their refusal would mean his resignation. The situation would have exasperated any leader, especially one whom Mrs Falconbridge calls 'amiable . . . void of pomp or ostentation, which his senatorial associates disapprove of exceedingly'.[39]

Nearly all the work of running the settlement fell to Clarkson, and he would have welcomed among others some professional accountants,[40] but the board preferred to send overseers. Thornton admitted this was because so many West Indian proprietors had taken up shares, making it plain they expected the company to concentrate on cultivating West Indian produce, especially sugar. Unfortunately, the board was not sure that their land was suitable for sugar, and indeed, when Clarkson planted a crop on the north shore of the river, it was devastated by termites. In fact the directors had no clear plans; no clear idea, as their chairman admitted, whether they were setting up a colony of Africans, of whites, of black immigrants, of British subjects, or a mixture of these.[41] They were uncertain of the kind of constitution they wanted their 'colony', as they called it, to have. They had, he said, 'formed their plan not on the very freest principles, but much on the system of the India Government'.

In January 1792, Clarkson's brother, Thomas, one of the directors, had sent him a long letter of advice.[42] There was as yet no government policy on non-white colonies, and Thomas had had to improvise one. The superintendent was of course to try and stop the slave trade. Kings, Thomas hopefully wrote to his brother, were to be 'convinced' by 'frequent conversations' of its evils, and when so convinced any king should 'issue an edict forbidding a trade in men and let him see that it is enforced'. There were in fact no such autocracies in the neighbourhood, and if there had been they could not have moved as rapidly from a slave-based economy to the plantation one based on growing export crops as the company envisaged.

Clarkson did his best to carry out his brother's instructions, organising four departments: for accounts, stores, for the plantations, and public works. But each councillor in charge of a department vied with the others for their employees' favour. The lack of a uniform wage structure meant that Settlers who felt overworked would allow themselves to be lured from one department to another by higher wages.

The currency complicated matters further. The directors had settled on Spanish dollars to be valued at five shillings each; labour and goods were to be valued in dollars, but the books were to be kept in sterling. Apart from the obvious dangers of confusion, the directors had ignored the medium of 'bars' in which the barter trade of West Africa had been conducted for centuries and which was the sole currency familiar to all. The settlement accountant, John Wakerell, was always in arrears with his paper work; Clarkson constantly dreaded his complete collapse from ill health and overwork. He had to convert local produce, valued in bars,[43] first to dollars, and then to sterling for the company's accountant in London. Moreover, unlike all other coastal traders, the Sierra Leone Company did not add an exact percentage of the cost of freight and insurance to each article. Instead, their invoices included one total sum for all extras. African traders refused to accept this unusual extra charge and as a result, the company often paid as much as 30 per cent too high a price.[44] Even worse, the difference of exchange on their various currencies lost them another 10 per cent on articles sold, as Zachary Macaulay established a few years later.[45] They were soon desperately short of capital.

Alliance of the Sharp Settlers and the Nova Scotians
The company's *Declaration* of 1791 had expressed a desire to have black men participate in government. Clarkson told them

before they sailed that no distinction would be made between black and white. But in 1792 the directors set up a government by a council of eight, all whites, all *ex officio* justices of the peace. The gaols were soon crammed with blacks committed for minor offences by Clarkson's self-opinionated fellow-councillors who often forgot even to report they had made a committal.

On 15 June 1792, Elliot Griffith, a Sharp Settler and now interpreter to Naimbana, and Thomas Peters, asked Clarkson, on reasonable enough grounds, that twelve black men should be commissioned to 'try causes and keep the peace'. This was the first significant alliance between the two groups of Settlers with a common fund of grievances.

Repeating their willingness to be governed by the laws of England,[46] they asked, understandably in view of events in North America and France, to be allowed to participate in government. Clarkson felt it was a good idea, especially since at the time all the white magistrates were sick, but he knew Peters hated his ousting him from the leadership (after all, the 1,200 or so Nova Scotians, who had originally looked to Peters, comprised about 90 per cent of the settlement) and he had heard he had sworn to drive the whites into the sea. Elliot Griffith he knew also as a white-hater and he realised the situation needed care. He replied therefore that he would require to approve their electoral rolls before any elections were held (he understood well that Peters and Griffith intended to get elected if they could), and afterwards to supervise their judicial decisions. In terms almost commanding he recommended they should nominate the captains of the fifteen companies they had been divided into for the Atlantic crossing. The radicals associated with the request answered that to conform to such stipulations would make them slaves again. It was an argument which soon became familiar in the years ahead.

Clarkson was determined not to give in, and was preparing to stand fast when for the second time death intervened to aid him, and Peters died on 26 June. For a time the matter lapsed, but it lingered in Clarkson's mind and it was probably he who suggested to William Dawes, his eventual successor who had arrived in September 1792, the idea of introducing a motion into council, 12 December, that he thought it 'most expedient for the distributing of justice the inferior magistrates should be appointed from among the Settlers, viz: every ten families in the colony should elect a Tythingman, whose duty should be to keep the peace and decide causes of less importance'.[47] Sharp's province had had this Frankpledge system and he had been urging Clarkson to adopt it. The motion was carried, and the constables, since April nominated by the governor were, from 31 December, to be elected by each head of the ten families that went to make up every tything.[48]

Clarkson's diary shows the other areas of conflict were: land, the money medium, and credit facilities.

The land question concerned more than mere allotments. Company policy, as laid down in Article 74 of the 1791 *Regulations*, reserved the waterfront for themselves. Since trade was to be their principal occupation, they needed the land there for quays and warehouses. But the Nova Scotians eschewed farming, and anyway at this juncture had no country land to farm. They were, however, as always, interested in trade; some had already acquired boats—since they had not landed destitute. They, too, therefore wanted access to the shore. In Nova Scotia the waterfront had been reserved for whites and they were adamantly determined not to be bilked twice.

Clarkson promised them equal rights on the shore, but the new surveyor, Richard Pepys, almost as soon as the governor left, on 30 December 1792, reserved the waterfront again for the company's buildings. Moreover, Dawes, the new governor, fearing the possibility of Temne attacks, took Pepys off surveying, to build a fort. This brought Dawes his first confrontation with the Settlers. They absolutely refused to give up the lot of one of their number in order that the fort could be erected on it. Here was the first serious constitutional crisis—a refusal to obey government.[49]

Distrust was increased upon learning the directors had changed their minds about the kind of town they wanted to build. Instead of a single conurbation surrounded by one agricultural area which was proving difficult to defend and which would mean increasingly longer daily walks to the farms on the expanding perimeter, they had come round to the concept of settling several groups of fifty families or so in a series of small townships, each surrounded by its own farm land.[50] Dawes was endeavouring to carry out this plan, but it meant that even the town lots and houses would be deranged, whilst the surveying of the country, or farm, lots, would have to be postponed for yet another year, though provisions were running low and the Settlers' allowances already halved.

Faced with rebellion, Dawes summoned a meeting on 6 February 1793, telling the Settlers their permanent town lots were now surveyed and that they must consequently relinquish the temporary ones on which they had been living. They replied by submitting an alternative plan of allotment,[51] and by stating: 'When placed on the lots we at present occupy, we were informed, they were merely for our temporary accommodation, and we promised, when the plan of the town was fixed on and surveyed, we would remove, but we were assured no public or other buildings would be erected between our lots and the sea . . .'[52]

They were referring to their talks with Clarkson, but his diary records only: 'I promised them they should not be excluded from the waterside.'[53] They had been assured of racial equality, however, and it was a matter of absolute principle that if there were lots on the shore, they should get them just as anyone else might. To Clarkson, however, his promise meant that the company, though it could build public buildings anywhere it liked, could not reserve all the coast. The Settlers may perhaps have originally misunderstood him—just as he, not comprehending their bitterness at being kept from the Nova Scotian waterfront, underestimated their demands—but they now asserted that the company having broken its promise, they considered their own cancelled. They would not move, therefore, unless new lots were set out running from the water's edge. They were free British subjects they said proudly, and they expected to be treated as such. Dawes unscrupulously replied it was not unusual for Clarkson to make 'prodigal and extraordinary promises'. Pepys, whom Clarkson had once befriended, added Clarkson had had no authority to make promises about land, which was untrue, and that he must have been drunk when he made them,[54] which was dastardly.

Finally, Dawes, flanked by Pepys and Zachary Macaulay, the second in council who had arrived about a month before, announced that farm lots would not be laid out until 1794. All this, of course, had settled nothing; by March 1793 unrest was widespread, and some had gone on strike.[55] They wrote to Clarkson who replied in a letter of 27 July[56] that he had made no promises the company had not authorised him to. He told them they must on no account break the law or the company would end. That would finish all hope of prosperity, in which alone lay their chance of getting an education and so of bettering themselves.

They had already seen these dangers, and instead of rebelling had sent a petition in June by Cato Perkins and Isaac Anderson to the directors. Article 15 of the 1791 *Regulations* empowered them to do this, but only after referring it to the council. The petitioners wanted to discover at first hand from the board exactly what Clarkson had been authorised to promise. The directors, receiving despatches from Dawes describing the complaints as 'frivolous and ill-grounded', tried to avoid a meeting. The petitioners insisted and, when at length admitted, told the board they had always believed in Clarkson. They asked for land on which to support their families rather than having to rely on company charity. Like the white traders in India who sought to end East India Company rule, they felt their interests were being jeopardised. They wanted to abolish company rule and get instead Crown government:[57] 'We *will not* be governed by your present agents in Africa . . . we want nothing but justice . . . we have been so often deceived by white people, that we are jealous when they make any promises, and uneasily wait till we see what they will come to!'[58]

The board asked for a written list of the broken promises, and received the following: thirty acres promised to man and wife and five for each child; tools and food provided at a reasonable price—which they estimated at about a 10 per cent surcharge—equal justice for black and white. Coming to the crux, they wrote: 'We are certainly not protected by the laws of Great Britain, having neither Courts of Justice, or officers appointed by the authority of this Government.'

They received no reply, returning home early in 1794. Matters had got worse in their absence; particularly, in April, the surcharge at the store was raised to 25 per cent, although the hundredors and tythingmen had complained about prices eight months before. The French war pushed up insurance and freight rates, whilst goods anyway became scarcer and dearer. The company already had heavy trading losses,[59] and was now forced to increase prices without raising wages. Later the surcharge on some goods was raised as high as 55 per cent, or more. Settlers began to hoard their specie, taking it up to Bunce Island to buy from the slave factory there. Higher prices could be had by barter than by money sales. The company's paper money encouraged a monopoly amongst a small group trading privately. They turned all articles into the few really profitable ones by barter, and then sold only those for specie.[60]

In October 1793 Dawes permitted a few Nova Scotians to open retail shops and at first sight this may seem liberal; but it was self-interest. Council minutes[61] show that the monopoly involved too much bother, especially in accounting, for which they had no trained clerks. At the same time the company stopped allowing black Settlers to have goods on credit. Trade, as the company well knew, depended on their giving credit, and their prohibition shows how desperate their finances already were. Even so, under the circumstances, racial discrimination like this was foolhardy. Continuing dissatisfaction over allotments led the council, on 1 September 1793, to offer twenty families a chance to settle on the Bullom, or north shore, of the Sierra Leone river, providing they relinquished their town and country lots in and around Freetown, and if they agreed to a quit-rent of one bushel of rice for each town lot and for each acre of country lot. No one accepted the offer. In August two more petitioners, complaining mainly of quit-rents, low wages and high prices, presented themselves before the directors.

Zachary Macaulay

Macaulay hoped some eminent Methodist could be sent out in order to establish discipline amongst them, 'for at present their government is pure democracy without subordination to anyone'.[62] Dawes went on leave in March 1794 and the more forceful Macaulay was now acting-governor.

With his unprepossessing looks and lack of conciliatory manners, Macaulay could be a formidable opponent. Clarkson, admitting his integrity, once said he was a man of illiberality who approved of arbitrary power.[63] He certainly disapproved of the American Revolutionary war on one hand, and the French Revolution on the other, feeling society was in danger, speaking of: 'the lawless, equalizing, atheistical principles which distinguish modern Democrats'. Looking for signs of these principles in Freetown, he naturally found them—as such people will—and when black Settlers criticised whites he saw it as insubordination. He dismissed two Nova Scotians[64] who, abused by a slave-ship's white crew working close inshore, had answered back. In June the hundredors and tythingmen sent him a 'warm remonstrance' over this action. Macaulay had the council resolve that it was most reprehensible, full of groundless accusations against the government and fomenting the very kind of disaffection it was their duty to prevent. Calling a public meeting, 20 June, he explained the dismissals, but the crowd abused him, threatened his life, beat up Richard Crankapone, the Nova Scotian marshal, and seemed likely to attack Government House. Macaulay began to encourage whites to keep aloof from blacks, buying a ship to take dissatisfied Settlers back to Nova Scotia. Having spent so many years getting away from it, none offered. Macaulay, however, prototype of later colonial administrators, could say they had turned down a reasonable alternative. One cannot have colonialism without self-justification.

Yet, as best he could, he was working to fulfil Clarkson's and Dawes' policy for more self-determination. Reading proposed regulations to the council he explained how he had laid them before the hundredors and tythingmen who had heartily agreed to accept them. Therefore, he said, they must be passed into law and considered as such, at least until the will of the directors, who had a right of veto, was known. He thus granted not only consultative powers but some legislative ones.[65]

In September and October 1794 the French sacked Freetown; amongst other things carrying off the coinage. Everyone had to use the company's paper money, exchangeable only at the company store. But the store was empty and the money worthless. Fortunately, after the pillage, a period of mutual co-operation ensued.

In March 1795, after the elections, Macaulay addressed the new hundredors and tythingmen.[66] What had done most to prevent progress, was a 'mistaken notion' of their rights. Free to dispose of their own property they had no right to the company's: 'Was it not that mistake which led you to oppose the allotments of the Town and to talk as if the land was yours and not the Company's?' It had led them, he continued, into keeping the company away from the waterside, into thinking that so long as work was paid for in wages the company had no right to ask more work for the land—he meant quit-rents. It led them into thinking schools and medicine were rights, that they were not bound to pay their debts (ie arrears of quit-rents), that they could help themselves to company property (some looting had occurred during the French raid). He read out the printed copy of the company's promises before they had embarked in Nova Scotia: 'Here is no word of credits, here is no word of schools, physicians, etc. Here is no word of wages bestowed without a return of labour. Here is no word of imposing on the Company such servants as you choose. Here is no word of being credited with goods till the produce of the land pays for it, as I have heard many people maintain was promised them.' At this point a Settler interrupted to say Clarkson had so promised; later Macaulay, always sternly just, minuted 'this is true'.

The company had promised black and white equal rights, he went on, and had kept it. Confusion over that had arisen when black Settlers confounded 'the privileges annexed to office with civil rights'. Harping on a theme familiar to West African nationalists between World War I and World War II, he said their salaries were less than white men's because they could not write, act, or think as well as whites. He had always filled posts with black people if suitable ones could be found.

As far as prices at the store went, they were not high enough and he intended raising them, so as to give to the company a real profit. The only grievance he admitted in this speech, remarkably foreshadowing many principles of late nineteenth-century imperialism, was that about land. Even here, he said, they had been compensated ten-fold by free provisions for nine months, by credit for goods, by free medicine and schools. In any case, they could have as much land as they liked providing they paid quit-rent for it.

Perfectly sincerely he concluded by expressing a hope that even from such a small beginning as this of tythingmen and hundredors 'a future House of Commons might arise to give laws to Africa'.

Dawes returned a few days later to find that some had been so aggravated by Macaulay's governorship they had obtained land at Pirate's Bay, from the Temne, and intended moving there in the autumn, where they would be outside company territory. These were extremists—all Methodists; most were content to get on with the work of reconstruction.

William Dawes

Macaulay now went on leave, and Dawes, more practical than Clarkson, more sympathetic and less ruthless than Macaulay, carefully refashioned the administration, building it on principles of mutual co-operation, and earning the trust of all save the radicals. He encouraged Settler participation in both legislative and executive spheres of government. In May the hundredors and tythingmen presented the council with a list of rules for their meetings.[67] Like the council, they had suffered from frivolous suits, and plaintiffs were now to pay their tythingman one shilling.[68] In June they politely asked the council to fix a ceiling on bread prices and to stop strangers selling meat retail—an act aimed no doubt at the Fula. The council obliged. In October (after the rains) they proposed a road tax, the settlement's first direct tax, whereby all under sixty years of age were to give six days work, or their equivalent, a year. They supervised it and maintained the roads themselves. On their initiative one hundredor and one tythingman, associated with any justice of the peace, were constituted a special court to hear petty cases,[69] and thus Nova Scotians received magisterial responsibilities. All was harmony, the council resolving such recommendations 'were highly proper and should be made to form part of the laws of the colony';[70] and so admitting hundredors and tythingmen to the kind of status later accorded to a legislative council.

Dawes, never well even on his first tour, suffered bad bouts of fever. He went home in April 1796 buying a house at Newtown, near Portsmouth. He had formed the necessary hyphen between the Clarkson's improvisations and the extreme professionalism of Macaulay. Looking back under Macaulay to the days of Clarkson and Dawes, Settlers came to think of them with nostalgia.[71]

Macaulay as Governor

In 1796 the Settlers elected no whites as hundredors and tythingmen. Extremists began, in the words of the directors' 1801 *Report*, to deny the laws of England and the governor's veto, to insist on judges of their own appointment and to aspire to the whole legislative authority.[72] John Garvin, an English Non-conformist schoolmaster sent out in 1793, and soon dismissed, had stayed on, venting the hatred of Non-conformists in England against the Establishment in Church and State, where he was soon joined by Jacob Grigg of the Baptist Missionary Society. They played on people's fears, saying that Macaulay was going to suppress the Nova Scotian preachers (Baptists and Methodists mainly), and shut their chapels. Sectarian strife died only when they were deported.

Macaulay, more determined than ever to give parliamentary democracy to Africa, worked away at forging a constitution, drafting 29 Articles, and showing them to the hundredors and tythingmen on 19 November 1796.[73] The draft would have given the vote to all over twenty-one paying a tax of over twenty cents a year. The fifth article proposed that: 'The Supreme power is

I

lodged in the general assembly of Sierra Leone composed of
three distinct and separate branches, viz: the Governor and
Council, the Senate, and the House of Commons, each having
a negative vote on the other two.' Each of the three districts
returned one citizen to the Commons; there were to be six
senators.

However, the December elections brought in largely illiterate
hundredors and tythingmen, deeply suspicious of Macaulay
and fearing he meant to enslave them, as Garvin and Grigg had
warned. When they asked the governor to explain his constitution, he decided to treat them with a high hand, feeling he was
independent of them and that they would not dare oppose the
execution of the existing laws. Any alterations, he reflected,
could only be done with his consent. He therefore decided to
put off constitution-making until men of moderation, less anti-
white, were elected.[74]

In January 1797, he announced that quit-rents would be
payable in July. The extremists, led by Nathaniel Snowball,
set up an illegal court on land not owned by the company at
Pirate's Bay. They cited to the court three loyal Settlers, requiring them to surrender the printed land grants issued by the
company. They asked Bai Farma for help in their rebellion.
Loyal Settlers feared their houses would be burnt. Macaulay,
never lacking in courage, gathering together the loyal Nova
Scotians and the Europeans on Thornton Hill, published a
notice threatening to hang any guilty of arson, even though,
still having no charter, he knew he might have to answer for it
at the Old Bailey.[75]

To forestall the malcontents, he reduced the number of writs
for the 1797 election. This was largely successful, though the
disaffection they had stirred up amongst the Temne simmered
throughout most of 1798.[76]

In January 1798 the new hundredors and tythingmen, mostly
'good men' he noted approvingly, petitioned for two chambers,
which he granted: one, of all the hundredors and one tythingman, the other a chamber of two hundredors and four tythingmen. They were 'to wait upon the Governor for the purpose of
forming rules and regulations for the use of the Colony' and

thus represented a significant constitutional step, often over-looked.[77]

The question of the quit-rents he allowed to lapse, however, judging it possible to collect only by force. But in January 1799 ordered by the directors to try again he announced that only those children whose parents had paid quit-rents could attend school free. This was unfortunate: discrimination like this separated the favoured, literate, assimilated black men from the illiterate, unassimilated, unfavoured ones. Governor Thomas Ludlam, his successor, later said the schools had divided the young people into different classes.[78] Perhaps Macaulay had meant to do that. However, he never did collect his quit-rents before he left in the spring of 1799.

Rebellion

In mid-February, just before he sailed, the hundredors and tythingmen demanded the appointment of two black justices of the peace and one black judge.[79] The council refused on the grounds that none had the necessary knowledge of English law and that there was no injustice in the present system, where the judge was assisted by a black jury.

In June, by which time Thomas Ludlam was governor, the demand was repeated; also, in returning a list of their legitimate officers, the overseers of roads, they took the opportunity of nominating Mingo Jordan, a teacher whose duty was to instruct such Temne children as the local notables sent for education, as their judge. John Cuthbert, a Baptist elder who had recently visited England, and Isaac Anderson, who had been one of the two deputies taking the second petition to the directors, were named as their justices of the peace. The council refused to accept it but promised to send the nominations to the directors.[80]

Getting no quick response, they met on 7 September, resolving that with the rest of the Nova Scotians, and the Granville Town dissidents, they were all proprietors of the 'colony' and that no foreigner should be allowed in, or have a vote without their consent. They meant to deny whites both sovereignty and franchise.[81]

In November the directors replied, stating English law was legal in the settlement and that JPs were appointed only by the Crown. Even if they wished, the board were powerless to appoint. The governor and council, because of its inflammatory nature and because quit-rents were already danger enough, kept this reply back until December. Even so, the new officers, in April 1800, again nominated a judge (James Robertson) and a JP (John Cuthbert).[82]

Only a few were extremists, but the council was powerless without legal authority. They were hoping, almost daily, for their long-delayed charter, as well as for British troops, both of which would give them greater strength. There was every reason to procrastinate, especially since, under the circumstances, nothing could be done except wait for the silent majority of moderate Settlers to come to their aid. For this to happen, matters had to get worse; they could count on no help there unless a direct attack was made on the government,[83] and this, for a long time, the extremists dared not risk. Through most of 1800, the council temporised. On 20 May Ludlam addressed some two dozen Settlers known to be averse to violence. He referred to current negotiations with the British Government, including an offer to hand the territory to the Crown. It was the only way of avoiding eventual bankruptcy and thus abandoning the Settlers outright. However, the rebels' unconstitutional demands might wreck the plan and frighten the government off. He reminded them that if the scheme succeeded, the king's authority, which the rebels so constantly demanded, would fall heavily on trouble-makers.[84] Undaunted, the hundredors and tythingmen, 'forbade' the holding of quarter sessions until new laws were made. On 25 September they promulgated these themselves, fixing prices, specifying fines for crimes, and denying the authority of the governor and council in anything but company affairs. People must obey or leave the settlement.[85]

Ludlam, next day, ordered the marshal to arrest the rebels and, in the excitement, shooting broke out. Some were taken. Anderson and Wansey, the ringleaders, escaped.[86] Only about fifty joined the rebels; most were for peace; even some of the radicals begged Wansey to surrender, adding that they had been seeking peace when they backed him. Those who escaped lingered outside the settlement, threatening to fight. King Tom sent word if they could not settle their palaver he would come and do so himself. Ludlam felt he must take the initiative and attack, weak though he was. On that day the Jamaican Maroons and their escort of soldiers arrived, in the very nick of time, to prevent defeat. Next morning the Maroons (and the forty-five white troops) landed. As much by their awesome reputation as anything, they persuaded the rebels to surrender.

The offices of hundredor and tythingman were abolished. Macaulay's exercise in parliamentary democracy had come to an end. Liberty for all was curtailed by the excesses of the few. Company government had been unjust, at times merely inefficient, unimaginative but never blameless.

The Maroons

In the eighteenth century Jamaica was the most important jewel in the imperial crown. There had been frequent slave risings on the island, but the planters' most lasting worry was the threat posed by the Maroons—free black communities living in the hills and officially granted their freedom by the Spaniards, when they left in 1655. By 1730, the time of the First Maroon War, a quarter of a million pounds had already been spent in trying to reduce them. Peace was patched up after eight years of inconclusive fighting, the treaty giving small areas of land for cultivation, and all the uninhabited parts of the island as their hunting grounds. This was a mistake; as numbers increased, land became insufficient, and their being required to live in their own hill towns prevented assimilation.

Many of their ancestors had come from the Gold Coast, from Asante territory, and had handed down their fighting qualities to their descendants. Taking no part in politics, they devoted their time to hunting, to returning runaway slaves— whom they despised and for whom, since the peace of 1738, they were paid £3 a head—and to selling sun-dried boar's meat which they brought down into the towns. They rebelled again in 1754 and in 1795, threatening the island's prosperity.

The West India lobby at Westminster was considerable, combining with the slave-trade interests of London, Bristol and Liverpool. Many large estates were bought on credit advanced from Britain, and there had been a tendency for holdings to become larger at the expense of the small planter. The metropole had perhaps a greater financial stake in the island than the plantation owners.[87] Thus, a continual and dangerous hazard in Britain's most important colony, the Maroons were of very much greater concern to His Majesty's Government than their pitifully small numbers might lead one to suppose.

Nominally in the charge of a white superintendent, they had their own generals, majors and captains, as administrative officers. Independent, clannish, unassimilated and bold, they were feared by slaves and planters alike. With Macaulay in Sierra Leone, the Jamaican legislature feared that the democratic principles of the French Revolution would lead to rebellion, like the rebellion of slaves in the French island of San Domingo in 1793. In 1795, the earl of Balcarres, the new lieutenant-governor of Jamaica, wrote to the duke of Portland, secretary of state, of a 'rebellion affecting the Empire at large'.

The immediate cause of the Maroon War in 1795 was an unpopular superintendent at Trelawney Town, who interfered with their women, and the flogging of two Maroons (for stealing pigs) by a slave, which was an intolerable insult. The real cause was land-hunger. The Maroons of Trelawney Town had modestly asked for another 300 acres, which was ignored. However, their popular superintendent, Captain James, Junior, was returned to them. A local JP reported they were content with that and all would be well if they were left alone,[88] but Balcarres, rightly mistrusting his militia, had already set out for the seat of trouble, when he met certain Maroon delegates hastening to patch up a formal submission. Unscrupulously perhaps, he had them put in chains, giving them three days to offer a formal surrender and accusing them of unprovoked rebellion. Earnestly desiring peace, 'General' Montagu, their aged leader, and thirty-seven notables did surrender. They were bound and put in prison, two being released (one was Montagu) to go to their comrades and persuade them to surrender too. But the Maroon community was divided, the younger generation despising the elderly, ineffective Montagu and his cronies. Thus, far from surrendering, as he advised, some 300 Trelawney Maroons, including women and children, fled into the woods. Whereupon no less than 1,500 European troops, some diverted from the San Domingo expedition, and 3,000 colonial militia were, at one time or another, moved up against them.

One more parley was held, when two Maroons hastened off to see Montagu, now in chains with the rest, and removed to a ship for greater security. This seemed like a prelude to banishment, so they called off the truce on 21 August, defeating the British on numerous occasions, being skilled bush-fighters. The ludicrous war was ended only when Major-General George Walpole cut them off from their food and water supplies.

The terms he made promised, in a secret clause, they would not be banished. They were given ten days, from 21 December, when peace was concluded, to deliver all the runaway slaves who had joined them, and they were to settle on whatever lands the governor and council decided.[89] This was thankfully accepted by the civil establishment, especially because the sugar harvest was imminent and all carts were needed for that rather than for supplying the military. But by 1 January 1796 only a handful had surrendered. Walpole, feeling the deadline too short, accepted the surrender of some 400 others, under the treaty, in January. In this, at the time, he seems to have had the governor's concurrence, because as late as 13 January the latter wrote to him: 'I think you may give them an opportunity until two o'clock tomorrow afternoon to come in, and then proceed against the remainder.'[90] Walpole took this to mean the Maroons were to come in under the terms of 21 December. He told Balcarres so: surrenders were being accepted 'under the treaty'. Even as late as 16 January the governor replied, giving him *carte-blanche*.[91]

Lord Balcarres, however, had powerful influences working on him. First, his council had never liked the treaty: six voting for accepting it, five against, and two abstaining.[92] Secondly, the duke of Portland sent him a confidential despatch which seems to have reached him on 15 January. This was followed by a private letter ordering him to secure the island against the possibility of any further rising, first by not restoring the rebels to their district, and secondly, 'by placing them in such a situation within the Island (if it cannot be done out of it, which would be preferable) as will, from its nature, incapacitate them from contriving further mischief.[93]

In April a joint committee of the council and general assembly, by twenty-one votes to thirteen, ruled the treaty was void since the runaway slaves had not been surrendered, and because those surrendering after the time limit could not expect the privileges of the treaty to be extended to them. They recommended deportation.[94] The governor therefore ordered Walpole to send all the Maroons to Montego Bay, and on 13 June 1796 informed Sir John Wentworth, Bt, lieutenant-governor of Nova Scotia, that he could expect them (this was his first intimation), and that it was not impossible they might have already arrived before the despatch.[95] The island was jubilant, voting £25,000 to buy land and settle about 550 Maroons in Canada. 'I have saved the Island', the governor wrote ecstatically.[96] The planters had finally broken the Maroons, and Jamaica remained free of any insurrection for over thirty years.

Walpole, of course, was disgusted. It was on 3 February that Balcarres had definitively told him no rebel still out could expect to come in under the treaty and it was then he had begun offering surrendering rebels their lives only.[97] He said he had been scandalously traduced and, with most of his field officers, felt the civil service had let the military down by making him seem to break his word. It was true the Maroons had not surrendered the runaway slaves, but they had disarmed them. They had delayed sending them, moreover, in good faith, believing that if sent in at that disturbed time, they would have escaped again.[98] He believed several Maroons had surrendered late because they or their families had been delayed by illness.

He resigned his commission, refusing the five hundred guineas subscribed by the Assembly to present him with a sword, entered the Commons and, producing petitions from the Maroons in Nova Scotia, managed to get the matter debated. It was poorly attended; only five MPs supported Walpole, and thirty-four supported the ministry.[99]

The Maroons in Nova Scotia

In Nova Scotia Wentworth did what he could, though the citizens of Halifax feared the Maroons' swaggering ways, their warlike reputation, their polygamy, cockfighting and boisterous festivals. They were put to work at ninepence a day on the fortifications whilst HMG decided what should be done next.[100] Perhaps they could settle permanently. Sierra Leone was suggested. Meanwhile about three thousand acres were bought, some the very land the Nova Scotian Loyalists now in Sierra Leone had found so inhospitable. Discipline was well maintained by the Maroons themselves, under their two white Jamaican commissioners. Offences were tried in the presence of at least three Maroon captains, the latter told what the conviction would be on a similar white offender, and judgement given accordingly. A Church of England chaplain and schoolmaster were seconded. Assimilation had begun.

Wentworth, who had no colour prejudice and indeed kept a black mistress, watched results eagerly, reporting to Portland he could discern no sign of malice or revenge, and that they made very good soldiers. They survived Nova Scotia's worst winter for nearly fifty years; despite their disinclination to wear shoes and stockings the governor was able to report with insouciance: 'I do not find that anyone has lost more than a joint of a toe or finger, and but a few of those.'[101] However, the Maroons were hunters and predators and their health suffered through lack of accustomed exercise. By the spring they were complaining that no tropical crops would grow. They sent two petitioners to London asking to be sent elsewhere.[102]

The Ministry wanted to prevent criticisms being aired on the floor of the Commons; the Treasury wanted to avoid financial responsibility; the Jamaican Assembly, extending its vote for their expenses in Nova Scotia until July 1798, sought relief from the financial burden which altogether cost them nearly £50,000. Ochterlony, the subordinate commissioner in Nova Scotia, had private dreams of being made their colonel in some tropical part of the empire where he could engage in deeds of martial splendour; consequently he discouraged them from working, hoping this would hasten their deportation. The other commissioner, W. D. Quarrell, wanted them broken up into smaller units and thus more easily assimilated. The governor, thinking they were all his friends, wanted them kept together. However, like everyone, he was in awe of their reputation and he temporised telling them if they would petition him they could be sent elsewhere: 'where their valour would make them happy and great'.[103]

Who was going to pay? The English Commons debated it, but turned it down. The Jamaican Assembly had had enough. The uncertainty was no inducement to farm—a calling they did not like anyway—and so Wentworth told them firmly they were not going away in the near future. Officials now, making the best of a bad job, began to find many reasons why it was in their interest to stay in Nova Scotia. The Maroons at Boydville were discovered to have been against moving all along, to be anxious to farm. Comparisons with the Nova Scotian Loyalists were now seen as fallacious. It was pointed out how many blacks lived prosperously in Nova Scotia who only thirteen years ago had nothing except a government ration. They now owned land and quantities of cattle. It was mainly the charisma of Thomas Peters which had persuaded some to emigrate. Other reasons were seen to be the unjust way land had been assigned to them and to the bad management of the province in making unsuitable arrangements when they first arrived. Wentworth told Portland that the Loyalists were quite different from the Maroons: ex-slaves, the former had had no idea how to provide for themselves and had joined the army where they got subsistence and 'gathered more dissoluteness than economical discretion'.[104] The clothing and provisions given them were now seen as a mistake—encouraging idleness. When unemployment arose the white Loyalists had been able to seek jobs elsewhere, but there were few places the Nova Scotians could have gone without danger of re-enslavement. Their departure had left behind the problem of the sick and infirm, whom hitherto the extended family system had supported in the traditional African way. Wentworth spoke feelingly of governments willing to spend thousands transporting blacks but unwilling to give him anything to keep them.[105] All this had been overlooked, he said, in the zeal engendered by the humanitarians. Many more had died in Sierra Leone, proportionately, than had succumbed amongst those staying behind. The Maroons, Wentworth went on, were very different. They were already well provided with schools and the opportunity of religious instruction.

1798 came around and with it a second petition to leave, sent through General Walpole. They despatched another shortly to Henry Thornton. The Ministry began to fear more awkward questions in the House; though Jamaica had voted money for 1798 it had not been paid by 1799 and Portland, authorising the Treasury to meet the bills, feared Britain might find herself responsible. Accordingly the under secretary approached the Sierra Leone Company early in 1799.[106] Everything was to be done as cheaply as possible, but when Wentworth reported not all Maroons wanted to leave, he received a curt reply from the secretary of state that it was not the policy of HMG to consult the Maroons at any stage, and they were not to be told of the government's decision until as late as possible so as to avoid trouble.[107] Hastily doing sums, the under secretary estimated it would cost about £10,000 a year to keep them in Nova Scotia, whilst it had cost only £30,000 in 1792 to ship the Nova Scotians to Sierra Leone. The Maroons, less in number, could be shipped for about one-third the sum—merely what it might cost Britain, if she could not get out of it, annually to keep them in Nova Scotia.[108] Scenting a bargain, Britain offered to pay for transportation, settlement and education, if the Sierra Leone Company would accept responsibility for administration.[109] Seizing their opportunity, the company pressed for a government subvention, for soldiers, and—again—for their long-delayed charter. Successfully receiving £7,000 to fortify Thornton Hill, a promise of troops together with an annual grant of £4,000, and their charter, they accepted the Maroons.[110]

By March 1799 arrangements between Portland and Thornton were well advanced, but the first Wentworth heard of it was from Portland's despatch dated 18 June. It looked for a while

as though the Maroons' departure from Nova Scotia was going
to be as precipitous as their arrival. The reasons for their going
were as remote from their own lives as ever. Transport was
delayed, however, and they did not sail for nearly another year.
They had agreed that each male would get three acres, each
wife two, each child one. They were to pay one shilling annual
quit-rent or, in lieu, half a day's work. No provisions were to
be given after six months.[111] Before they landed they were asked
again to acknowledge acceptance of these terms. Many refused;
having been duped in Jamaica in 1795, they had resolved never
to sign another agreement.[112]

The Maroons in Sierra Leone

Landing at midnight, 1 October, they quelled the Nova
Scotian rebellion. A presumably grateful company later voted
$400 to those who had borne arms. This came to $2 70c
each.[113]

The Maroons had now shattered the canard that they were
out to destroy legitimate government. In Jamaica they had for
years returned runaway slaves and acted as the planters'
reliable and efficacious ally in slave rebellions. They despised
slaves, loved fighting, and had begged General Walpole and
the British Government to be allowed to create a territory for
their families, part of the British Empire, somewhere in the
tropics. Despite careful explanations by the Sierra Leone Company, they sailed from Halifax with that intention. Landing,
they could hardly have found a situation more to their fancy,
a countryside more like their precipitous Cockpits than the
magnificent slopes behind Freetown.

Very many, of course, were illiterate. The company tried to
assimilate them, settling them, not on the Bullom Shore as
intended, but at Granville Town. At first the Nova Scotians
were almost afraid to work beside them, armed as they were,
and quick to take offence and level their weapons. To curb
polygamy, bachelors were henceforth permitted only one wife
and a marriage register begun. A superintendent, George Ross,
who had brought them from Nova Scotia, and a JP were
assigned them. In 1802 Robert Johnson, a Maroon colonel,

was appointed a commissioner of the Court of Requests. They did not make much progress with their farms in the mountains, allotted in March 1801, because they received them too late for that season's planting and anyway house-building required most of their attention at first. If they wanted extra work they could find it as labourers at the very attractive pay of two shillings and sixpence a day. They were not destitute, however, many when they left Jamaica carried loot gathered in their raids; according to Quarrell, several were 'pretty rich'.[114] In any case the Temne, encouraged by certain exiled Nova Scotians and the slave traders, attacked from the west in November 1801, and it was decided to move the Maroons for safety into Free-town, Granville Town and its crops being abandoned to the enemy. Many now gave up farming and became craftsmen instead—especially carpenters. In November and December they spent a happy week or two firing the deserted Temne towns and plantations to the west of the settlement, whence they had driven King Tom. Governor Dawes, having acquired land there, gave each Maroon a portion, and they employed Nova Scotians to clear the ground for them, enjoying their own role as guardians and sentries.

In March 1803 they were given 103 town lots, strategically placed under Fort Thornton, their rallying point in time of danger. Although they agreed to a quit-rent in Nova Scotia, they saw eye to eye with the Nova Scotians and now 'Major' Jarrett objected to it in an 'inflammatory' manner. Ludlam, easily the company's most constructive thinker so far, pointed out that the rent brought in less than £100 a year, and none would have pushed it in the first place if they had dreamed it would end in rebellion. He was now against it, reminding the directors that after the lull in 1797, their request to have the rent collected, in 1798, had led to the confrontation. In any event it was five or six times as high as that in America. People feared that if they could not pay it, it would make them slaves. Few objected, on the other hand, to prices at the company store, or to not appointing their own judges, but all hated the quit-rent. Now that the fearsome Maroons were added to the opposition, it had better be very considerably reduced.

In fact, ostensibly as a reward for Settler loyalty in the Temne War, it was abolished in 1803.[115]

There now occurred three events, important to the settlement in general and the Maroons in particular. In 1807 the British Parliament made the slave trade illegal within the empire. On 1 January 1808, Sierra Leone passed from the hands of the Sierra Leone Company, and became a Crown colony. On 16 March that year, an order in council established a vice-admiralty court in the colony for the trial and adjudication of slave ships and their cargoes brought in as prizes. Recaptives were looked after by the Captured Negro Department: by 1812 they already outnumbered the Settlers.

The British Government introduced a new charter in 1811 which, making slight constitutional changes, required an oath of allegiance to His Majesty. The Maroons, having enough of oaths, and being accustomed to getting their own way, encouraged by Charles Shaw who had led the fighting in Jamaica, refused to subscribe. Never thinking the government would dare to offend them, some were surprised when, having gone over to the Bullom Shore, they were declared outlaws. In fact Governor Charles Maxwell, now enlisting recaptives into the army, used them as a counterpoise to the Maroons, as the latter had once been to the Nova Scotians. It was a bitter lesson they had to try to learn. Some did return, to humbler circumstances, but though several held quite high office, like John Thorpe, who had learnt to read in Nova Scotia and eventually became sheriff in 1818, many never became assimilated, building their own Maroon church, and petitioning their old friend, General Walpole, to get them sent back to Jamaica.[116] In 1840 one of them, Mrs Mary Brown, bought an old schooner and went back home with some of her friends including Thorpe. Sixty-four went the following year, but that generation was old now; few were left. Those born in the colony and its environs looked on it as home. The 1865 Jamaican rebellion, and its brutal suppression, was no encouragement.

In April and May 1819 five companies of the Second, and all of the Fourth West Indian Regiment had arrived. The Fourth and some of the Second were discharged there, adding

1,030 to the population and considerably diluting the purely Maroon element in the West Indian contribution to the colony. The Royal African Corps was disbanded, too; henceforth, recaptives were drafted into the five companies of the Second West Indian Regiment, now stationed in Freetown.

The Recaptives or Liberated Africans

Recaptives, unlike Nova Scotians and Maroons, had never seen a white man until they were embarked on a slave ship; and of course, they had no corporate identity. As Professor Porter has said: 'apart from colour identity there was not much else that was common between the Settlers and the newcomers'.[117] They were suspicious of everyone. The Reverend Henry Düring of the Church Missionary Society, has left a harrowing picture of the first village in the mountain district, Leicester (founded in 1809), formed to take the overflow from Freetown: 'Most of those with whom I had to do were sick with the Dysentery or else large Ulcers of which a great many died; but my greatest difficulty I had with them was that they mistook every act of kindness for certain signs of being sold again as soon as cured . . .'[118]

Unfortunately, until about the 1830s, there was not much contact between the Settlers and the liberated Africans, who were regarded by the former as 'illiterate, heathenish and barbarous'.[119] Until about 1850 the gradations in Freetown society depended very largely on Settler descent and on participation in, and conformity to, western cultural patterns. There were few schools for children of recaptives. They were, in any case, very often apprenticed, working during school hours. Adults and apprentices could only attend Sunday schools. This separation hindered their assimilation.

The British, generously devoting large sums to naval patrols during and after an exhausting and expensive war, fell down, as before, when it came to succouring and rehabilitating. Including the fiascos of the 'Black Poor', Nova Scotians and Maroons, nowhere perhaps was failure more pronounced than here.

Between 1808 and 1814 four men governed Sierra Leone and

the policy of government towards liberated Africans varied with each one.

Thomas Perronet Thompson, an ex-soldier, saw Freetown as full of libertine ideas. Dollars, he felt, reminded the inhabitants of the American Revolution and he changed the currency to pounds, shillings and pence. Freetown became Georgetown. He found the Nova Scotians obstinate, was inclined to favour Maroons and recaptives, especially the latter who seemed obedient. He abandoned the scheme of apprenticeship, which Ludlam had begun and which the Abolition Act allowed, and began to settle them in colony villages. Here, he hoped, they would not be polluted by the Nova Scotians in Freetown, and they would become the spearhead of civilisation into the interior. They would, incidentally, be a perimeter defence against attack. Edward Columbine, RN, during his sixteen months of governorship, reinstated the apprenticeship system but the influx grew so fast, all could not be absorbed. Many went of their own accord to independent villages. Governor Charles Maxwell, who succeeded in 1811, like Columbine used enlistment and apprenticeship as much as possible, but he reported home that those who had gone to the mountains had become self-supporting; thus any who could not be apprenticed or enlisted, should be made farmers. Whitehall refused to say anything definite to this, except that he was to spare no effort to reduce the numbers of persons to whom government had to give rations.

By 1811 there were some twelve hundred recaptives in the colony, but 1812 almost doubled that figure. By 1814 the vice-admiralty court had emancipated about six thousand, and three-fifths of the population were recaptives. It was Governor Charles MacCarthy (1814–24) who saw clearly and logically what had to be done and, with Church Missionary Society help, did it. The CMS became responsible for the administration and cultural transformation of the villages, and the government subsidised them, a Liberated African Department (the Captured Negro Department renamed, 1822) being established in Freetown to see to their welfare.

In MacCarthy's view the villages had failed because they

were not Christian and their agriculture did not produce enough to support even themselves. He gave 1,000 acres of Leicester Mountain to the CMS for schools to teach recaptives to be self-sufficient. In 1817 he got British approval to divide the country into parishes, each with its own clergyman who would both instruct and manage his village, representing central government in the local administration.[120] Grants from Britain for the Liberated African Department greatly increased. In 1815 the total expense of administering the colony was £29,000. Next year it was £41,000, increases covered by British Treasury grants. In 1823, it rose to £95,000; in 1825, the first full year after his death, it dropped to £39,000. From 1816–24 the average annual expenditure for the Liberated African Department alone had been higher than that. New villages were built. Leicester (1809), Wilberforce (1810) and Regent (1812) were the only ones recognised by the government when he took over. Before 1820 he established government authority at ten more.

Each recaptive was given food, clothing and certain tools by the central government. By 1819 they were getting a regular ration of rice, palm-oil and salt. In 1823 over two-thirds received government assistance. Only at Regent was more than a third of the population self-supporting. At Wellington, Hastings and York (founded 1819) the entire population depended on government. His parish plan was working well with schools operating, parishes defined, and superintendents appointed. Yet two years after his death things had decayed. Indeed they began to go downhill after 1821; first because in that year the governor of Sierra Leone became administrator-in-chief of the West African Settlements and was often out of the colony. Secondly, the CMS, who had never managed to recruit more than a few missionaries in England, by not providing sufficient or adequate personnel, began a period of deteriorating relations in their partnership with the government. They preferred to concentrate on their Susu mission in the northern rivers territory. Missionaries felt, too, that one should not try, as the superintendents had, to serve Church and state at once. Soon after MacCarthy's death the CMS asked to be relieved of the

K

superintending. Governor Charles Turner replaced them with government managers, especially West Indians who would know how to grow cotton and coffee. To MacCarthy baptism was 'an act of civilisation',[121] to Turner civilisation meant the ability to produce exports.

In the twenty-seven years after MacCarthy there were twenty-eight administrators, each left to himself in the matter of liberated Africans. Recaptives were sent to the villages after three months on public works in Freetown. Many arrived when the season for planting was over. They worked for other recaptives, already established, drawing water and cutting wood, and doing farm work for a year or so. Then they set up on their own, employing their own newly landed recaptives. The Liberated African Department tried to settle them evenly over the colony, clearing the bush and laying down a line on which houses were to be built, whether or not it was a good, healthy or convenient place to live. There was no inducement to stay; newcomers soon abandoned their huts to join fellow-countrymen elsewhere. What began as a cradle of civilisation, after 1825 grew into a base merely for judicial and naval operations against the slave trade. Governor Dundas Campbell, arriving in 1835, found there were no schools at all for newly arrived recaptive children, and that the apprentice system was flagrantly and continually abused. As far as she had one, Britain's policy from 1825 to 1850, was for greater and greater economy and less and less involvement. Settlers and liberated Africans were left to look after themselves.

In a glutted market wages were depressed. From 2s 6d a day at the time of the Maroons' arrival, they had gone down to 4d. Many never got a paid job all their working lives. Nine-tenths were unemployed. Between 1807 and the end of 1836, the records showed that 56,563 were landed. Yet the colony's population was only 33,628. Twenty-three thousand had vanished. Some, seeking the employment their numbers denied them in Freetown, had gone to work as domestic slaves for chiefs in the interior. It was said that Gallinhas slavers in the 1830s (Gallinhas and the Bights were the only significant West African centres by now) shipped 10,000 slaves annually (mainly to Havanna). Many were Mende who, liberated in Freetown, soon found their way home. In the early 1840s the King's Yard had never been so crowded; to relieve pressure, groups of several hundred were from time to time despatched to the Gambia where a Liberated African Department was set up in 1836. Men died quicker than women; the Liberated African Department's chief clerk estimated there were three men to every two women in the colony. Ships' cargoes show even greater imbalance of the sexes. A typical sample of 425 slaves contained only 40 women and 80 girls. No population could survive under these circumstances.

Ironically it took almost twice as long for a prize crew, beating to windward from the Bights of Benin and Biafra, to bring recaptives into Freetown for adjudication than a slave ship needed to cross the Atlantic. Hundreds landed weak and ill. Sent to Kissy hospital, which entailed a pitiful three-mile walk, many died almost as soon as admitted. Mortality rates are harrowing, even at this distance in time. Of 4,417 liberated in 1835, 1,154 died within three months. There is no doubt that the main cause of the 23,000 missing persons in 1836 was death.

Governor Dundas Campbell was amazed at the way they helped one another. Many lived on what they could grow, in times of need relying on the willing charity of neighbours.

Nearly every group in any colony village had its own head-man. This was the earliest form of their political organisation, taking part in prevention and punishment of crime. Benefit societies, too, took on political and judicial functions.[122] Though in theory British law operated, it was often administered in modified form, 'country fashion', all very like their own village life, left some knew not how many hundreds of miles away. Then came the institution known as the Seventeen Nations which developed in the 1840s beginning at Waterloo, when the headman or 'king' of the Freetown Yorubas, or Akus, was sent to pacify rioting Yoruba and Ibo. It was a council representing all seventeen tribes at Waterloo, redressing petty grievances, assisting in administering justice and keeping order. The idea spread through other villages until liberated Africans were most successfully filling the void Britain had failed to provide for, controlling their own affairs for the rest of the century.

The apprenticeship system, enlistment into the services, and the colony village scheme all helped recaptives to adjust to the dominant Settler culture in Freetown. In 1853 when Britain passed an Act declaring liberated Africans British subjects, like the Nova Scotians, they were tacitly recognising the direction social change had taken in the colony. Creole society had been born.[123]

The Creoles

Trade provided the key whereby liberated Africans entered creoledom. The villages remaining agricultural, by the late 1830s migration of liberated Africans to Freetown had begun. Companies arose, men banding together in the Freetown market to buy or sell. Some traded a hundred miles up-country with European goods bought from shopkeepers, or at auctions of condemned slave-ships, returning with rice, country cloth, sheep and goats. It was they, not the British, who diversified the economy. Very often these were Yoruba who were skilled traders and whose own culture included large cities; Freetown did not seem strange to them. In trading and securing property with their savings, they followed the Nova Scotians. Having no prior knowledge of English with which to communicate, Krio was born, mainly a mixture of English, German, French, Yoruba, Ibo, Portuguese and local languages. Making money, they sent their sons to England for education. Returning, they married into élite Settler families. By the 1870s old distinctions of class were almost obliterated, though nothing was done to bring the indigenous inhabitants of the colony into society. Having risen in the world by cleverly adopting European ways and rejecting those African ones which conflicted with them, this is not surprising. Like European travellers and writers, Creoles despised most African institutions as keeping people back in ignorance. James Africanus Horton, one of their most prolific writers at this time, envisaged the British and other empires falling as Rome had fallen. In time would come the turn of the Africans—providing they gave themselves up to hard work and inventiveness as had the people of Europe and the Creoles.

Traders gradually settled inland. The timber trade, begun in 1816 by an Irishman John McCormack, attracted several Maroons into the creeks of the Bumpe and Ribbi. Employing gangs of up to 300 men, it raised wages to sixpence, and many got employment for the first time. Money seemed plentiful in the colony. However, the forests were soon worked out; timber was replaced by groundnuts in the north, first exported in 1837 by Charles Heddle. Smaller Creole traders followed him along the rivers Scarcies and Mellacourie; 1839 was a significant year. A group of Yorubas decided to return home, having prospered sufficiently to buy a trading ship, which they sailed to Badagry with passengers and goods. As in the West Indies, black men had received neither official help nor encouragement in diversifying the economy. Dissatisfied recaptives were attracted by calls to their homeland. They were not keen to take up the official emigration schemes now sponsored in the West Indies. In any case freed slaves there were discouraged by planters and government alike from working outside the sugar industry. Freetown Creoles henceforth were likely to be drawn along the coast. Many young men got clerkships and by mid-century Creoles were to be found from the Gambia to Fernando Po. When the American 'Mende Mission' opened in the Bum river in the late 1840s, an area hitherto little penetrated by Creoles, there was an increasing influx into the Sherbro. At first timber, then palm-kernels were exported. The latter, easier to trade in and needing less capital, attracted many small traders from the nearest colony villages in the south, like Kent. Intrepid Creole women hawked goods from town to town. In 1861, to keep out France, the Colonial Office annexed British Sherbro, though unwillingly.

In the Muslim north, traders did not penetrate so far inland and were put off in the 1880s anyway by the Sofa raids. None the less much of the colony's trade was with the northern rivers area and the 1860s and early 1870s was an era of considerable prosperity. All was well, so long as there was peace and merchants continued prosperous, but in 1865 civil war broke out. The British refused to authorise intervention; in any case many did not want it, afraid the Sierra Leone tariffs would be extended to the area. French tariffs were lighter and nineteen Mellacourie traders in 1865 were induced to petition France for protection. More and more traders went into the northern rivers' trade, landing their goods where no duty was payable; Freetown's revenue suffered.

Worse, perhaps, in 1873, Governor John Pope-Hennessy abolished all import duties save on tobacco, arms and liquor. Colonial revenues dipped sharply. In any case world prices were falling and West African ones with them. To anxious Creole traders the solution seemed to be: annexe the hinterland and adjacent rivers, and apply a tariff, thus forestalling the French, retrieving the revenue, directing lost trade back to Freetown, and establishing peace in those parts. In 1875, Sierra Leoneans petitioned for the acquisition of the river Scarcies, and of the coastline from Freetown southward to Sherbro.[124]

Soon, tribal wars upset the Sherbro trade too, upon which so very much of the colony's prosperity depended. Sir Samuel Lewis in 1879 prepared a pamphlet, *The Wants of Sierra Leone*, later published. Perhaps the most influential Creole at that time, he argued the colony could live only by trade and, having no great waterway to the interior, the best method of counteracting tribal wars and French encroachment was territorial expansion.

In 1885 three main centres of war near the coast were disrupting Freetown trade.[125] In an effort to put pressure on the government the leading Freetown merchants—both British and African—founded the Sierra Leone Association, but HMG was still not ready to accept new military or financial responsibilities. However, learning the importance of influence at Westminster, they resurrected the Freetown Chamber of Commerce which from 1890–6 supplied local information to the African committees of the chambers of commerce in Liverpool and Manchester, which those chambers had set up to bring pressure on the Colonial Office. At last, in 1890, the latter, becoming alive to the French activities all round the colony's hinterland, authorised treaty-making with as many chiefs as possible to the north and east. Finally, in 1896, the Protectorate Ordinance was proclaimed.

The period 1870–1900 has been called the apogee of Creole civilisation and ascendancy.[126] In almost every walk of life there were trained and qualified Africans. In 1872, Governor Pope-Hennessy wrote to the secretary of state that the two most intelligent men in the legislative council were African, so were the best scholar on the coast, the most intelligent clergy and the clerks in the public service. Very likely; the Sierra Leone civil establishment in 1865 had been described as a 'wretched poverty stricken machinery'.[127] There was a vigorous, intelligent and responsible local press, whose correspondence, articles and leaders, compare favourably in every way with English newspapers today. Indeed their world news coverage was often better.

Class and status were soon validated by political power. In 1853 a Sierra Leone Committee of Correspondence was formed to press for 'the constitutional privilege of representation'.[128] Five years later the Merchants' Association petitioned the secretary of state to set up an elected house of assembly in Sierra Leone. Change did come. In 1863 a new constitution divided the old council into an executive and legislative council, the latter to include some unofficial members. The first two were Charles Heddle and John Ezzidio, elected by the Merchants' Association. Ezzidio was a recaptive. In 1893 a comparable step was taken in local government and Freetown became a municipality.

The economic supremacy of the Creoles was now challenged: by adverse world trade; by a change in the policy of mercantile houses which, as medicine made the coast safer for whites, abandoned the Creole retailer and set up their own agents; by the influx from about 1900, of Lebanese and Syrian traders who soon learnt to undercut them; and by the Creoles themselves who, rather than apprenticing their sons to trade, preferred, when prosperous, to turn them into professional gentlemen —lawyers, doctors, etc. Further, the opening of the protectorate by education and commerce, and the change in the government's attitude to the Creoles modified the social stratification in Freetown. By the 1890s the government had decided to insulate the protectorate as much as possible from Creoles, who were no longer the instrument of civilisation and colonisation. The interior, under a system which eventually came to be known as Indirect Rule, was to remain uncreolised under its own rulers.

CHAPTER 5

Colonial Expansion

Eighteenth-century Changes in Britain and in Temne Country
The eighteenth century was a period of transition and change; for Britain an age of partial release—in trade and commerce, from monopoly and government control; in politics, from benevolent despotism; in industry, by the industrial revolution.

Adam Smith's *The Wealth of Nations* attacked slavery at length; not on humanitarian grounds, but because it denied the sacred principles of a free labour market. His book came out when the American Revolutionary War was driving the first nail into the coffin of protectionist mercantilism. Thus some have seen Abolition as the logical outcome of economic development. The 1807 Abolition Act, the 1832 Reform Bill, the ending of slavery in 1834, the 1836 equalisation of East and West India sugar duties (and hence the end of protection for West Indian planters), and the Corn Law repeal of 1846, were part of the same thread: the forward movement of the British industrial classes and their intellectual spokesmen, confident that, given free trade, Britain could become the workshop of the world. Clarkson, however, though he agreed, more or less, with Smith's doctrines, saw slavery crying out for humanitarianism; saw himself not so much an economist as an instrument of God.

Society in Europe was under considerable strain as a result of the industrial revolution. There was a struggle for existence, whether the prize was social status, economic gain, or political power. A few romantics like Byron, Shelley and Schiller, looking for tranquillity, dropped out. Some like Goethe's Faust, even Marx's struggling proletariat, tried to master nature.[1]

Others, like the Swedenborgians, a number of whom were connected with the Sierra Leone Company,[2] wanted reconciliation
with nature, seeking Utopia in Africa. Granville Sharp's settlement was founded on the romantic notion of brotherhood in a
state specifically not out for gain. Geographical discoveries
quickened interests already roused by the concept of the 'noble
savage', and Edmund Burke's speeches in Warren Hastings'
trial and impeachment, 1787–95, opened people's eyes to the
concept of commercial connections implying a trusteeship.
Lord Mansfield's judgement in 1772 freed 14,000 slaves in
England and brought the black man's problems on to many a
doorstep. It is no coincidence that the first modern missionary
societies were founded at that time.[3]

Zachary Macaulay looked to Africa for refuge in case French
Revolutionary principles overthrew England. He saw it his
duty to pass on 'civilisation'—English law and all its respects
for property. After all there was no doubt who stood at the
Lord's right hand; as a prayer issued to foreign ships entering
British ports in the cholera epidemic of the 1830s made plain:
'O Almighty God who hath visited the nations near us with
sudden death of thousands, spare we beseech Thee, this Thy
favourite land.'[4]

The eighteenth century was a time of change for the Temnes
also, a period of great disaster and decline. In Port Loko, the
Susu ousted the Temne and Loko rulers in mid-century, controlling its trade and politics. In Yonni Temne territory the
Fula assumed a dominant role which exists today. Elsewhere
Mandinka Muslims from the new Islamic theocracies in Futa
Jallon, established themselves as mori men and virtually controlled the territory they occupied. On the coast the Europeans
sent in agents. Gumbu Smart, a Loko and factor for English
slave traders who built up a Loko settlement in Masimera
country, dominated Temne commerce and politics there. The
bunduka as agents of the French went out along the Rokel
grabbing trade for their masters. The booming slave trade
attracted the Mende into Temne territory, too. Civil wars dis-
tracted them, involving Masimera, Port Loko and Bombali
peoples, raging for many years.[5]

The arrival of the Sierra Leone Company was another disaster. The treaty of 22 August 1788 acknowledged the usual dues paid for ships' watering, but if a vessel merely anchored, a duty of ten 'bars' was to be paid 'to the free Settlers'. This was the first time any 'stranger' had taken a share in the duties; it was an ominous moment.

Incredibly the company remained in total ignorance of the local system of landlord and stranger until after Naimbana's death in 1793, and thus paid him neither the requisite 'dashes' nor due respect.[6] Nor did they get him to settle their internal squabbles, as they should have, and inadvertently insulted him and his people.[7] Only when he died, and the young men of Robana—Naimbana's town—accused the company of poisoning his son, did Macaulay find they had none to speak for them.[8]

The need to fill the various offices, chiefly and in the Poro Society, vacant on Naimbana's death, was partly the cause of the young men's unrest. Society was already dislocated by western contamination. Disbursements in cash for rents, 'dashes', customs, services, and purchase of local produce upset the hierarchy, by introducing to a wage economy and to office young men who would not otherwise have received them. Elliot Griffith, a former valet in London, became Naimbana's secretary, and was appointed as the company's interpreter—a position well-known for its potential in graft under nineteenth-century imperialism. He now led the young men.

Macaulay was told by a Temne that free men had become more independent of their chief since the foundation of Freetown and the old chiefs were very indignant.[9]

The Land Question

All problems were dwarfed by the land question. Frequent and inconclusive palavers were held, and in the end the Temne went to war over it. Naimbana never signed the Sharp Settler treaty of 11 June 1787, though he 'ratified' it on 12 July.[10] He put his mark on the 22 August 1788 treaty—a replica of the previous year's, with suitable changes of names—but he told Falconbridge in 1791 he had been hastily drawn into disposing of the land, which he had no right to sell, and he must get consent of all his headmen before allowing strangers even to live amongst them.[11] None the less the 1791 directors' *Report* spoke of land 'actually purchased and given up by the native chiefs ... so that it is an English territory'. Expropriation had begun.

The Temne were very patient; even when avenues were cut through their rice plantations and the bush which protected their villages.[12] The new Bai Farma, crowned in 1794, intended to exercise his rights, however. Objecting to not being called to settle the riot on 20 June 1794[13] and the one after the French raid when the company's stores were looted, he felt justifiably furious when asked to confirm the company's possession.[14] He wanted to return the 'payment' for the land, with the idea of dissolving the contract and having instead the usual agreement for an annual rent.

Macaulay regarded a landlord's rights as 'interference' and sent James Watt, an ex-West Indian planter, to tell Bai Farma: 'we were now there, and that we had nothing to lose, and that they had better consult their own interest and not provoke us too far'.[15] King Tom told the governor unequivocally, in December 1796, no man had a right to alienate any part of the country and any sale was unlawful and thus void.[16] Macaulay, with a weak claim, fell back on bluff and bluster, saying it was a matter of indifference what their private laws might be.[17] When the Nova Scotian quit-rent malcontents approached King Tom, understandably he gave them sanctuary. The Wesleyan Methodists and the Lady Huntingdon people proposed to appoint one of themselves king after the Temne manner, and have him advised, like Temne kings, by a council, which brings to mind both the Egba United Board of Management at Abeokuta in 1865, and the Fante Confederation of 1871. All were adaptations of traditional rule to modern demands,[18] where westernised Africans advised traditional rulers, so as to stop British encroachment. A series of palavers were held all through 1798, and at one of them the governor showed King Tom various 'deeds of sale'. The king replied correctly that former agreements did not bind him, the country fell to him on his being crowned, and he would make his own bargain. Macaulay again showed the documents saying they had 'fairly bought the land'. Tom was furious, but could do nothing.[19]

In 1799 relations worsened, the king's men raiding cattle across the western boundary and the Settlers, without the governor's knowledge, arming themselves, entering Temne territory and seizing the culprits. The king retaliated by driving away the Kru and other labourers who daily went to work in Freetown.[20] When the Nova Scotians rebelled in 1800, King Tom said he was coming to settle them—as was his traditional right—but the Maroons arrived.

Augmented by Maroons, defended by Governor William Dawes' fortifications (he was an engineer), the administration forced the Temne into a final settlement of their eastern and western boundaries, upon pain of making Bai Farma have King Tom de-stooled. The boundaries cut into Temne culti-vated land. All the worst prognostications of slave traders and disaffected Nova Scotians seemed to have been realised. The company's ultimatum was a challenge to Bai Farma's authority, amounting to a declaration of war; the settlement had paid no rent and refused to pay tribute to its landlord; Settlers gave sanctuary to runaway Temne slaves, and they had built fortifica-tions—obviously for a good reason. On 18 November, in desperation and led by Nova Scotian fugitives, the Temne attacked, but were driven off.

King Tom retreated north. The secretary for war despatched 65 additional troops from Goree. Friendly chiefs sent a large force too, but in their poverty the company had to send it away. This was a mistake. King Tom had gone to look for allies. In January 1802 it was learnt that two local Temne,[21] Mori Kanu of Scarcies and Mori Bundu, a bunduka Fula married to one of the late Naimbana's daughters, living at Foredugu on the Rokel,[22] had joined him. Mori Kanu was partly occupied elsewhere, ever fishing in troubled waters, and did not come in the end, but on 11 April some 400 men from Koya attacked the settlement, accompanied by about 40 Susu. They were driven off in about half an hour.[23] King Tom fled to Malaghia. Mori Kanu now came down early in 1803, greatly alarming the Settlers who respected his men's fighting qualities and saw that he had an eye on making the western peninsula his own. All the white soldiers were sick, provisions were short because farms had been abandoned as the Temne advanced, the fort was still unfinished and the stores and water line undefended. Fortunately the Temne, suspicious of Mori Kanu, did not join him, and he abandoned his scheme.

Meanwhile, Captain William Day, RN, arriving early in 1803 as governor, rebuilt Fort Thornton, remounted the cannon, built another battery at Falconbridge Point and persuaded seventy settlers to join his volunteers.[24] Feeling safer, he thought it time to abandon 'temporising' language, for a more commanding tone. He wrote to Mori Kanu telling him on what terms peace would be acceptable. On the principle of divide and rule he offered peace to Bai Farma and King Tom. Mori Kanu lost no time in using his influence trying to crown a friendly chief on the Bullom Shore land rented by the company. Ignorant of country custom as usual, they nearly surrendered this trump card to him which, if he had been able to play it, would have severely damaged their economy, their commissariat and their defences. Just in time they learnt of their rights and installed the friendly King George Gbana. A few days later Fenda Modu at Wongapong, friendly since visiting Macaulay in 1794, sent his son Dala Sambo, a well-known warrior, with fifty men to the Bullom Shore. He pointedly asked Mori Kanu to leave, and he went off quietly.

Day left at the end of 1803, returning in January 1805, dying in office that November. By then the settlement's external threats were over (the problems henceforth internal, as Acting Governor Ludlam reported), the company at last possessing a legitimate title—by right of conquest. Peace was signed in 1807, the boundary being fixed at Robis near modern Hastings. After that Koya rulers did everything they could to avoid friction with the colony; when neighbouring chiefs planned revenge for the Abolition Act, they sent King Tom to pledge Koya's loyalty. The Bai Farma died soon after, discredited for having lost land to the English. His three councillors succeeded him. The Naimbana died in 1825, King Tom Kant-

tineh then became regent until his death in 1832, to be followed by Bai Bureh who died in 1838. Bai Bureh's death was a turning point: after him a twenty-one-year interregnum followed, the Koya people refusing to install a new set of rulers because of the disgrace the last ones brought.[25]

Crown Colony

With remarkable persistence the company spoke of its territory as a colony. Ludlam replying to Nova Scotian rebels in 1800 wrote: 'I must do my duty to the English Government and bring to justice all who rebel against it.'[26] The government, too, in that vague proprietorial way which developed the British Empire, sometimes felt the territory was part of its dominions. In 1802 they required the company's forces to occupy Gambia Island, to keep out the French.[27] The governor obliged, more imperial than the directors at home, who stalled, and better able to see that, commanding the mouths of the Quia and Bunce rivers, it drew much trade; in the hands of any other power its occupation might encourage the Temne to attack Freetown again.[28] The company's impending bankruptcy merely accelerated a natural process, when Freetown became a Crown Colony on 1 January 1808.

At this time, the government relied heavily on the African Institution for advice. Wilberforce was vice-president, Thornton treasurer, and Thomas Clarkson and Sharp amongst its directors. Until 1812 Macaulay was its honorary secretary. Governor Perronet Thompson's instructions, on Macaulay's advice, stated that HMG wanted Sierra Leone to play a leading part in the civilising mission. The influence its growing strength and commercial importance would give it over neighbouring chiefs was to be 'exerted in composing their differences'.[29] He was to patronise every scheme for improving Africa and to favour the introduction of suitable people to teach the inhabitants. From the beginning colonial policy was therefore to send people outwards.

Macaulay had plans far in advance of his times.[30] Seeing how mixed were the methods of government in the West African factories and forts, aiming at uniformity he suggested a 'presidency' at Sierra Leone, which should govern the other territories too. Naval commanders should be sent to explain Abolition to coastal chiefs, who should be encouraged into legitimate commerce. An agricultural seminary should be set up, a vice-admiralty court established in Freetown; Britain should acquire the Dutch forts on the Gold Coast and send over a West India regiment; Bissau should be taken from Portugal to extinguish her slave trading; the interior should be explored; consuls should be established on the coast. These suggestions were not incorporated into Thompson's instructions, but they followed later, the Sierra Leone experiment suggesting to Britain their wisdom, or at least their practicability.

Treaties

The first seven years of Crown-Colony government were ones of improvisation, a consequence of transition in Sierra Leone and war in Europe. However, MacCarthy's administration (1814–24) was an era of prodigal philanthropy. Between 1818 and 1827, fourteen treaties were signed with neighbouring chiefs,[31] when full and entire sovereignty was acquired in the neighbourhood. In 1825, however, HMG had set its face against further acquisitions of territory or sovereignty. Refusing to ratify Governor Charles Turner's treaty of 1825 over what is today called Turners' Peninsula, the secretary of state informed him that HMG was unwilling to consent to arrangements which might look like territorial aggrandisement. Financial crisis at home, growing protests at unprofitable expenditure, and the unflattering report of the parliamentary commissioners who, sent out in 1825, reported in 1827, led to retrenchment. Looking back on the major-general's exploits,[32] the commission reminded the House that the object of the West African settlements was entirely peaceful. Treaties with people who were small and weak and who might be continually asking for protection were politically embarrassing. Retrenchment had come in, and with it a period of practical philanthropy intended to develop a self-supporting liberated African population which led eventually to assisted emigration to the West Indies and to the non-extension of responsibility on the coast.[33]

Events in England and Sierra Leone combined to hinder any coherent policy. From 1828 followed a decade in Britain where there were six ministries and eight secretaries of state. Interest raged round home matters. Sierra Leone had ten governors or acting governors, six of whom held only very brief spells between 1828 and 1830. Neither Alexander Findlay nor Henry Campbell, the two holding office longest, could work in harmony with colleagues. A select committee in 1830 recommended most of the Sierra Leone establishment should be withdrawn and that liberated Africans in future should be sent to Cape Coast or Fernando Po. Britain contemplated handing the colony to the resident merchants, as in Cape Coast.

From 1828 to 1845 only six treaties were signed; none ceded sovereignty. Frustrated in their imperial designs, governors began acquiring indirect influence by friendly agreements in which chiefs promised not to go to war without first having the governor mediate. Domestic slaves were an important part of their economy, and governors had recognised this. Maxwell issued a proclamation as early as 26 February 1811 on the matter, reassuring chiefs they would return runaways. Treaties of friendship to this effect with Marampa and Port Loko rulers, 23 September 1831, were an embarrassment to the Colonial Office, however, since slavery was not recognised in British territories. Instructions were issued that they were to be annulled. Even so this was not done until 1841.[34]

Then came a period of anti-slave-trade treaties; with one exception[35] the first batch of twenty-one referred to places north of the colony. Only two ceded sovereignty—both in 1847. Most were like those the Niger expedition signed: abolishing the slave trade, permitting the entry of Christian missions, with country law and Poro not applying to British subjects who in turn were not to engage in local wars. Paths were to be kept open, with unrestricted trade for the British; the queen, if she wished, might appoint an agent for the territory.

After that, partly overlapping the previous one, came an era of intense naval anti-slave-trade activity. Here only the first three treaties, all in 1847, cover the north, because in 1848 the Report of the Court of Mixed Commission in Freetown

L

stated that, except for the Rio Pongo, the slave trade there had been put down.[36] Attention moved southwards, and seventeen treaties were signed there. No sovereignty was acquired between 1848 and 1860. By then all the principal chiefs of the Bullom and Port Loko districts, as well as some elsewhere, had signed peace and trade treaties.

In 1832 Governor Alexander Findlay told the secretary of state[37] that neither North Bullom nor the Sherbro should have been let go because retention of sovereignty would have put a complete stop to the slave trade. Dr Robert Madden, appointed as commissioner to report on West Africa, in 1842 actually recommended annexation of these territories. But the Sherbro at the request of their chiefs was annexed only in 1861, and even then solely because an enthusiastic governor, given permission to annexe one small town, Bendu, to keep out the French, exceeded his instructions. The great attraction was its prosperity. A civil commandant was immediately appointed; troops and police stationed there. It quickly became the colony's largest source of revenue.

In that year Koya too was acquired—by a series of tricks. Raiding Tombo Island, which was British, the Temne were required to pay £500 reparations. Being unable to raise the money, Bai Kanta was made instead to lease the colony a ten-mile-wide strip eastward. Worse, though he was told it was a lease when he put his mark on the treaty, the colony declared it ceded to the British Crown.[38] The secretary of state accepted it only very reluctantly though not because of the chicanery. It was the increasing territorial complications on the west coast as a whole which alarmed him. New territories needed managers, barracks, troops, police, customs posts and regular mail services. It was time to stop. Thus the 1865 Select Committee which recommended withdrawal from everywhere, except possibly Sierra Leone, advising that all further extension of territory or assumption of government, or new treaties offering protection would be inexpedient, was merely bestowing parliamentary benediction on a policy practised off and on, at least officially, for some forty years.[39]

The Colonial Office, the Foreign Office and the Merchants
The Colonial Office preferred to avoid rather than to make
decisions, however. The Cabinet hardly ever discussed West
African policy, except in times of emergency, and even though
large numbers of papers circulated, little interest was roused.
What policy there was, was almost entirely that of the secretary
of state and, since Sierra Leone was virtually financially independent, she received far less attention than other British
settlements. Governor Dundas Campbell, appointed in 1834,
was given no written instructions at all—though he had a talk
with the secretary of state. He was told to refer to instructions
already in the colony. On arrival, he found these had been sent
to Sir Neill Campbell—not even his immediate predecessor—
in 1826! Even then, they indicated no policy, outlined no
plans.

The Foreign Office, on the other hand, believed, with
Wilberforce and Buxton, that the way to extend 'civilisation'
and Christianity was to extend commerce. That could be
achieved only if traders had security for life and goods. Thus
the Foreign Office, implying protection extended beyond the
limits of the settlement, went further than the Colonial Office.

Much could be done by a determined administrator.
Governor Findlay, forbidden to extend active rule, began in
1831 a policy of acquiring indirect influence by treaties of
friendship with nearby chiefs, in return for a stipend, providing
peace was maintained and colony traders unmolested. Later
governors enlarged this treaty area until in the mid-nineteenth
century it stretched along the coast to Rio Nunez and inland
to Mende and Limba countries. Even so, many alliances were
merely nominal, the chief being too far away to receive his
stipend or to be admonished, in event of failing to keep the
bargain.[40] By 1873 there were at least seventy-three of these
treaties, offering stipends from £10 upwards.

Local traders and administrators followed the practical
approach of the Foreign Office. Under MacCarthy, merchants
complained revenue was not spent on anything of use to them.
What they needed, and asked for, were customs houses, stores,

wharves, breakwaters, a colonial surgery and communications to the interior. Major Charles Callwell's *Small Wars* (HMSO, 1899), probably the first official manual of bush fighting, held it axiomatic (p 5) 'that the trader heralds almost as a matter of course the coming of the soldier and commercial enterprise in the end leads to conquest'. Few Sierra Leone exports, save ginger and arrowroot, were grown in the peninsula; gum, ivory, hides, palm-oil, rubber, timber and groundnuts were brought down from the interior, or collected by Sierra Leone traders going inland. The colony simply did not have resources within itself, on which the immense importation of labour through the Liberated African Department could be employed locally. As traders spread out, clashes were bound to occur. By the 1840s the timber in the north was worked out and groundnuts took its place, smaller traders following Charles Heddle's example there. By 1850 there was a considerable Creole settlement at Kambia on the Scarcies. In the east the boundary was extended by unofficial movement of liberated Africans from Waterloo into adjacent villages, and by timber traders who, denuding the banks of the Rokel, turned to the Ribbi and southwards. By 1850 Mabang was a centre of the timber trade and Thomas Ellis, a Maroon, had the main factory for it. By 1854, having pushed up the Rokel they were also trading in the Masimera chiefdom. In 1840 the Church Missionary Society opened a station in Port Loko, where many Creole traders were found. Soon the American 'Mende Mission' went on to the Bum river, so far scarcely penetrated by Creoles. In the 1850s and 1860s there was an influx into the Sherbro, settling round the 'Mende Mission' and the other American mission (1855), the United Brethren in Christ. Timber was exported; in 1829 it had formed 69 per cent of exports, though by 1860 it made up only 6 per cent. Palm-kernels had replaced it, again pioneered by Heddle. These were easier to trade in than timber and attracted hordes of small traders. Creoles soon penetrated into Upper Bumpe and six had their stores plundered at Senehun in 1862.

French Intervention in the North
In the first half of the nineteenth century the northern rivers

area fell into the economic and cultural sphere of Sierra Leone. The Rio Pongo was never a place for any great trade other than slaves, but the Nunez was more significant, though trade fell off after disturbances in 1850 and, particularly, after 1865 when the French built a fort there. By then Sierra Leone's major northern centre was the interconnected system of creeks around the mouths of the Mellacourie, Fouricaria and Bereira, about sixty miles north of Freetown, forming a safe anchorage at a favourite terminus of the Futa Jallon caravan route. The Freetown Government had concerned itself with the peace of these rivers since the 1820s, Kenneth Macaulay, as acting governor, obtaining cession of Matacong and a coastal strip, though London had disavowed it. At Heddle's suggestion new treaties were made in 1845 giving protection to the property of British subjects, and these provided the basis for British influence for the next twenty years.[41] The early 1860s saw considerable economic growth. There were no customs and profits were high; from 1865 Bordeaux merchants began to come in. In the early 1860s the Susu captured Kambia, directing the caravans from the Scarcies to the Mellacourie, to the latter's delight. From 1861, however, south of the lower Mellacourie region, Temne and Bullom of the Samu chiefdom were trying to displace the Susu who had come in from Moriah—between the Fourecariah and the Mellacourie—and occupied factories on the south bank. British and French merchants, caught in these wars, appealed to Sierra Leone for protection, without really expecting it. These traders next tried to get Paris to 'protect' the coastline which was intended to fend off British encroachment and a possible Sierra Leone tariff. Governor Faidherbe refused. French hesitation was only temporary; in 1867, having signed a treaty two years previously with Maligi Toure, a claimant to the Moriah chieftaincy, they established a military post at Gbinti, cutting off Sierra Leone's territorial expansion there and establishing a 'protectorate'.

The chiefs along the Nunez, Pongo and Mellacourie opposed the French advances, feeling Sierra Leone had commercial 'treaties' with them. These were frequently local arrangements which the Foreign Office accepted but did not ratify, being a

recognised method of keeping the roads open and of providing
a period of time for adjustment from slaving to legitimate
commerce; in fact, of acquiring control without annexation.
When the chiefs appealed to Sierra Leone to drive the French
away, the Colonial Office consulted the Foreign Office who
replied there was nothing to stop the French; Britain certainly
did not own those rivers, and the stipends were for providing
peaceful trading conditions only. No kind of protection against
other powers was implied. In 1865 HMG repudiated, in a
secretary of state's despatch, the 1826 annexation of Matacong,
though it was never publicly proclaimed invalid.

British Jurisdiction Extended
The Temne tried to drive back the recaptives who crossed into
Koya. So long as they were outside the colony they were an
embarrassment and Governor Richard Doherty (1837–40)
several times endeavoured to get them to return. In the end
he recommended buying Koya, but as Sir James Stephen, the
under secretary, pointed out, even if the colony did expand
they would still have a frontier and there would still be clashes
on it. Lord Russell referred the question to Madden, who also
recommended extension. Even so the government refused to
act. In 1841 Governor Sir John Jeremie tried to solve the
problem by an act of the Sierra Leone legislature for preventing
and punishing offences committed by British subjects within
certain adjacent territories. HMG disallowed it on the grounds
that they were not competent to legislate for offences outside
the colony. However, 6 and 7 Victoria, c 94, an Act to Remove
Doubts as to the Exercise of Power and Jurisdiction by Her
Majesty within divers Countries and Places out of Her Majesty's
Dominions, gave authority to send for trial to a British colony
such malefactors, 'as if the said crime or offence had been
committeed within the jurisdiction of such Supreme Court'.
There followed an Order in Council, 1844,[42] designating Sierra
Leone and Cape Coast as such colonies. Submitted to the
Committee of the Council for Trade and Foreign Plantations
for a legal opinion, it was pronounced invalid, the queen
having no such right unless chiefs actually ceded their territory.[43]

Britain therefore advised Governor Macdonald to make treaties whenever he could. Even so, the question arose as to whether recaptives were British subjects; the law officers thought not; hence the Act of 1853,[44] hastened on to the statute book by the fact that certain recaptives had been selling their fellows into slavery. This was followed by another in 1861[45] dealing with the prevention and punishment of crimes by British subjects in Sierra Leone, 'and for five hundred miles east of the Colony', against the indigenous inhabitants. Nothing in the Act was to be construed as giving Her Majesty any title to dominion or sovereignty.

The great and everlasting worry of the Colonial Office was finance. Thomas Elliot, assistant under secretary, blamed the Treasury in 1864 for the real source of 'darkness and confusion' pervading African finances, because it consistently overruled every effort made in his office to make some settled plan. Not getting enough financial aid from the Imperial Government, the Colonial Office endeavoured to have each settlement financially independent as soon as possible. They were interested in West African trade only because on trade one could levy duties. From 1860–75, however, West African imports into Britain were a very small part of imports, and those from outside British jurisdiction were larger than from within. Colonel Harry Ord's report for the Parliamentary Select Committee, 1865, as well as other witnesses, made it clear the settlements could not continue without considerable assistance. The 1864 Asante campaign had been expensive in lives and cash. Britain was scarcely likely to agree to any kind of expansion, much less a military one. Governor Samuel Blackall told the committee the best way to protect British trade was by treaties of commerce, not treaties of protection. The latter led to friction and fighting amongst neighbours in which Britain became involved. After the 1865 report there was a lull for a decade in annexation activities.

However, when the ruler of Mouricariah complained that the French, by putting a high tariff on British goods as they had in Senegal, were stopping his trade with Sierra Leone, that was different, the Colonial Office decided a definite understanding should be made concerning the rights of occupation and sovereignty of Britain and France.

Formal and informal empire were partly interchangeable. Commerce strengthened political influence; politics aided trade. From 1867 there were continuous attempts to define spheres of influence, not for purposes of expansion, but to protect revenue. Governor Cornelius Kortright, seeking to annexe the Scarcies river area in 1876 was refused, but was given permission to conclude trade agreements if it would help revenue, and thus ensure that the Colonial Office need not ask the Commons for money.[46] In the following year HMG sanctioned a proclamation that Matacong was still British under the 1826 treaty—despite the despatch of 1865 repudiating it— so as to ensure the collection of customs there. An acting governor, Judge James Huggins, seeing that if the coast opposite the island were not also British, traders would simply move there and avoid duties, in 1877 summoned the Samu Bullom chiefs to Freetown where they ceded a coastal strip from Scarcies to Mellacourie, including Gbinti, which they claimed never to have given to the French. Lord Carnarvon refused to ratify it. But the following year Rowe was told to do so—the first territorial acquisition since 1861. Early in 1879 the Scarcies was proclaimed subject to Freetown customs.

In 1882 an Anglo-French Convention, never formally ratified, was accepted by both sides. It gave the Mellacourie to France and the Scarcies basin to Britain. Three subsequent agreements in 1889, 1891 and 1895 supplemented this. In 1904 the Iles de Los were ceded to France and in 1912 details of the French Guinea frontier adjusted.

The south was full of war in the 1870s.[47] Doctor Samuel Rowe, acting governor, and as energetically eccentric as ever, led an expedition to Moyamba to stop raids spilling over into British Sherbro. At Senehun the Mende, fined 10,000 bushels of rice, promised to stop hiring out warriors and the Bullom undertook not to employ them. George Stephen Caulker of Shenge and Richard Caulker of Bumpe, originators of a raid, were made to cede their right to collect customs. Since British policy was now to acquire as much coastline in the neighbourhood of their settlements as possible, Rowe was applauded at home for being like Sir John Glover in Nigeria: able to lead successful expeditions into the interior without vast expense and without losing his head as did some governors who, construing broken promises as carte blanche for wholesale annexations, gave the secretary of state nightmares. Even so, Rowe implied in his talks that if peace was not kept, annexation was not inconceivable.[48]

In 1882 to avoid having the colony squeezed at both ends by France, arrangements were made to try and settle a common frontier with Liberia (previously raised in 1861–3 and again in 1879), and at the same time Jahrah and his chiefs ceded a half-mile strip of coast as far as Mano. The following year treaties were made with Krim country and further strips ceded. The whole coast from the Scarcies to Mano was now attached to the colony. In 1886 Liberia accepted the Mano as the boundary; readjustments being made in 1911.

Susu and Temne rivalry for Kambia disturbed the northern rivers trade, involving chiefs in the French sphere as well. Wars in Yonni Temne and in Upper Mende countries kept traders out. The 1887 Yonni expedition brought peace which Governor James Hay determined to perpetuate by cutting and policing a road thirty miles inland from the coast, running eventually from Kambia on the Great Scarcies, to the river Mano. It was, in fact, an unofficial delimitation of a sphere of influence which had never been officially recognised. After 1890, when they were raised, the Frontier Police patrolled it.

In 1890 the European powers signed the Brussels Act. Article 1, *inter alia*, declared the most effective way of counteracting interior slave trading was by the 'progressive organisation' of the administrative, judicial, religious and military services in all territories 'placed under the sovereignty or protection of civilised nations', and by establishing strongly occupied stations in the hinterland. Dividing the hinterland with France, yet alert to French dangers, Britain despatched two travelling commissioners through Loko, Limba, Yalunka, Upper Mende and Kisi countries, making treaties of friendship and binding signatories not to make agreements with other

European powers without the governor's consent.[49] In 1891 Hay toured the interior, scattering police at Taiama, Mano, Bumpe and Tikonko. In 1893 an expedition against the Sofas opened up Kono and Koranko country.

The 'Native Affairs' Department

In Rowe's time London recognised that the governor had to do nearly everything himself and that public service was an 'Augean stable'.[50] Two years later, in 1877, Acting Governor Huggins had to patiently explain to the secretary of state that in West Africa the chief is always landlord to the occupier; treaties were never looked on as giving rights of ownership or property in the soil; sovereignty was never given except to another nation and major decisions were taken only in full council.[51]

Clearly, little had changed since Clarkson's day; the settled area of influence extended scarcely further than in the eighteenth century, when occupied by European and American slave traders; money was still as scarce as either good public officers or official knowledge of indigenous societies; Sir Richard Burton, whom a senior Colonial Office official pronounced better qualified to judge African character than probably any living European, had just pontificated: 'I do not hold the black to be equal to the white.'[52] There was still less freedom of action, and more crass ignorance available for policy making than is often imagined.[53]

The trouble was that simply being there was no longer enough. Neighbours could no more be either ignored or bullied into acquiescence, as Macaulay had the Koya Temne. Government had been drawn in deeper and deeper: to protect British subjects trading in war-torn areas; to bolster precarious revenue by developing new trade routes and defending old ones—both entailing expansion of imperial jurisdiction; to investigate complaints by chiefs of lawless behaviour on the part of Sierra Leoneans; to preserve the coast and the hinterland from the French; to undertake moral obligations towards faithful allies.

Happily, after 1852, arrangements for all this fell to a Togolese, sent to Freetown for education, who had married into a Koya ruling house. Thomas George Lawson, himself of chiefly family, after six years' temporary government service, was made government messenger and interpreter. It was an astute appointment. He was convinced British expansion was a good thing and he proved a firm and stable element in an era when from 1852 to 1871 there were only three substantive governors, though stop-gaps came and went bewilderingly. There were five between 1872 and 1877.

Ever since the Sierra Leone Company days there had been a deliberate policy of encouraging Muslim settlers and traders. In 1869 Winwood Reade, erratic explorer and devotee of Burton, travelling the caravan route to Falaba—which especially seemed the key to the Sudan—predictably reported how caravans were exploited by Sierra Leoneans whilst in Freetown. As a result in 1871 an assistant interpreter and protector of strangers was appointed. Next year Mohammed Sanusi was made Arabic writer.

By his voluminous correspondence, by the trust he engendered amongst chiefs, by his constant presence, however, Lawson grew into a department, appearing as such in the *Blue Book* of 1879 as the Aborigine's Branch, where he ran the colony's foreign policy on a budget of merely £5,000. By now Rowe was governor, and he liked to engage in military operations. Civilians like Lawson were eclipsed, and anyway from 1879 Rowe urged the appointment of a white man. Not surprisingly none suitably qualified could be found for three years, and even then there was no continuity.

When Lawson retired in 1888 Governor Hay separated the branch from the secretariat, keeping it under direct control, in 1891 renaming it the Native Affairs Department, and appointing James Parkes, a Creole, as superintendent. However, Creoles were being squeezed out of trade and public service now. Competition in Europe brought white retailers into the colony, where trade anyway was harder to find as the Fula caravans were diverted northwards by the French, the cable and parcel post supplied people with direct links with Europe and, after about 1900, the Syrian and Lebanese traders arrived, spreading, like the earlier Creole pioneers, over the country and also along the new railway. As one resident Englishman put it, Creoles baulked in trade, in territorial expansion and in the public service were like minnows behind a dam.

The Protectorate

In 1890 two expatriates, George Garrett and Thomas Alldridge, were appointed travelling commissioners in the hinterland; the Frontier Police were formed, officered by expatriates. Scattered thinly, they were ill-disciplined and oppressive; Garrett and Alldridge were overburdened with complaints. In that year, too, the Foreign Jurisdiction Act empowered the Crown to exercise any jurisdiction claimed in a foreign country as if by right of cession or conquest. In 1892 Parkes drew up a plan for administering the interior: whereby the government assumed its long-neglected responsibilities. He proposed proclaiming a protectorate, taking over the Frontier Police's political authority,[54] the latter being gradually disbanded. Five political agents should take over their duties and have limited juridical powers as well. When London found the agents would be Creole, the plan was turned down, because 'we could not depend upon them', and because, it was said, five suitable ones could not be found![55] In 1893 sovereignty was proclaimed over a district lying between the Great Scarcies and Port Loko countries.

Governor Frederick Cardew who arrived in 1894 travelled the hinterland indefatigably, trying to decide how best to transform a British sphere, ruled by sovereign chiefs, into a protectorate which, it seemed, had to be administered by Europeans, not Creoles. In 1895 he set off again. Palavers were held to discuss suppressing the slave trade and 'fetishism', but the route was governed principally with a view to discovering the most practical line for a railway, the first in West Africa and begun in 1896. Cardew increased the Frontier Police, dividing the country into five districts under expatriate inspectors. In 1895 under the Foreign Jurisdiction Act an order in council declared the Crown had acquired jurisdiction in foreign countries adjoining the colony, and empowered Sierra Leone to legislate accordingly for the protectorate. Almost exactly a year later, on 31 August 1896, a 'protectorate'—whatever that might be had never been defined—was proclaimed,[56] though none explained how jurisdiction had been obtained. When Sir Samuel Lewis pointed this out in council, Cardew indignantly ruled him out of order. Many chiefs with no treaty with Britain now found themselves ruled by one of the five district commissioners appointed to each of the five districts guided, but not bound, by English law, and responsible to the colonial secretary in Freetown. These DCs and, especially, the Frontier Police who were expensive, costing almost £20,000 in 1896—nearly a fifth of the revenue—had to be provided for. So did the railway Cardew had begun, which was to tap the rich oil-palm belt in Mende country. The governor, refused a British Government grant, decided on a house tax (five shillings yearly), though Parkes advised against it, to be collected from 1 January 1898.

The Rising of 1898

The house tax, imposed on three of the five districts[57] was only the spark. Joseph Chamberlain told the House of Commons it was 'a general rising against white rule'.[58] The main causes were: the loss of chiefly authority and prestige; the abolition of the slave trade and the sanctuary domestic slaves found in the colony; the Frontier Police in whose ranks were many runaways. The chiefs' loss of authority, particularly judicial authority, was especially hateful, being the mainstay of their power; deprivation also meant a serious loss of revenue from court fines. Abolition brought further losses, since lucrative tolls from slave coffles ended—especially in Kasseh which lay on the route to the Susu market. The 'Frontiers' had no authority to interfere in the government of the chiefs, only to protect traders, patrol the roads and, if possible, avert the outbreak of local wars. However, the ordinance permitted chiefs to be flogged, a tremendous insult for any ruler in front of his people, but worse if carried out by a former slave, now in police uniform.

The district commissioners curtailed chiefly activities considerably. Their judicial powers included: all civil and criminal

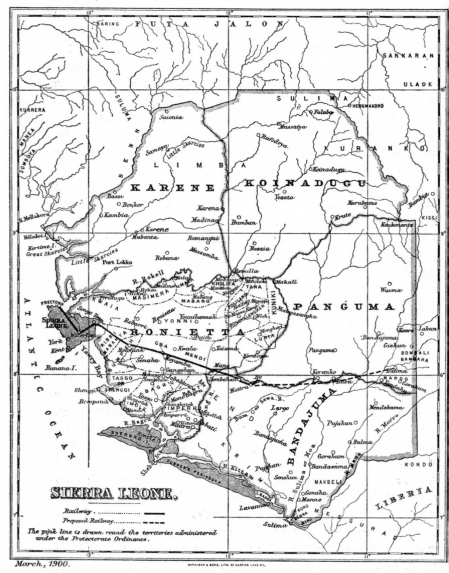

SIERRA LEONE.

Railway ....
Proposed Railway ....

The pink line is drawn round the territories administered
under the Protectorate Ordinance.

March, 1900.

HARRISON & SONS, LITH. ST. MARTINS LANE, W.C.

Map 8

cases involving 'non-natives', all land cases, cases of witchcraft, factional and tribal fights, slave dealing, murder, rape, Alligator, Leopard and other 'society' cases. They could arbitrarily adjudicate on anything, even matters of customary law, if likely to cause a breach of the peace. Young, inexperienced, speaking no local language, they knew little about local affairs—the *sine qua non* of good government and, especially, good police work.

Missions were a subordinate cause, encouraging young men to despise their animist, illiterate elders. This was not so important a grievance in the north, where Islam was strong, but there were many missionaries in the south.

There were two risings. The first, in February 1898, began in the Temne north; the second, in April, was amongst the Mende in the south.

Cardew, on tour in 1896 to explain his tax ordinance, mistook passivity, and the good breeding that in Africa accords strangers politeness, for consent. In fact in December 1896 a number of Temne chiefs, including Bai Bureh of Kasseh[59] who led the Temne rising, wrote to Captain Wilfred Sharpe that they would be unable to observe the new laws or to pay the house taxes, asking that adjudication in country matters should not be taken from them, reasonably suggesting they settle their own affairs; only if unable to do that, should they take them to the DC. In February 1897 the Bai Sherbro and the chief of Mano (Kittim) led a group of chiefs to Freetown to protest to Cardew. In June, Temne chiefs powerful enough to get invited to the Freetown Jubilee celebrations, drew up a petition, expressing fears about their status, lands, and judicial powers, waiting two months in the colony so as to be able to present it personally to Cardew when he returned from leave. They explained their poverty, prices for protectorate produce being low and domestic slaves, if worked too hard, liable to run to Freetown. Debarred from dealing in slaves, they had no gold mines, no quantity of palm-kernels or rice as surplus for sale.

In December 1896 sixty-four chiefs and leading men of Sulima had tried to get Sir Samuel Lewis to act on their behalf against the ordinance. Though he agreed with them, he refused. He declined the following October to present a petition against it from the Port Loko area, referring it to the governor, as he did a complaint from the south-east in January 1898. Parkes, to whom chiefs turned more and more for advice (which made him unpopular in Government House) warned that 'considerable tact and patience' would be needed if the tax were to be collected during the coming dry season. He confirmed prices were low in the protectorate, wisely suggesting at one time that, rather like Lugard in northern Nigeria later, a form of tribute should be collected instead. Even the Colonial Office suggested the tax be lowered, but Cardew's reaction was to inform Chamberlain, 8 October, that the chiefs could well pay and that in any case they would never be able to combine to resist![60]

Cardew and the British never understood the system of *kruba* or war-chiefs, persistently calling them 'mercenaries'. Bai Bureh was the son of a war-chief who sent him to Pendembu Gwahun, a well-known training school for warriors. He was successful and acquired the sobriquet *Kebalai*: one whose basket is never full—who killed so many. A *kruba* would be called in by other chiefs to help in wars in return for certain rights of plunder, including that of enslaving prisoners. It was a professional calling and only war-chiefs could travel foreign chiefdoms collecting warriors. By 1890 much political authority in Temne country was in their hands, knitting chiefdoms into a broad alliance. Bai Bureh's leadership of the rising lay in his warrior status, not his chiefly one.

Captain Sharpe, DC of Karene (in which Kasseh lay), began to collect tax in late January 1898 at Port Loko. Chief Bokhari Bamp said he could not allow the sixty or so Sierra Leone traders to pay taxes without fear of reprisals, and he would not help to collect it. The traders rightly pointed out that paying it would imply ownership of their houses, leased merely from the chief, their landlord. Cardew had not made it clear whether the tax was to be collected from the sub-chiefs in the towns or from what the British called paramount chiefs, so Sharpe illegally arrested not only Bokhari Bamp and the traders but four sub-chiefs, installing as ruler, Sorie Burki, said to have been a slave's son. The chiefs, sent handcuffed to Freetown, received sentences of hard labour for a year at least. Their discovery that the colony was not paying the tax confirmed suspicions that it was capricious and unjust. There is no doubt that DCs were collecting the tax stupidly and arrogantly. Edward Blyden said they felt they had 'nothing to learn from or to respect among the natives'.[61] Chiefs resented being ordered about by young men anyway.

Bai Bureh's warriors having kept Sharpe continually under surveillance from the bush, the latter, fearing an attack, determined to arrest him. One company of the West India Regiment was despatched from Freetown, the administration hoping once the military arrived, resistance would collapse. The regiment was quite unsuited to operations like this; the single company left Freetown, with 540 carriers! The fact that the Frontier Police had never been properly trained and that the two forces had never practised any combined manoeuvres, made their unsuitability now obvious even to the administration. The Colonial Office, with War Office permission, authorised Cardew in April to recruit for a new imperial force to be called the West Africa Regiment, a more mobile force, officered by regular army officers.

All through March the Temne, attacking Port Loko, held the initiative, avoiding direct confrontation, firing often from professionally constructed stockades made of banana stems, the squashiness of which stopped bullets effectively. Bamboo was sometimes inserted as a firing hole, and the grass and bush fired on either side of the advancing British. Soon, as the *Daily Telegraph* correspondent reported, most of the huts which Cardew intended taxing had been burnt down.

With the marines of HMS *Fox* and *Alecto*, the 1st Battalion of the West India Regiment and the 3rd, sent up from St Helena, a detachment of Royal Artillery from England, together with the Sierra Leone Royal Artillery, Royal Engineers, Frontier Police, and Court Messengers, a force of about 2,500 was in the field, supported by another 2,000 carriers. Most of the time more than half the troops were needed to protect the carriers and their supply lines.

The carriers were recruited by the tribal headmen in

M

Freetown, who now became important citizens. Bai Bureh sent
spies to Freetown to get engaged as carriers and evidently he
was in easy and frequent touch with many there, including
white men, whom he interviewed.[62] He manufactured his own
'Dane guns', using empty British metal cartridges to make
bullets. He captured British carriers, selling them as slaves to
the Susu and with the gold bought guns from English merchants
in the Mellacourie. His staff officers were former Temne
Frontier Police. He was eventually tracked down and taken on
11 November 1898, near Roballan. Cardew wanted to try him
for treason, but he was not a British subject. He never was tried,
being exiled to the Gold Coast, returning in 1905 to rule again
as the Bai Bureh of Kasseh. He died in 1908.

In Mende country chiefs had also suffered from 'Frontiers',
bullies as usual, taking names like Darea-Gbo: 'I will flog you
till you cover your feet', or Jepeh-Gutu: 'short talk under
torture'. Chiefs who hesitated to pay the tax were now handcuffed or robbed. Besides the abolition of the slave trade, there
had also been a Poro Ordinance, which took away the right of
that society to put a prohibition on harvesting, particularly
palm-oil. It was done partly because Sierra Leone revenues
were suffering from the shortage of oil-palm exports from Mende
country.

Mende chiefs and Poro officials knew how bad things were
in Freetown since many carriers had been killed or captured
in the Karene campaign against the Temne and the government had to hire Mende ones. Sierra Leoneans were hated in
Mende country because they enriched themselves at the expense of the Mende (hence the Poro prohibition on harvests),
exposed Mende secrets, notably the Wunde, Poro and Leopard
Societies, and helped missionaries anglicise villagers. It is said
that a general massacre of Sierra Leoneans was decided on at
a Poro meeting. Another source suggests it was the Wunde
Society (centred in Kpa Mende territory, round which Mende
nationalism could have grown up) which gave the order for the
rising. More powerful than the Poro, it transferred the blame
afterwards. Few chiefs receiving the Poro leaf dared refuse the
order, though it is said one chief put it in the fire!

The rising began 28 April 1898 and from the first took a horrifying course, different from the Temnes'. The latter restricted themselves to fighting British forces.[63] The Mende murdered all Europeans and all Africans in European dress they could find. Several hundred perished in the first few days. Beginning in the Imperreh district it soon overran Turner's Peninsula and all seaports southward to the Liberian frontier. Others advanced inland, pillaging the Bum countries, Bagru territory and Ronietta District. Some attacked Frontier Force centres, coming even into Bonthe and Waterloo. Under Alexander Dumabaye, mission-educated son of a former Bullom chief of Mando, their 'Admiral', they attacked coastal places in the colony.

Unlike the Temne, they had only cutlasses, swords and sticks and knew little of European military skill. Consequently they suffered heavily in the subsequent campaign. Moreover, the British, learning by their mistakes, now used African warriors like Chief Gberi of Bonge, whom they did not have against the Temne. British troops were no good without African allies, and were seldom trained for bush fighting until they got to Burma and Malaya in World War II. An outstanding exception was Colonel Alfred Ellis, 1st West India Regiment, who trained his men in the bush. Bai Bureh had been his ally in fighting Karimu of Samaia, where both men had learnt a lot from one another. The regiment had returned to the West Indies, however, and a few months later in 1894 Ellis died, his methods unappreciated.

Creole society was very despondent. Any hope that they would be acceptable as leaders either to the British or the chiefs in the protectorate had gone.[64]

Opposition had been social, political, economic and religious. In reports, the humanitarian aspect was usually emphasised, to give expeditions a popular colouring at home—and to give governors the same. In fact, abolition of social customs was not in itself a cause of any rising. Cardew said a desire to return to fetishes was one of the true causes, but he failed to see what it was all about.

The mercantile interest held that 'it is not practical to shoot

your customer', nor to destroy African society and the chiefs.
They wanted to have Cardew forced to resign.

The Eastern Frontier

With the protectorate under control, the government turned
its attention to disturbances on the Liberian frontier. The
Liberian government could not control the hinterland and
wars spilled over into Sierra Leone, not unnaturally since the
frontier had been defined without regard to ethnography. The
Kissi were particularly ill-positioned, finding themselves under
British, French and Liberian jurisdiction. In 1896 and 1898
the government sent troops over the border. Even after the
1903 agreement there were still disturbances. In 1905, with
Liberian permission, a military expedition was sent against the
Kissi chief, Kafura, whose forces were attacking the frontier
road. Supplies and villages were purposely destroyed and two
companies of troops stationed on the border. In 1902 the headquarters of the West Africa Frontier Force (formed in 1901 from
the Frontier Police, as a battalion of the WAFF originally
created in 1899 by Lugard in Nigeria) moved to Daru on the
river Moa.

Modern Tendencies

By now the railway was well advanced: Bo in 1902; Baiima
in 1905; Pendembu in 1908; Makeni, on the branch line, in
1916. Wealth began to flow along it, and the Hut Tax, as it
came to be called, went up steadily at the rate of about £2,000
a year. Exports at £1,500,000 in 1912 were treble those of
1897; customs at £301,140 in 1912 were also trebled since 1900.
In the south-east until the coming of the railway, commerce,
centred on Bonthe, was river-borne. Creoles and Europeans
had factories at the major exchange points which lay at the
heads of navigation. The railway siphoned off this trade—and
so, later, did the roads, and the branch line at Makeni.

With the almost ceaseless warfare ended in the protectorate,
widespread economic change occurred. No plantations by expatriates were permitted, and no indigenous entrepreneurial
class, comparable to the Ghana cocoa farmer, grew up.

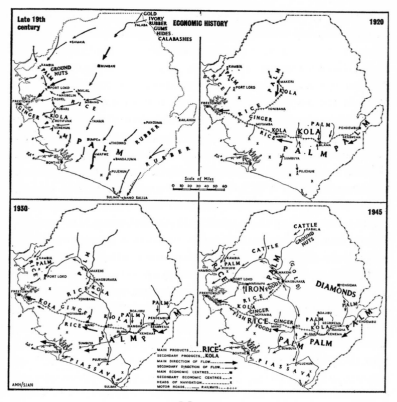

Map 9

Farmers engaged in palm-kernel production which was, until after World War II, the principal small-scale agricultural export.[65]

Palm-oil products sustained the economy, earning annually over £1,000,000 until the 1930 collapse. Between 1910 and 1930 the export value of kola rarely fell below £200,000 per annum; sometimes it represented 25 per cent, or more, of total export revenue. Other agricultural exports were of minor value.

The most important source of wealth was to be the alluvial diamond deposits, fortunately discovered as the slump began to bite in 1930, and first mined three years later by the Sierra Leone Selection Trust in Kono (Yengema). By 1938 they were the largest single export item, representing 37 per cent of total exports of £2.3 million. The other major economic development was the opening in 1933 of the large iron mine at Marampa, Port Loko District, producing, in 1938, 28 per cent of exports. Although urbanisation in the protectorate was limited, no town in the 1931 census having more than 2,500 inhabitants, the relative ease of travel (though no road to the protectorate was completed until World War II), the sophistication of the larger towns, the introduction of a cash economy, meant that chiefdom institutions needed revision. In 1931 forty-four of the sixty-five towns with over a thousand inhabitants were in the south and east, twenty-seven of them in the oil-palm producing districts of Kenema and Kailahun. The Mende were being drawn into modern society earlier, and in a greater variety of ways, than the Temne and others in the north. The new roads and railways in the south gave towns an economic importance previously lacking. On the other hand, French trade at Conakry, diverting the northern caravans, had spelt almost instantaneous decline for several northern centres. The rise of Makeni, Bo and Blama saw the eclipse of Port Loko. The north's break with tradition, therefore, came later, with the gold rush and the Marampa mine. When it did, by its nature it plunged them more completely, if they chose to try it, into urban life, which was more likely to upset traditional society.

Mende chiefs, being secular leaders, were probably better able to adapt, and help their people do so. The sacred Temne chiefs in the north were a little more remote from everyday life. There were more missionaries in the south, and the first protectorate lawyers and doctors were Mende. Sierra Leone, like so many African countries, was developing a modern-traditional, north-south, Muslim-Christian, dichotomy.[66]

The tasks of altering the Protectorate Ordinance to keep abreast of these changes, and of arranging for political representation in the protectorate were first undertaken in the 1920s.

CHAPTER 6

Modern Political and Constitutional Change

Nineteenth-century Society and Politics

Social and political balances, already disturbed in the eighteenth century, altered beyond imagination in the nineteenth, the pace quickening as the decades went by. In the twentieth the brief period of colonial rule in the protectorate produced more changes. The advantages Creole missionaries and civil servants had in local languages, relationships and customs soon passed away. In the 1840s Creoles returning to Nigeria had spoken Yoruba or Ibo, the language of the country where so many had been born. By the 1870s their returning sons had only a smattering of the vernacular. By 1900 Creole missionaries knew no more than those recruited in Britain. In any case Britain had begun to lose confidence in Creoles and missionaries as agents of social change.

The Colonial Office began to have doubts about the Creoles generally. Secular agents were needed now, men with experience of industrial society which the Creoles lacked. Scientists, technologists, teachers, doctors, nurses and railwaymen were recruited. Sir Samuel Lewis, the distinguished Creole barrister, began an agricultural scheme on his estate, Christineville, Waterloo, where the dozens of mainly Mende labourers he employed were given technical training.

Hill Station, 'ugly but necessary',[1] was founded for the expatriates in 1904. Often uncultured, obstinately suburban, negrophobic, they created their own world and lived determinedly in it. Many Creoles understandably developed a strong feeling of injustice. It all seemed remote from the times when, from the 1800s to the 1880s, the Niger Mission had been staffed almost entirely by them, when even the bishop, Samuel Adjai Crowther, had been a recaptive (after he was ousted in 1890 there was no African diocesan bishop again in Nigeria until 1953), when, in the early 1890s, Creoles had occupied nearly half the senior posts in the public service in Freetown.

In the hinterland, prolonged warfare and the concurrent rise of professional warriors introduced new governments, heads of clans often being replaced by military commanders—charismatic figures like Bai Simera Kamal, Canna Gboh, Macavore and Bai Bureh who transcended mere tribalism and formed larger political units, a fact not unnoticed by modern political leaders who sometimes recall these heroes in their public speeches. These politico-military fore-runners of today's military junta in Africa introduced an increasing specialisation into administration and warfare. Traditional chiefs were often relegated to obscurity, sometimes even exiled. War leaders used their booty to feed, pay, and attract followers, and also traded it for war material. They captured slaves to sell, to work their plantations, or to fight in their armies. Specialist craftsmen were employed: warriors to teach the new arms drill and tactics, following the adoption of modern weapons and the presence of a foreign, technologically superior enemy; blacksmiths to repair weapons; leatherworkers to make armour; and mori men to inspire patriotic fervour, settle disputes and impart magical strength and discipline to the cause.

Society was being restructured on all sides, a fact of which the colonial government on the coastal peninsula and at Bonthe, seemed almost oblivious. At first they were preoccupied in working out their own salvation; later, as modern colonialism developed, establishing a 'relationship of dependence',[2] they were concerned with law and order and with material wealth: 'All that needs now to be done,' said Sir Harry Johnston airily to the Foreign Office in 1895, 'is for the Administration to act as friends of both sides, and introduce the native labourer to the European capitalist.'[3]

Fortunately, there were other white administrators, not of the old school, though they did not come into the ascendancy until after World War I, and really only after World War II. Paul Shuffrey was assistant district commissioner in Pujehun, before World War I. In 1918 he became private secretary to Governor R. J. Wilkinson. He had come to Sierra Leone because he knew 'that the work would be worth doing'. It was worth doing; he discovered 'the more you know of and care for native customs and ideas the better you will do your work'. But he found himself out of sympathy with the administration, and often as private secretary, lost his temper with the governor which, as he admitted, was very difficult for a private secretary to do in a decent manner. In 1918 he wrote to a friend:

> Fortunately I am not on the council [ie Legislative Council] or I should certainly distinguish myself by voting against the Executive . . . I am bound to say that in the British Empire administration could not be much worse. It is probably useless to generalise about its defects. . . . But the fault that strikes me most often is the utter neglect by the heads of the Executive of native social conditions. Changes are going on in the life of the people—changes of vital concern to the revenue—which are entirely ignored by the rulers.[4]

The 1799 Charter
When the Crown took over from the Sierra Leone Company in 1808, it preserved its constitution unchanged until 1811, the directors' authority passing to the secretary of state.

The company's charter, eventually received on 6 November 1800, had two parts. The first provided for the company's land tenure rights, vesting the Crown's supposed rights on the peninsula in the directors' hands, with power to 'buy' more when needed. The second part dealt with government, giving the directors powers to legislate, appoint a governor, and three in Council. The hundredors and tythingmen disappeared. Courts of justice were set up but because the settlement had instituted the trial by jury system already, it only formulated what was being done. Governor and Council continued sitting as judges in criminal cases.[5] The biggest change was the strengthening of the judges' power. Freetown was given a mayor and aldermen, who sat to try civil cases by jury. The mayor and

aldermen were not elected, being nominated by the governor
and Council, to whom appeals were made. Only in cases involving over £400 were appeals allowed to the privy council.
In no other colony of coloured people under Britain was so
large a measure of self-government attempted for generations.

The main change in the charter of 1811 was that the governor was empowered to raise a militia to fight under military
discipline, in or out of the colony.

Dependencies 1821–88

In 1821 the British Parliament, abolishing the African Company for the Gold Coast Forts, transferred their dependencies
to the Crown. At the same time all Crown territory on the
West Coast was put under the government of Sierra Leone. At
Governor Charles MacCarthy's suggestion a new constitution
was drawn up for Sierra Leone, increasing his council from
three to nine, including two stationed on the Gold Coast. The
Freetown Court of Recorder was empowered to hear all cases
from the dependencies, two members of council sitting with the
chief justice (an office first occupied in 1811) as assistant judges.
The mayor and aldermen lost their judicial powers, but the
governor's status was enhanced by being given a right of veto
in Council and the rank of chancellor, in order to hear chancery
cases. In 1827 the united government of the coast was disjoined,
the Gold Coast being handed, in 1828, to the merchants. The
office of governor-in-chief was abolished, Sierra Leone and the
Gambia being given separate lieutenant-governors. Though the
governor and Council in Sierra Leone kept the power of legislating for the other colonies, they had no executive authority
there, however. In 1843 the Gold Coast was again placed under
Sierra Leone and remained so until 1850. The same letters-
patent of 24 June 1843 which placed the Gold Coast under
Sierra Leone's control, separated the Gambia. In 1866, a
period of retrenchment followed; the administrations were
merged again, Lagos and the Gold Coast finally breaking away
in 1874, and Gambia in 1888. These continual mergers had an
unfortunate effect on Freetown, developing a habit of looking
along the coast instead of to the interior.

The 1863 Constitution

The letters-patent of 1843 which created the Gambia a separate
territory had also established their Executive and Legislative
Councils. Ironically Sierra Leone had to wait twenty years
before receiving what the once-subordinate Gambia had been
granted.[6] Her 1821 constitution remained virtually unchanged.
The first direct tax, a house and land tax, was imposed in 1851,
but Sierra Leoneans still had almost no representation in government. However, since 1811, when the governor's Council had
consisted of the chief justice, the colonial secretary, and 'one
unofficial member from among the most considerable of the
Protestant inhabitants', it was usual for the business interest to
be represented in the legislature.[7]

In the absence of local representative institutions, petitions
to the secretary of state were the only outlet for the aggrieved,
as petitions to the directors of the Sierra Leone Company had
formerly been the only hope of the Nova Scotians. However, it
has been remarked before that complainants without power, at
a range of 3,000 miles, were in a weak position.[8] Now, the new
constitution wound up the predominantly official council which
had advised the governor on all public business, and divided it
into an Executive Council, normally composed only of officials—
ie public servants—and a Legislative Council to which a
minority of unofficial representatives could be nominated.[9] The
governor was instructed, when making his nominations, to take
account of 'the wishes of the more intelligent of the community', but this was not intended as a step towards early
self-government. The Legislative Council was meant to as-
sociate a select group of notables with the enactment of local
legislation and to provide a more regular channel for local
complaints to be brought before colonial and imperial authorities. It was essentially a device for the more efficient government of an expanding colony, not a step to the concession of
representation. Elected representatives, pleaded for by the
Sierra Leone Committee of Correspondence, formed in 1853
for the purpose of getting that constitutional privilege, were
not conceded. The petition to the secretary of state in 1858

from the Mercantile Association for an elected house of assembly was ignored, but Governor Samuel Blackall did ask the thirty-nine largest importers to choose a nominee. They suggested John Ezzidio, a recaptive Nupe, who was accepted. However, the secretary of state did not favour the elective principle, writing to the governor in 1870 that he was expected to choose representatives himself from amongst those most likely to support government. The Legislative Council was never meant to be a debating chamber; unofficial members according to the duke of Buckingham's Circular Despatch, 1868, were expected to 'cooperate with the Crown in its general policy and not oppose the Crown on any important question without strong and substantial reason'.[10]

Sir Frederick Rogers, permanent under secretary at the Colonial Office since 1860, said he was utterly opposed to democracy which he called yielding to the populace, this being his reaction to the Reform Act of 1867. When Blackall forwarded a long list of procedural rules for the new Legislative Council, Rogers had doubts about 'the adoption in a Legislative Council of the parliamentary precedents—it tends to introduce certain pseudo-constitutional fancies of their position'.[11] He saw no harm in it sitting even behind closed doors if this would stop 'speechifying' by unofficial members addressing the public rather than the agenda.

The Municipal Council

The powers of the Municipal Council, established by the 1799 charter, had always been strictly under government control. As time passed, this increased. Every September the governor's Council chose the mayor and aldermen, usually Europeans,[12] from the Freetown citizens. In 1844 Governor William Fergusson, an Afro-West Indian army doctor, first governor of African descent, had John Ezzidio appointed an alderman, and in 1845 made him mayor. In 1849 and 1850 no mayor was appointed. In 1851 Thomas MacFoy, another Afro-West Indian, and harbour master, was appointed; then, for over forty years, no one. Municipal government, provided for in the 1799 charter, had never been introduced.

In 1864 the Chamber of Commerce was reconstituted. Its president, Alexander Walker, a Scottish trader, proposed that the Municipal Council should be revived; so did James Africanus Horton, the distinguished army doctor, in his book *West African Countries and People*, published in 1868. In the 1880s the Freetown press joined the chorus, asking for an elected city council to give the community at least some control over its affairs. In 1883 a public meeting was held, where it was argued municipal government would mean municipal taxes. Enthusiasm waned. In the 1890s the Colonial Office saw a revival would be advantageous, since it would relieve colonial revenue of municipal expenditure. Hence a municipality ordinance was drawn up in 1890, providing for a council with a majority of government nominees, with power to levy rates. It was abandoned, however, when its opponents pointed out that it merely reintroduced a disguised house and land tax (abolished in 1872) without providing self-government. Finally, an ordinance was passed in 1893. Prepared by Lewis it carefully avoided a house tax; instead, revenue was to come from licences: for traders, vehicles and professional men; and the government handed over wine, spirit, canoe and other municipal licences together with responsibility for markets, water-supply, drainage. Twelve of the fifteen councillors were to be elected, the remaining three were to be appointed by the government. Elections were held in August 1895. Rates (a disguised house tax) could be levied if licences did not bring in enough revenue, but by doing it this way the government did not carry the stigma of imposing them.[13] The city council had to do so in 1898, collection beginning in 1899.

The Protectorate

English law was not introduced into the protectorate. The foundation of the administration of justice there was the Protectorate Courts Ordinance (no 33 of 1901), the Protectorate Courts Jurisdiction Ordinance (no 6 of 1903), and the Protectorate Native Law Ordinance of 1903. Government and administration was designed to preserve indigenous institutions, the district commissioner in each of the five districts sharing power with the paramount chief, a term now used to describe the principal chief (at least according to British reckoning). It was not until 1913 that the Legislative Council actually legislated for both colony and protectorate.[14] Doubts were raised about this later, since people in the protectorate were not British subjects.

The 1898 rising shaped the course of development of the Legislative Council because Britain felt either that its membership should be broadened to include representatives from the protectorate, or that the influence of its unofficial members must remain subordinate to the official majority for an indefinite period; the protectorate interests could not be left to the representations of colony men. Sir Samuel Lewis actually discussed the possibility of protectorate representation with Sir David Chalmers, the Scottish barrister heading the commission of enquiry into the rising. Chalmers agreed that the principle of introducing a few chiefs into the Council was most desirable but said he could see no early prospect of finding representatives who would be both suitable and capable of understanding the proceedings, even the language.

From 1896 to 1921 Britain governed the protectorate with five administrators, their assistant district commissioners, and one court judge. In 1921 they divided the area into ten districts ruled by ten district commissioners, ten assistants, and three provincial commissioners for respectively the northern, central and southern provinces. The role of the traditional authorities was largely to keep law and order. Their main responsibility, so far as directly assisting in the ever-quickening social and economic changes, was limited to recruiting labour for public works, and to tax collection—subservient functions, rather than distributive ones.[15] Even their jurisdiction in cases involving African traders was, as the numbers increased, taken from them and given to the district commissioners in 1937. However, a 1926 Public Health Ordinance enabled a chief to be designated as a health authority, giving him minor responsibilities in health, sanitation and medical services. Other measures of this sort were concerned with road making, agriculture and education, but all were *ad hoc* and were never part of any systematised modernisation plans for the protectorate. In 1935 the senior district commissioner, John S. Fenton, criticised this system as out of date, advising that the time had come to put new life into tribal authorities.

Following the Nigerian Native Administration example, which Fenton went to examine,[16] a reorganisation was made in 1937, and the three essentials of the Nigerian system applied to Sierra Leone, namely: separate financial institutions known as chiefdom treasuries were established for each unit of administration; each chiefdom unit was granted tax authority; paramount chiefs and other tribal authorities were given power to enact by-laws and issue orders regarding social services and development. As in Nigeria the chiefdom unit was designated a Tribal Authority, the paramount chief being held ultimately responsible for the performance of statutory duties of the Native Administration.

Chiefs could now receive a regular salary. Their former sources of income, notably stipend payments, the 5 per cent rebate on hut tax collected, and the fines and fees from the Native Courts, were handed over to the new Native Administration. These, with the new four shillings chiefdom tax and the five shillings house tax[17] (making nine shillings per adult male) constituted the major portion of Native Administration revenue. However, not all chiefs wished to give up their traditional emoluments. They were allowed to continue in the old ways, and in 1947 there were still 90 out of a total of 211 chiefdoms which were 'unreformed'—ie without treasuries.

The balance of revenue, after paying the chiefs' new salaries, was to be spent on social services. Thus the colonial government attempted to reconcile the preservation of traditional authority with the needs of social and economic changes. The difficulty was that chiefs could not be won over unless a large portion of revenue, sometimes almost 60 per cent, was reserved for their emoluments. At the same time many clung to their traditional rights. This was the cause of political opposition during the 1955–6 riots after new taxation had been introduced.[18]

Modern Politics

Modern politics began in 1909 when the urban élite in Freetown founded the Rate Payers Association, its main function to
contest elections to the Municipal Council. Other groups were
soon established, all expressing at least incipient nationalism:
the Aborigines' Protection Society (1919), the African Progress
Union (1919), the Sierra Leone branch of the National Congress of British West Africa (1920), the Young People's Progressive Union (1929). Even primarily occupational groups,
such as the Civil Servants Association (1907–9), and the Sierra
Leone Bar Association (1919), were of some political signifi-
cance, the leaders and members frequently belonging to the
outright political groups, even holding office in both.

The protectorate's first political organisation was the Committee of Educated Aborigines, which in 1922 began by
formally welcoming a gubernatorial visit and including in the
speech references to non-representation in the central legislature. The western-educated élite in the colony—the National
Congress of British West Africa, Sierra Leone branch—were
doing the same.

The skilled artisans in Freetown also protested. The first
trade union, the Carpenters Defensive Union, had flowered
briefly in 1895, but in 1919 the railway workers struck over
delayed payment of promised war bonuses, and in 1920 they
founded the Sierra Leone Railway Skilled Workmen Mutual
Aid Union. This was the first sign of coherent movement
amongst wage earners. Trade unions grew only slowly; by
1940 there were seven registered, by 1942 eleven.[19] Government
response was equally sluggardly. Only in 1939 did an ordinance (no 31) establish machinery for registering unions.
Ordinance 14 of that year at last provided machinery for
arbitration in strikes. Number 35 was the Workmen's Com-
pensation Ordinance.

Strikes, as South African nationalists find today, are the best
way to educate the illiterate masses politically. The 1919 railway strike, and the subsequent stoppage by the daily paid
Public Works Department staff, were boycotted by the Free-

town élite, alarmed at the breakdown of law and order. Middle class, assimilated, prosperous, after the manner of Sir Samuel Lewis, the latter were constitutionalists rather than democrats.[20] However, by the time of the 1926 railway strike the Sierra Leone branch of the National Congress of British West Africa were more experienced politically and, hoping to use these wage-labourers at least temporarily to their advantage, collected money on their behalf. Of course, they had no plans (perhaps no notion of how) to include them in their movement.

The rural elements were inevitably less articulate than even the urban labourers. None the less, there were riots in Moyamba in 1923–4, in Kambia in 1930, Pujehun 1931, Kenema 1934, and elsewhere. As in 1955–6, violence was not really aimed at the colonial presence directly, but at the chiefs, the main government agents. Often it was organised through traditional societies, like the Poro. At least once, in the 1931 Idara rebellion, so called from its Muslim leader Idara Contorfilli, it was religiously inspired. Coming at a time of economic depression, when neither government nor chiefs would ameliorate their tax demands, it became an instrument of political expression. Machetes and even a few guns were issued and the people told not to pay their taxes to the chiefs and not to heed colonial government.[21] None of these risings gave birth to any lasting political movement.

Government reaction to protest was for a long time to slow down the pace of integrating the educated élite into its decision-making bodies. Administration was seen as depending on a capacity for negotiation, on the working of a bureaucratic machine, on the experience acquired by an English public-school education, followed by army or university and then by long years as a colonial civil servant. Westminster-type democracy and independence was not yet on the horizon.

The years after World War I, however, were a period when many younger Europeans began to have doubts. Doubts about the hitherto unquestioned virtues of Christianity and of western civilisation itself which perhaps might even be bad for Africa. Anthropologists now studied indigenous societies *in situ*. J. Northcote Thomas, the government anthropologist, came out

N

to Freetown and made a survey in 1919. Captain R. S. Rattray, on the Gold Coast, was showing how African political life could not be separated from the social and religious. The International Anthropological Institute was founded in 1926, Hanns Vischer, its first secretary, having begun work as a missionary in northern Nigeria before joining the Nigerian political service. In 1926, Oxford and Cambridge began the Tropical African Service Courses, which assumed recruits could actually be taught about the peoples they were going to administer. As the world's economic depression widened, the free trade principles on which Lord Lugard's 'dual mandate'[22] had rested became a dead letter. Liberalising movements in Britain were altering the old relationships between master and man. A sensitive young man like Paul Shuffrey, a family business keeping him in touch with reality, could scarcely help losing his temper in the Government House of that era.

The 1924 Constitution

In 1922 the National Congress of British West Africa, welcoming the new governor, Sir Ransford Slater, asked for the introduction of an 'elective franchise'. The chamber of commerce sought more direct representation of commercial interests, whilst the paramount chiefs drew attention to the anomaly presented by a Legislative Council legislating for a protectorate which had no direct representative on it.

Slater had doubts about the elective franchise, partly because it was not Colonial Office policy, and partly because, though they might claim to represent the 'sons of the soil', the National Congress was representing little more, as they virtually admitted, than the intelligentsia.[23] In any event they asked, outrageously, for five African members to represent the colony, giving altogether seven directly representative of the colony's 85,000 inhabitants as against only three for about 1½ millions in the protectorate.

After consideration, a new constitution gave a Legislative Council of twelve official and ten unofficial members. Of the latter, two represented commercial and general European interests; three elected members represented, respectively: Freetown, Sherbro and the Rural Areas (ie the colony villages outside Freetown); two members were nominated for the colony and three for the protectorate. The latter were paramount chiefs, two from the Mende and one from the Temne (one from each province). The Executive Council remained unchanged and purely European until 1943 when one representative from the colony and one paramount chief were appointed. Elections, first introduced here, were entirely for the élite; there was a literacy qualification as well as an income one. Only 1,866 persons found themselves eligible to vote!

The Creoles offered several objections to this arrangement: that the chiefs were too closely tied to the protectorate administration; that the chiefs did not necessarily represent their people, being nominated as they were and in view of the current strained relations between chiefs and people owing to alleged misuse of power;[24] that it would be illegal for British-protected persons, and aliens under the 1890 Foreign Jurisdiction Act, to legislate for British subjects. In fact they were afraid of the ultimate destruction of Creole ascendency in the Legislative Council.

A new generation of literate chiefs began to take office in the 1930s, many having known each other at Bo school and formed friendships transcending tribal politics. Others, whose parents had become rich enough to pay the secondary-school fees also received a western education. These two groups in the protectorate began organising their own quasi-political activities.

Dr Milton Margai, grandson of a Mende chief and son of a wealthy merchant educated at a United Brethren in Christ School, was frequently called in by older chiefs for technical and political advice. Partly at his instigation in 1940 the chiefs began a series of annual chiefs' conferences. These were spontaneous in that no British officials were present. The first met at Moyamba.

Most educated protectorate men automatically went into government service. Meeting frequently in provincial towns they could develop plans. In 1929 several, including Dr Margai and A. J. Momoh, a civil servant, with a number of educated paramount chiefs, formed the Protectorate Educational Progressive

Union, to provide scholarships for protectorate boys, offset the protectorate's educational backwardness, and give intelligence a chance wherever it might occur.

The educated soon formed another group, the Sierra Leone Organisation Society, ostensibly educational but meant to encourage political awareness. Its founders were Dr John Karefa-Smart and a number of teachers, nearly all from chiefly families. Mostly government servants, however, they were more vulnerable than self-employed professional or business men to government pressure.

In 1944 Paramount Chief A. B. Samba, member for the northern province, expressed in the Legislative Council a hope that chiefs' conferences would soon be officially recognised. In 1945 the government, pursuing a colonial policy which reflected changed attitudes in post-war Britain and anticipating further demands for greater representation in the protectorate, established two consultative bodies. At the lower level was the system of District Councils, each with two representatives from each chiefdom, one of them a paramount chief, the other appointed by the Tribal Authority, which in practice meant someone acceptable to the chiefs, since their interests prevailed in the Tribal Authority. They were a second tier in local government, created when Native Administrations proved unsatisfactory. From 1950 on, they developed into fully executive bodies, but only after fierce competition with the Native Administrations. In 1950 four additional members were added to represent wider interests in the district. Though their administrative expenses were considerably lower than the NAs, they suffered from very severe limitations in planning efficiency and in the execution of plans. They were handicapped because government officers could not over reconcile themselves to the fact they were not traditional, disliked them for not being a proper part of the old system of indirect rule and, possibly, saw in them some aspects of western civilisation about which they had grave doubts anyway.[25]

The second and higher body created at this time was the Protectorate Assembly whose sole function was to advise the government. Twenty-six of the forty-two seats were reserved for

paramount chiefs, indirectly elected by the NAs and District
Councils. The remaining seats were for eleven officials, one
representing the Creoles, one European business interests, one
missionary interests, and two educated protectorate Africans
selected by the NAs.

The educated, protectorate élite—notably the Sierra Leone
Organisation Society, whose deputy president was Dr Margai—
criticised this allocation for discriminating against them.

The 1951 Constitution

In February 1947 in a circular despatch on local government
the new Labour secretary of state intimated his wish to bring
African territories to responsible self-government, stressing the
need to develop efficient, representative, local government.

Once it became apparent that more than mere advice was
to be expected from the Legislative Council and Protectorate
Assembly very considerable interest was aroused as to representation. After consulting both, Governor Sir Hubert Stevenson
informed the secretary of state, in October 1947, that the 1924
constitution was no longer appropriate, that it had an unduly
high proportion of nominated to elected unofficial members
and that the representation of the protectorate, containing
90 per cent of the population, was entirely disproportionate.
The time had come to redress the balance between colony and
protectorate, and in particular to ensure a majority of elected
members as well as to provide opportunity for the protectorate
to take 'an increased and increasingly effective share in the
management of the affairs of the country'.[26]

The struggle between the different elements in the political
system lasted until 1951, when the constitution was promulgated. The paramount chiefs were firmly in favour of the
Stevenson proposals. The younger, educated, protectorate men
in the SOS saw that they were going to be excluded from any
chance of election to the legislature since election was through
District Councils and the Assembly—both controlled by chiefs.
The Creoles feared the built-in majority for the protectorate.

It was only the persistent friendship of Dr Milton Margai
with the chiefs that prevented an inevitable break between the

protectorate westernised, middle-class élite and the chiefs. Even so, violence broke out in several places in the south in 1948, 1949 and 1951. In the end the new élite's representation was increased. The governor implored Native Administration and chiefs 'to move with the times like the rest of us', and the following year, 1952, Tribal Authorities were reconstituted to provide one member for every forty tax-payers. Native Administrations were more closely scrutinised by the central government, and unviable ones amalgamated.

By 1951 Sierra Leone had the only constitution in British West Africa to retain an official majority. This was now changed: unofficial members were raised from 10 to 23, officials reduced from 11 to 7. Elected members from the colony were increased from 3 to 7, and the protectorate for the first time returned elected representatives, 12 chosen by the District Council, 2 by the Assembly. There were also the 2 nominated members representing trade and commerce. At the same time the Executive Council, previously consisting of 5 official and 3 unofficial members, was reconstituted with 4 official and not less than 4 appointed members, nominated by the governor from the elected members of the Legislative Council. In fact, the governor nominated 6 for a period of 5 years.

The 1951 constitution also made it possible for the unofficial members of the Executive Council to take over responsibilities for government departments when the Legislative Council considered it appropriate.

Party Politics
When Dr Margai in 1950 announced his intention of standing in the Freetown by-election to the Legislative Council, he was castigated as a 'cradle baby',[27] not intelligent or experienced enough to represent Freetown. Creole delaying tactics and propaganda of this sort antagonised irrevocably the up-country westernised élite. The Creole-protectorate split was forcing together on one side the two articulate protectorate groups, the chiefs and the handful of educated élite, and on the other hand, a motley collection of Creole organisations. In August 1950 representatives of all save one of the colony political

groups came together to form the National Council of the Colony of Sierra Leone, with Dr Herbert Bankole-Bright, doyen of Sierra Leone politics who had had the distinction of being called a harmful demagogue as long ago as 1926 by the governor,[28] as its leader. Its election manifesto for the 1951 Legislative Council elections said: 'We object to foreigners [ie protectorate people] prepondering in our Legislative Council.'

In the protectorate, Dr Margai, who had just retired after twenty-two years as a medical officer, was the most widely accepted leader. It was he who, in September 1950, had moved in the Assembly that the government be asked to implement the revised Stevenson proposals as quickly as possible. Relations between protectorate and Creoles seemed to make compromise impossible.

In mid-1951, when a number of leading political figures in the protectorate decided to dissolve the SOS, and create the Sierra Leone People's Party, there was little thought of any save Dr Margai leading it. Typically, it was he who persuaded the founding members not to call it the Protectorate People's Party, insisting on a national format. Other leading figures (Albert Margai, Siaka Stevens) had also been active in the SOS and A. J. Momo had been a founder of the 1929 Protectorate Educational Progressive Union. The chiefs remained in the background, the leading figures being educated élite, including Kande Bureh, Temne headman in Freetown and a former teacher whose followers were the younger, urbanised, ordinary Temne who had elected him in preference to some member of the traditional hierarchy. Beyond enlisting a few big men in each locality, the SLPP undertook little political activity in the protectorate. In general, this remained its policy for over twenty years.

Many of the educated SLPP leadership were still interested in supporting chiefs at the national level. Though its manifesto in the 1951 elections contained some sops to chiefs, this was not enough to induce them to elect all candidates favoured by the party. Eight out of the twelve District Councils returned chiefs. The Assembly, thanks to Dr Margai's influence, however, returned two non-chiefs: Albert Margai (later knighted and also made prime minister after his half-brother's death) and Siaka Stevens, a representative of the trade unions and, later, president of Sierra Leone.

In the colony the National Council won five seats, as against the SLPP's two, but outside the colony it had not even tried to win support.

No one was quite certain what the chiefs who had been elected were going to do. The governor, Sir George Beresford-Stooke, after some discussion with the two parties at a private meeting, called for a vote, and all but one of the members from the protectorate voted to support an SLPP government. Thus the SLPP had fifteen supporters and the National Council had six. For the first time in history, protectorate people controlled the legislature. As leader of the majority party Dr Margai was able to choose the unofficial members of the Executive Council who would, in time, take over government departments, ie become ministers of state. He chose a group which balanced tribe and region as far as possible: Albert Margai, to whom the educated in the protectorate looked; Siaka Stevens, a northerner, and a trade unionist; Chief Bai Farima Tass, an important northern chief; A. G. Randle, half-Mende member for a colony constituency; M. S. Mustapha, a Muslim Creole and member for Freetown East.

In April 1953 these members became ministers and took up their portfolios. In 1954 Dr Margai was accorded the title of Chief Minister in recognition of his special responsibility and standing as leader of the other ministers of the majority party.

The 1957 Election

In 1954 the government set up a commission for electoral reform under the chairmanship of Dr Bryan Keith-Lucas, Nuffield College, Oxford. It discovered, naturally, that the younger educated protectorate men favoured extending the franchise. It discovered, too, that most chiefs favoured it as well, though to some extent this depended on whether or not they were literate.[29] Accordingly the commission recommended a two-stage progression to universal suffrage. The first, in time for the next election provided for a taxpayer franchise (ie all adult males) in the protectorate, and an income and property franchise in the colony. It also recommended paramount chiefs should be given separate representation and that non-chief members of the District Council be directly elected, not appointed by the Tribal Authority. All this was accepted.

The Protectorate Assembly was abolished in 1955, on the grounds that the Legislative Council had now superseded it.

In 1956 a unicameral body, of 57 members, plus a speaker (with 4 officials and 2 nominated members), was set up by order in council. The 51 elected members were to comprise 12 paramount chiefs, one elected by each District Council. This partly eliminated the direct competition between westernised middle-class protectorate people and the chiefs.

Independence, 1961

The 1957 election confirmed the ascendency of the SLPP, and of the protectorate educated men within it.[30]

No less than 19 of the 25 successful SLPP candidates came from professional or near-professional occupations in which at least secondary-school education was required. Sixteen of them were, however, chiefs or members of chiefly families.[31] Chiefdom politics was understandably nearer the electorate's interest in the protectorate than national politics.

When the wheeling and dealing was over, the SLPP emerged with 44 of the elected members of the House of Representatives, as the unicameral body was called. Secure from Creole—or any other—threats, the party leadership began to fall out. In 1958 there was a struggle, which had, indeed, been apparent as early as 1956. Dr Milton Margai, with his quiet, introverted manner, was challenged by the more rumbustious Albert, his half-brother. The latter eventually left the SLPP and with Siaka Stevens as deputy leader, founded the People's National Party. It attracted many young men of middle-class background, as well as those in the SLPP who were uneasy at continuing chiefly dominance. Even young Creoles joined.

But early in 1960 Mr Alan Lennox Boyd,[32] until October 1959 secretary of state, visited Freetown, and Sir Milton Margai (knighted in 1959) issued invitations to leaders of all political parties to attend an SLPP round-table conference to discuss constitutional proposals for independence. All agreed to put up a United National Front, so that the new party was dissolved before it could test its strength. The opposition leaders, accepting that Sir Milton should head the government after independence, and thus waiving their earlier insistence on having elections before independence, asked for, and obtained a promise that they would be given portfolios after independence.[33]

Meanwhile in May 1960 it was decided that the governor should no longer take the chair at Executive Council meetings, which should now be occupied by the premier, whose title should be changed to prime minister. At the same time the Executive Council became the cabinet, and it was arranged that Sierra Leone should become independent on 27 April 1961.

At the Constitutional Conference, London, May 1960, the United National Front had been successfully maintained (Britain intimating she would not hand over to any except an established government) until almost the last minute, when Siaka Stevens announced himself unable to sign the independence constitution document.

The All Peoples Congress

Siaka Stevens as a Limba and as a northerner no doubt distrusted Mende preponderance in the SLPP and the United Front. Moreover, the 1957 election being fought almost entirely to pursue tribal interests, most protectorate people seeing creoledom as their great enemy had united to defeat it. When the UPP began to break up in 1958, northerners became even more restless in the SLPP.

Many saw with disgust that, though the opposition parties had for years been working the protectorate and colony up against the SLPP, their leaders were now willing to accept office in the United Front. Creole leaders resented the protectorate dominance of the SLPP and indeed all non-Mende seem to have been disaffected. Thus when the disillusioned Siaka Stevens founded the All Peoples Congress in mid-1960 on his return from London, many hastened to follow him, seeing it as the right place for tribal and group interests to be served.

The latter was an important factor. Tribal demands were indeed accommodated within the SLPP, but more radical group demands were not. Mr Stevens had especially hard words to say about his erstwhile leader in the PNP, Albert Margai, who accepted office under Sir Milton and, it was noted, when the PNP broke up as Mr Stevens left it, led his Mende PNP followers all safely back into the SLPP fold.

Not only Mr Stevens' old PNP northerners—the Limba, Susu, Loko and Mandingo—followed him, but disaffected young Creoles, politicians and intellectuals as well as young men in the lower levels of the wage scale, like lorry drivers, who could not support the SLPP's upholding traditional values and authorities which they had broken away from. The 1955–6 northern riots had shown that there were many there who no longer respected their chiefs as they had done until very recently. (A combination of the nature of a Temne chief's office, the influence of Islam, the slower penetration of westernisation in the form of education, wage employment, cash crops and transport, had all slowed down the disintegration of the old ways in the north.) It has been estimated that in the three years 1952–4 as many left to mine diamonds as had departed in the previous eighty years to seek wages.[34] Since it was a seasonal job—the rains making alluvial mining impracticable—they returned more frequently to their villages than permanent work would have permitted. They brought back disruptive ideas about wealth, morals, law and order which soon spread, because perhaps as many as one man in five had in the end tried his luck amongst the get-rich-quick, relatively lawless crowds in Kono.

After only two months' existence, the APC showed its phenomenal strength in winning the Freetown City Council elections taking two of the three seats by substantial majorities, and only losing the third by less than thirty votes. A realignment of political tribal groupings set the pattern for the 1960s. Confrontation was now the APC against the SLPP, all non-Mende tribes endeavouring to bring down the SLPP. The 1962 election saw the SLPP retain power, thanks to overwhelming Mende support; even so it was a close thing.

A new era had indeed dawned with the APC's symbol of a rising sun. None of the APC leaders had gone beyond secondary school; all had earned their living in clerical or trading occupations; half of them came from families without any particular standing in either traditional or modern society; their median age was nearly twenty years less than that of the SLPP leaders. They took a non-aligned, Pan-African view of foreign affairs, and spoke of founding 'a welfare state based upon a socialist pattern'.[35] It was perhaps, a young man's party, with much of the simple, high, idealism of youth, but even so there now confronted the loosely organised coalition of traditional and westernised notables, a tribally based movement of younger, radical commoners.[36]

The 1962 Election

Sierra Leone's election of 1962 made history in tropical Africa in that it was the first to be held in an independent state where parties were able to compete unhindered, though it is true that the APC found it advisable to have their local headquarters in the larger towns where there was not only the advantage of reaching larger audiences more cheaply but also the harassment by the SLPP-dominated chiefs' courts was less blatant. None the less, they won twelve of the eighteen northern seats.

Generally the SLPP candidates had to look after their own interests, the vans provided for each district being monopolised by the ministers, each person being expected to see to his own deposit and out-of-pocket expenses, and to campaign pretty much on his own. However, the northern chief who told his people that though he was an SLPP man he would not force anyone else to support that party seems to have been an exception. In the Western Area, where there were no chiefs, Hunting Societies and 'Companies', were used by both sides to bring in voters.[37] Generally the APC presented more of a united front, candidates helping each other, and the party at times successfully persuaded voters to support the party rather than an individual.

Official SLPP candidates won less than a majority of ordinary members' seats, and only eight more than the two allied

opposition parties (APC and Kono-based Sierra Leone Progressive Independence Movement). Here the constitution came
to their aid. As a distinguished Canadian scholar has pointed
out,[38] Sections 58 (6) (a) and 58 (8), empowered the governor-
general to call upon the leader of the majority to become prime

Map 10

minister. But once called, a man was in a position to distribute
patronage, using his powers to create a majority for himself,
thus providing *prima facie* evidence of the correctness of the
governor-general's decision. Sir Milton was called and all
fourteen Independents now declared support for the SLPP.[39]
    For the first time in the House of Representatives, most

northerners were now in opposition. For the first time, therefore, southerners dominated the SLPP parliamentary party.
Regrettably, perhaps, the six APC–SLPIM members who were
sons of paramount chiefs, eventually crossed to the SLPP.
Within two years of crossing one was elected as a paramount
chief, an event unlikely had he continued to oppose the SLPP
government. Otherwise, however, Sir Milton's tactics of conciliation—used so successfully against the Creole's original hostility in 1951—was unproductive. Most APC members felt they
were in Parliament to protect the ordinary man, and thus to
change the ruling oligarchy, not to join it. They suffered considerable harassment in several chiefdoms, and had at the
same time to watch their step carefully. Sir Milton had put
Siaka Stevens and several other APC leaders in gaol just before
independence. He said later he was not prepared to let young
men destroy what he had built, and no one believed it was an
idle threat. He was not a bully, however, using as little coercion
as possible. His reliance on chiefs at the local level meant not
upsetting them. Local government was left virtually unchanged
between 1956 and his death in 1964,[40] even though more than
half the revenue still went on chiefs' emoluments and administrative costs, and the District Councils became more and
more corrupt. What little democratisation the colonial power
had introduced into local government was halted.

Sir Albert Magai

When Sir Milton died the governor-general, for reasons which
have never been entirely cleared of suspicions of coercion, sent
for Albert Margai. His career as prime minister falls into three
stages.[41] First, for over a year he was trying, not very successfully, to consolidate his position as leader of the SLPP over
such rivals, or potential rivals, as Dr John Karefa-Smart, M. S.
Mustapha, Kanda Bureh, Y. D. Sesay, and Salia Jusu-Sheriff.[42]
He also endeavoured to establish his party outstandingly above
the reach of the APC. In both these he had little real success.
His response was to try to create a one-party state, thus safeguarding himself and his supporters, and striking off down a
path often trodden by modern African leaders. This met stern

resistance from his own party, from the judiciary, the civil service, the university, most of the Creole élite and many ordinary people, to say nothing of the APC and, perhaps especially, since it caused the prime minister to go softly, from his electorate in the northern constituencies during the District Council elections in May 1966, when the APC was so very successful. He then conducted a short holding operation which led up to the 1967 election and the subsequent military *coup d'état*.

It was unfortunate that many senior civil servants happened to be Mende. Moreover, after his ministerial purges only three northerners were left in the Cabinet. Tribal divisions became steadily stronger, especially perhaps when, having catastrophically lost the city council elections in 1964, the prime minister endeavoured to eradicate APC influence at all levels. The fact that the commanding officer of the Royal Sierra Leone Military Force, Brigadier David Lansana, was a Mende and the army Mende-dominated was unfortunate, too, since the unlikelihood of any forceful restraint seems to have encouraged excessive abuse of constitutional practice by Sir Albert[43] and his closest supporters, as well as corruption. It should be noted, however, that when he proposed to bypass the constitution (which, in certain entrenched clauses, required him to call an election if he were to make radical alterations to it) in order to secure his one-party state by substituting a national referendum, even the SLPP caucus jibbed and he had to drop the plan.

The 1967 Coups d'État

At first the APC leadership seemed to favour the principle of a one-party state, and some were willing to enter a coalition with the SLPP. The APC constitution spoke of building the unity of the nation under a unitary form of government. But finding how the country felt, the party changed its view. Meanwhile, Sir Albert began to campaign for the creation of a republic. Here again, the entrenched clauses came into operation, requiring a two-thirds majority in the House, a dissolution and a second passing of the Bill by the new House. In any event, the five-year rule required an election in 1967.

Elections for ordinary members were held on 17 March and for chiefs on 21 March. Sir Albert went to the polls probably with more confidence than was justified, despite certain precautions taken by the SLPP to encourage success. Tribal feeling ran high, and by election day a state of emergency had been declared for all districts except Pujehun. The SLPP suffered heavily because of its usual lack of even rudimentary grassroots organisation, which fell far short of that of the APC. In the Northern Province the APC won all but one of the contested seats; in the Western Area (former colony) it gained every contested seat, and in Kono it gained two out of four contested seats. It even picked up one in the Southern Province in a district where Temnes happened to outnumber Mendes. All told the APC gained thirty-two seats, the SLPP twenty-eight and the Independents six.

The SLPP had gone to great trouble to get their candidates returned unopposed in as many constituencies as they could. Even so, they had success in only six, where rivals had been eliminated on minor faults in their nomination papers. None the less, outside Mende country they had been virtually eliminated. They won only one contested seat in the north, and none in the Western Province. In those areas the APC had polled nearly 75 per cent of the votes though ballot-rigging concealed a true, and higher figure.

Everyone was waiting for the final results, but the government-controlled media purposely delayed. Since it was very close, the question of the paramount chiefs' elections on the 21st became vital. Their position gave rise to some doubt; hitherto, not permitted to campaign under party labels, they had supported the government, rather than a party. They could, unlike other members, be deposed from office as chiefs, and it was therefore held that their constitutional position was different from that of ordinary members of the House of Representatives.

Sir Henry Lightfoot-Boston, the Creole governor-general, called upon Sir Albert Margai and Siaka Stevens to form a coalition. The latter, consulting his MPs, and exercising his political acumen, refused.

Next, four of the Independent members wrote to the governor-general saying they were willing to support either party, but not the SLPP led by Sir Albert. Two of these had been counted in the official SLPP total of returned members, so that their action now gave the APC a clear majority, if the chiefs were not taken into consideration. Sir Henry, therefore, invited Mr Stevens to State House and swore him in as prime minister on 21 March.

The force commander, a Mende, surrounded State House with troops and proclaimed martial law. The north, where celebrations had been in full swing for days, was shocked. Two days later widespread violence seemed likely. Senior army officers arrested Brigadier Lansana, and declared the formation of a National Reformation Council, composed of themselves and of senior police officers who had joined the military on 23 March.[44]

Thus the first peaceful transfer of political power in post-independence West Africa was forestalled, to the shame and humiliation of thousands, and to the fury of the north who felt robbed, especially when they saw that half of the eight-member National Reformation Council were Mende. The APC leaders and most intellectuals and professional men declared a boycott of the Civilian National Advisory Committee established by the NRC, which, however, the NRC scarcely used, preferring to rule by decree, consulting their civil servants.

The NRC promised to hand over to the politicians as soon as the situation became favourable, undertaking to do all in its power to bring about civilian rule in the shortest possible time.[45] In fact it was reluctant to do so and thus, being largely Mende-dominated, linked with the traditional and the middle-class élites, and having taken over from an elected government with genuine popular support, it was not welcomed in various quarters.

There were rumours that the ambitious NRC chairman, Lieutenant-Colonel Andrew Juxon-Smith, was planning to declare himself president of a republic, but the non-commissioned officers staged a counter coup on 18 April 1968. This surprised no one who knew the army well. Other ranks had felt neglected even before the first coup; pay, conditions of service and promotion prospects have all been subsequently improved. On 26 April Siaka Stevens was again sworn in as prime minister, heading an APC, SLPP, Independent coalition.

The Republic

Siaka Stevens came to power enthusiastically supported by his own northerners, by the less-educated wage earners, by ordinary farmers and by the Creole intelligentsia.

He faced a severe financial crisis, however, left by the last civilian regime. Mounting unemployment, inflation, a slow rate of investment, a serious lack of industrial development, and other scourges so tragically common in the developing world, all beset him.

A bankrupt Produce Marketing Board had brought a drastic reduction in agriculture. Over £4·2 million was needed in 1968–9 for debt repayment and servicing. Diamond smuggling was costing £3 million a year. The railway had been losing £500,000 annually. There was only one doctor for every 19,000 inhabitants.

The government began an immediate rescue operation, taking over from the NRC's 'stabilisation budget' of 1967, which had been aimed at stopping the outflow of reserves, shrunk by February 1967 to £5·5 million—the equivalent of only two months' imports. With minerals accounting for 85 per cent of exports, a high priority was given to agriculture, especially palm products and (mainly swamp) rice; it was hoped to become self-sufficient in the latter staple within a few years. Improvements in cattle and poultry were taken in hand, iron-ore and bauxite mining continued to be expanded, all with a view to diversifying the economy and reducing the cost of living, which the government saw as two of its priorities. The railway was phased out in 1968. By 1968 agriculture was contributing 30 per cent of the gross domestic product.

Industrial production, concentrated on import substitutes, only employed some 5 per cent of the population. In August 1969 a Retail Trade Act prohibited foreigners from undertaking certain kinds of retailing such as cement, poultry, insurance, garages, printing and laundry. One great problem was the inadequacy of credit facilities available to indigenous business-men, and so a National Development Bank was founded which soon announced the formation of a National Trading Company to encourage Sierra Leonean participation in business, follow-ing the Retail Trade Act.

The main exports at present are diamonds (nearly £30 mil-lion a year), followed by iron ore, palm-kernels, coffee, bauxite and cocoa.[46]

In politics, the Mende, playing the role hitherto cast for others, found themselves with only two of their people in the Cabinet. Ominously, by-elections in November 1968, in Mende country, produced SLPP victories and tribal clashes; there were rumours of an impending mercenary invasion to restore Sir Albert from voluntary exile. In December, after further tribal disputes between Temne and Mende workers at the Marampa iron mines, the Mokanji Hills bauxite mines and the Bonthe District rutile mines, workers not belonging to the ethnic group of the locality were forced to return home. Final by-elections in March 1969, following on various election peti-tions, exile, or other disqualification of candidates, gave the APC forty-eight of the total seventy-eight seats. The National Coalition Government gave way to an APC one in June.

In December 1969, when events permitted more normal activities, the prime minister announced the government's in-tention of taking a controlling 51 per cent interest in four ex-patriate mining companies, the main objective being the Sierra Leone Selection Trust, the diamond company. It was national-ised in late 1970, but no further steps were taken against the others.

Possibly internal APC affairs were preoccupying the prime minister, where a familiar struggle had developed between the founding members and the youthful newcomers. The 'old sweats' who had suffered imprisonment and worse in former days were unwilling to step aside for more radical youths. A few days after the party convention in May 1970, Ibrahim Taqi, a Temne, was dropped from his post as minister of information. He and some young SLPP formed a new party, the National Democratic

Party, which criticised the prime minister's increasing reliance on the Creoles and was especially apprehensive of the prime minister's attempts to reconcile the Mendes. In July they were joined by another influential Temne, Dr John Karefa-Smart, a rumoured rival to Mr Stevens since he had first joined the APC in 1965. They accused the prime minister of seeking to become an autocratic executive president. In September, a state of emergency was declared—the second since the prime minister took office. On 20 September the dissidents, incorporating the NDP and selecting Dr Karefa-Smart as chairman, founded the United Democratic Party. Violence occurred in the north as well as in Freetown. In October it was banned and the leaders detained.

Meanwhile, the army was flexing its muscles again under the new, Temne, Force commander, Brigadier John Bangura. On 23 March 1971 the military opened fire on a cabinet meeting from the adjacent Paramount Hotel. The coup was unsuccessful. Two cabinet ministers, K. A. Daramy (a Susu) and C. P. Foray (a Mende) were allegedly involved in the plot, and were dismissed.

By now Sierra Leone was the only African territory where the queen of England was still head of state. On 19 April 1971 Sierra Leone became a republic with Mr Stevens as executive president. Sori Ibrahim Koroma, a Temne founder member of the APC, was vice-president and prime minister.[47] The president approached Salia Jusu-Sheriff, now leader of the SLPP, with a view to forming a coalition. Conciliation has always been the president's policy, and although the SLPP refused there were no signs of any plans for a one-party state; the president not being a radical, nor a communist, as has been suggested. Relations with Russia and China have indeed become closer, but not at the expense of the Commonwealth.

The president has come to rely increasingly on the Creoles, even to the extent of giving them more representation; the Creoles, ironically, have been driven further and further into the arms of the APC—the 'up country' party—by the anti-Creole attitudes of the Mende SLPP and the Temne UDP. Also, they needed the president's protection from the left wing of his party. Conversely, as educated provincial men became disillusioned, the APC, with few highly educated men to call on at the best of times,[48] has had to rely more and more upon Creole professional and middle-class expertise. There would be little chance of preserving this co-operation should the APC's left wing ever succeed in pushing through a one-party state, or acquire leadership of the party.

Perhaps the final irony is that the APC and the chiefs are now in harmony (though not, of course, everywhere). Politicians in Africa have proved fragile, even ephemeral, but chiefs have remained steadfast, watching, often unmoved, the rout of those they once voted for—and got their people to vote for. A politician's success in Africa depends greatly upon whether he lives up to his promises, as the 1962 Sierra Leone election shows. Three-quarters of the ministers succeeded in retaining their seats at that time, though only a third of the backbenchers did. Apart from greater access to transport and other party organisations and funds at election time, their success was partly due to their having been better able to provide benefits and patronage for their constituencies. If a party cannot produce the goods, then it has lost the chiefs' support, and with it, that of much of the country.

No really satisfactory form of local government other than that involving chiefs has been found in Sierra Leone. Chiefs resent party offices in their towns, but in fact no party has as yet managed to establish anything even remotely resembling a grass-roots organisation. So long as villages remain cut off by lack of communication, radio and education, and so long as the parties are crippled by lack of money for agents and propaganda equipment, then the chiefs will continue to be an essential part of the political apparatus of the ruling party, and Sierra Leone politics will remain a matter of localism.

The president therefore needs the chiefs. They, too, need him above all, because some of his younger followers wish to abolish traditional offices. Friendly relations between the chiefs and the president, and the Creoles and the president, are perhaps the essential ingredients for peace and prosperity, especially if he can succeed in harmonising the Temne and Mende political and traditional leaders. All this implies holding his own party together too. It is not an enviable task.

The 1973 Elections

The latest general elections, those of May 1973, resulted in the APC holding ninety-two of the ninety-seven seats in the enlarged House.[49] No less than forty-six of these were returned unopposed by the time nominations closed. Most former ministers were re-elected and of the five non-APC seats, three were in the Freetown area and two in Bo. It is less easy in those two large towns to indulge in intimidation, and the president does not deny that violence occurred. He was especially disturbed at the deaths caused by police shooting in Freetown. The SLPP allege many of their candidates were prevented from submitting nomination papers, whilst many who had succeeded in doing so later withdrew, claiming they would have been in physical danger if they had stood.

The electoral commission declared several nomination papers null, including that of Salia Jusu-Sheriff, leader of the SLPP opposition. The twelve paramount chiefs as usual declared for the majority party.

After an interlude of British overrule it looks, therefore, as if northern influences may predominate again. Despite the importance of land in African life, the government has been concerned essentially with people. National boundaries, in the European and 'Great Power' sense, always seemed a trifle irrelevant in Africa. The author recollects the delightful surprise of a distinguished French botanist, nearly a quarter of a century ago, at the bureaucratic furore engendered by his eccentric wanderings between French Guinea and Sierra Leone in search of his beloved flowers. Africans have always felt free in that sense at least; local languages, villages and even families straddling the artificial frontiers. The president today maintains, and indeed has inherited, more than merely friendly relations with Guinea. He and the core of his party, and his country as well, are part of that broader culture.

European administrative and political concepts are in the process of re-acculturation. Foreigners who criticise this have simply failed to comprehend the vigour of African culture, the dignity and integrity of daily life (how many towns in the so-called developed world can exist, like much of Africa, without a police force?), the adaptiveness and common sense of traditional West African rulers—traits their own civilisation has unfortunately mainly lost.

Since the euphoric days of independence the future, given a modicum of mutual co-operation, can scarcely have looked brighter. Food and raw materials have been valued more fairly since the whole world's ecology was seen to be related and suddenly perceived to be precarious. A little more priority is now given to intermediate technology, which is concerned with improving indigenous techniques, the production of wind, water and solar energy and the intelligent use of local labour. Industrial nations have realised one can gain no nourishment from a motor car, nor keep warm by burning bank notes. As the shah of Iran has observed, the era of exploitation is finished.

Notes and References

INTRODUCTION

1 Colonial Office, London; Public Record Office CO 267/235, Despatch 182 (9 November 1878), enclosure no 8, paras 31, 36. Published as Africa Confidential Print 163 of 1878. See also *The West African Reporter* (Freetown) (1 Jan 1879; 23 July 1881; 24 Sept 1881); *The Freetown Express* (19 Jan 1883); Colonial Office Confidential Print 879/14, sections 8, 11, 15.

2 John Hargreaves, *The Prelude to the Partition of Africa* (1963), p 221.

CHAPTER 1

1 The first Earlier Stone Age date for West Africa, so far, is that of the Acheulian culture of the Jos Plateau, given as more than 39,000 years before the present.

2 Oliver Davies, *West Africa before the Europeans* (1967), p 133. See also pp 19, 20–2, 93–8, 149. For fuller accounts see especially William Hance, *The Geography of Modern Africa* (1967), pp 165–73.

3 Frederick Johnson Pedler, *Economic Geography of West Africa* (1955), pp 15–17. The term Neolithic is generally agreed to be unsatisfactory, being capable of ambiguous interpretation. But like other unsatisfactory terms—Negro, Bantu, etc—which the white man has imported—we seem to be stuck with them at least for the present. By Neolithic I mean to imply food production, though I am aware that in West Africa, or at least in places, direct evidence of food production is sometimes hard to come by prior to the introduction of iron. The term Late Stone Age is therefore sometimes used.

4 Davies, op cit, pp 176ff.

5 John D. Clark, *The Prehistory of Africa* (1970), p 205, suggests that perhaps they attacked the rain forest especially c1000 BC. Subsequent desiccation, ie in historical times, has probably

been largely the result of man's destructive activities, especially bush-firing, over-grazing, over-cultivation. See A. Mabogunje, 'The Land and Peoples of West Africa', *History of West Africa*, I, ed J. F. A. Ajayi and M. Crowder (1971), pp 7–9. The Kamabai level yielded a carbon date of 2560±115 BC; the upper level a date of AD 340±100; see Frank Willett, 'A Survey of Recent Results in the Radiocarbon Chronology of Western and Northern Africa', *Journal of African History*, XII, 3 (1971), 350.

6 T. Shaw, 'The Prehistory of West Africa' in *History of West Africa*, I, p 62; John Atherton, 'The Later Stone Age of Sierra Leone', PhD thesis (University of Oregon, 1969), pp 13–16, Chap 3 and pp 84, 149.

7 See *The West African Archaeological Newsletter*, Inst African Studies, Ibadan, No 6 (1967), 28–31 for those in the Gaura chiefdom, Gola forest, Sierra Leone. See also Davies, op cit, p 235; Atherton, 'The Later Stone Age', pp 94, 104; Atherton and Kalous, 'Nomoli', *Journal of African History*, XI, 3 (1970), 303–17.

8 These have been found in Guinea and are also amongst the collections of the Sierra Leone Museum, Freetown.

9 Thomas M. Newman, 'Archaeological Survey of Sierra Leone', *The West African Archaeological Newsletter*, No 4 (1966), 19. Bunumbu has been dated tentatively as early in the Christian era.

10 Davies, op cit, p 277. Such circles and monoliths are found in Sierra Leone in the Gola Forest.

11 Eg Ulli Beier, *The Story of Sacred Wood Carvings from One Small Yoruba Town* (1957).

12 Mabogunje, op cit, p 28.

13 David P. Dalby, 'Languages' in *Sierra Leone in Maps*, ed J. I. Clarke (1966), p 38.

14 W. Rodney, *A History of the Upper Guinea Coast 1545–1800* (1970), p 6. The Cocoli have been identified as a branch of the Landuma; Paul Hair, 'Ethnolinguistic Continuity on the Guinea Coast', *Journal of African History*, VIII, 2 (1967), 253.

15 D. J. Siddle, *Patterns of Rural Settlement in Sierra Leone*, PhD thesis (Durham, 1968), pp 49, 149.

16 Davies, op cit, p 313.

17 Also spelt Djalonke. *Nke* is a Mande suffix meaning 'man of'. Yalunka were thus men of Jalon, and today represent the

original stock fused with the Susu. For the Temne account of Bai Farma see: E. F. Sayers, 'Notes on the Clan or Family Names Common in the area inhabited by Temne-speaking People', *Sierra Leone Studies*, OS 10 (Dec 1927), 21. David Dalby, 'Distribution and Nomenclature of the Manding People and their Language' in *Papers on the Manding*, ed C. T. Hodge (1971), pp 1–13, speaks of the unusually confused question of the relationship between Manding and other so-called 'Mande' languages, partly arising from the terminological difficulties surrounding the use of such similar terms as Manding(o), Mande, Mende. Fluctuations in nasalisation have accounted for a large number of variations in form: Manden, Mandin, Mande, Mani, Mali. Also the French form Malinka has been used to embrace all Mandinka and Maninka peoples as well as all 'fringe' Mandinka. Mandinka, with its suffix -*ka* used to derive adjectival stems from toponyms, strictly means: 'belonging to, or originating from the Manding heartland'. The English term Mandingo has been ambiguously employed in the past to denote Gambian Mandinka, Mandinka, Maninka, Manding, or even the whole 'Mande family'. Dalby suggests a scale of relationships between Manding itself and each of the component language-groups within the 'Mande' family, namely:

level 1   Manding (Mandinka/Maninka, Bambara, Dyula, etc)
     2   Vai, Kono
          Ligbi, Huela, Numu
     3   Soso, Yalunka
     4   Soninke (?)
     5   'South West Mande' (Mende, Loko, Bandi, Loma, Kpelle)
     6   'Southern Mande' (Mano, Dan, Guro, etc)
          'Eastern Mande' (Samo, Bisa, Busa, etc).

The word dyula, besides describing one of the three regional and ethnic forms of the language, is also used in West Africa to mean a Mande-speaking itinerant trader.

18   See Chap 3 below.

19   Sayers, op cit, p 21. He equates the Kagbo, Kanu and Mansare: 'all branches of, or alternatives for, the great Keita Clan'.

20   Robin Horton, 'Stateless Societies in the History of West Africa', *History of West Africa*, I, p 81.

21   See especially Chap 3 below and particularly the section on the Mende wars.

22 R. H. K. Willans, 'The Konnoh People', *Journal of the African Society*, 8, no 30 (Jan 1909), 130–4.

23 Max Gorvie, *Our People of the Sierra Leone Protectorate*, nd, p 24. Gorvie says the elders were called Massaquoi generally. Rogers (qv p 11 above) derives from the name of an English slave trader.

24 *Adam Afzelius' Sierra Leone Journal 1795–6*, ed Alexander Peter Kup (Uppsala, 1967), pp 156–8 and references. Rodney, op cit, p 11, notes that a section of the Yalunka were called Sulima (men of the sharpened teeth), a feature which distinguished the Baga on their arrival at the coast. See pp 24, 32.

25 See especially Horton, op cit, p 110, for refutation of what has been called the 'Hamitic Myth'.

26 Cf Massaquoi, Mansa Dansa, etc. Mande influence in Sierra Leone has been diffuse. It is discussed more particularly in Chapter 2.

27 A. P. Kup, *A History of Sierra Leone, 1400–1787* (1961), pp 124, 132. Arthur Abraham, 'Some Suggestions on the Origins of Mende Chiefdoms', *Sierra Leone Studies*, NS 25 (1971), 30–6. E. A. Ijagbemi, 'A History of the Temne in the Nineteenth Century', PhD thesis (Edinburgh, 1968), p 9. Sayers, however, felt the Kamaras had come first; see Chap 2, p 42 below. For the Mani see Alvares d'Almeida, *Tratado Breve dos Rios de Guine*, ed L. Silveira (Lisbon, 1946), Chap 15.

28 D'Almeida, op cit, Chap 15; Kup, *A History of Sierra Leone*, p 166.

29 Fernando Guerreiro, *Relacão Anual das Coisas que Fizeram os Padres da Companhia de Jesus nas suas missões nos annos de 1600 and 1609, pelo Padre Fernão Guerreiro*, 3, ed A. Viegas (Lisbon, 1930–42), pp 255ff.

30 Rodney, op cit, p 44.

31 Very possibly an arm of the river Sierra Leone.

32 See pp 24–26 above.

33 See p 22 above.

34 Thomas Winterbottom, *An Account of the Native Africans in the Neighbourhood of Sierra Leone*, I (1803), p 3.

35 For further discussion see Kup, *Adam Afzelius*, p 85, and especially Ijagbemi, op cit, p 7; also pp 112, 123, 163ff below.

36 H. Baumann and D. Westermann, *Les Peuples et les Civilisations de l'Afrique*, quoted by Rodney, op cit, p 16.

37 Kup, *A History of Sierra Leone*, p 123.

38 This is an English name, when looked at from Freetown. The

French, further north, called the area the *Rivières du sud*.

39 Rodney, op cit, pp 16–24 and references.

40 Kup, *A History of Sierra Leone*, p 179 and references, and p 139. Sierra Leone was a term whose meaning varied until the twentieth century.

41 And gathered together later by various authors, such as Dapper, Ogilby and Barbot. John Barbot's *A Description of the Coasts of North and South Guinea*, 1746, is especially valuable.

42 The Kru today are a heterogeneous group, comprising, among others, the Quoja and the Quea. The latter sixteenth-century Europeans associated with the Cobales, living between the Gallinhas and Cape Mount. The Quea, Quoja and Cobales were probably all Vai speakers; certainly O. Dapper's list of Quoja words are Vai (see Rodney, op cit, p 50, especially n 4). D'Anville's map of 1749 marks 'Folgia D'ou sont sortis les Carous', and 'Royaume de Qoja ou des Carous'. John Ogilby's *Africa* (1670), p 381 said the Gola-Vy, High Quoia and Folgias very closely resembled the *Karou*. According to S. W. Koelle, *Polyglotta Africana* (1854), p 3, *Karo* = Gallinhas. See also Hair, op cit, pp 256–7.

43 Buré was sometimes written Borea by contemporary Europeans. Sherabola lived to be over one hundred, dying about the middle of the seventeenth century.

44 British Museum, Cotton MS, Otho E viii f 27r. Cf also Westerman and Melzian, *The Kpelle Language in Liberia* (Berlin, 1930), p v: 'The languages most related to Kpelle are Mane and Gio in Eastern Liberia and Mende in Sierra Leone. All the languages mentioned thus form a linguistic unit, which may be called the Kpelle-Mende group.'

45 Rodney, op cit, p 55. Early Portuguese records of the Mani refer to their skill at sea; the Kru have long been famous as sailors and for bravery. Today they are divided into small commonwealths, each with an hereditary chief. There is no reason to suppose they had any different organisation then and they would certainly not have thrown in their lot with the Mani any longer than it suited them. The Cobales may possibly have lived in 'Coya', 'thirty leagues' inland on the Cape Mount river. See Paul Hair, 'An Early 17th Century Vocabulary of Vai', *African Studies*, 23, 14 (1964), p 133. If so, they were Vai.

46 'Who were the Manes?', *Journal of the African Society*, Nos 19, 20 (1919, 1920); Ogilby, op cit, p 401. See also n 44 above.

47 Kup, *A History of Sierra Leone*, p 166.
48 See, for example, William B. Fagg, *Afro-Portuguese Ivories*, Batchworth Press, nd, *passim*.
49 See Rodney, op cit, pp 63–4.
50 The Temne show a marked disinclination to weave.
51 Bai Sherbro of Yonnie in 1896 was said to be the thirteenth king of Yonnie, and perhaps his line goes back to this time (*Chalmer's Report*, II, p 120).
52 Jean Barbot, *A Description of the Coasts of North and South Guinea* (1746), p 123.
53 See, for example, Kup, *A History of Sierra Leone*, p 148.

CHAPTER 2

 1 A. P. Kup, 'Early Portuguese Trade in the Sierra Leone and Great Scarcies Rivers', *Boletim Cultural da Guine Portuguese*, 17 (1963), 107–24.
 2 Yves Person, 'Samory and Resistance to the French' in *Protest and Power*, ed R. Rotberg and Mazrui (1970), p 80. The expansion of diyula commerce has been held to date from the fall of Ancient Ghana, when Islamic Soninke were dispersed south and east; Jenne's rulers' conversion to Islam about the twelfth century is said to mark the achievement of diyula dominance there. See *Colonization and Migration in West Africa*, ed Hilda Kuper (University of California Press, 1965), pp 42–3. See also Chap 3, p 81, n 5 below.
 3 E. F. Sayers, 'Notes on the Clan or Family Names common in the area inhabited by Temne-speaking Peoples', *Sierra Leone Studies*, OS 10 (Dec 1927), 14–122.
 4 Ibid, p 96.
 5 Ibid, p 76. This event seems to have overlaid the origins of Bai Farma, the Mani. Despite traditions to the contrary, he was not a Fula.
 6 Z. Macaulay, *Journal*, MS MY420, 30 June 1793, Huntington Library, San Merino, California.
 7 Amadu Wurie, 'The Bundukas of Sierra Leone', *Sierra Leone Studies*, NS 1 (Dec 1953), 14–25.
 8 Nicholas Owen, *Journal of a Slave Trader on the Coast of Africa from the year 1746 to the year 1757*, ed E. Martin (1930), p 92. The Jong was also known as the Tia.
 9 *Karamoko* = teacher.
10 Sayers, op cit, pp 61, 70.

11   D. J. Siddle, 'Patterns of Rural Development in Sierra Leone', PhD thesis (Durham, 1968), p 224. For the Sofa see pp 71, 82.

12   Public Record Office, Colonial Office (henceforth CO), Confidential Print (henceforth 879) 24 No 332, pp 8–10.

13   Alexander G. Laing, *Travels in the Timmanee, Kooranko and Soolima Countries* (1825), pp 264, 280, 283, 351, 380, 450ff; CO 879/14 No 159, pp 12, 29.

14   *Adam Afzelius' Sierra Leone Journal 1795–6*, ed A. P. Kup (Uppsala, 1967), pp 6, n 7, 54, 57, 94, 108, 119, 122, 132, 163.

15   R. H. K. Willans, 'The Konnoh People', *Journal of the African Society*, 8, No 30 (Jan 1909), 130–44; and Vol 31, No 8 (April 1909), 288–95.

16   Alexander Gordon Laing, *Travels in the Timmanee, Kooranko and Soolima Countries* (1825), pp 400–12.

17   Thus: *Alimami, Santigi*, or the word for 'sacrifice'—*saraka*, or 'dead ancestors'—*fureni*. See Ruth H. Finnegan, *Survey of the Limba People of Northern Sierra Leone* (1965), pp 14, 15; and R. Finnegan and D. J. Murray, 'Limba Chiefs' in *West African Chiefs*, ed M. Crowder and O. Ikime (University of Ife Press, 1970), pp 409–13. Also Thomas J. Alldridge, *A Transformed Colony* (1910), p 296.

18   *The Royal Gazette* (Freetown), 24 Feb, 13 Oct 1821.

19   E. A. Ijagbemi, 'A History of the Temne in the Nineteenth Century', Chap III.

20   And thus exhibiting a religious syncretism which Orthodox Muslims abominated; hence their flight from the *jihad*.

21   And in this century was superseded by the Alimami (or Alikali) of Port Loko, when the British made the latter paramount chief.

22   Ijagbemi, op cit, Chap 3 *passim*.

23   *The Royal Gazette* (Freetown), 10 Feb 1821. (Even so, Moribu introduced the turban as part of his regalia.)

24   According to Christopher Fyfe (*A History of Sierra Leone* (1962), p 283) he was 'a Susu of the Turay [Toure] family'.

25   Algernon Montagu, *The Ordinances of Sierra Leone* (1857–81), Treaty No 25, 18 April 1837 (wrongly dated 1836, for which see Ijagbemi, op cit, p 200). Bai Mauro died in 1832.

26   See p 169 below.

27   PRO Colonial Office 267 (Governor of Sierra Leone Despatches) 203, despatch 29, 18 March 1848.

28   Ijagbemi, op cit, p 54.

29   See p 66 below.

30 Alexander Bai Kanta was installed, youngest son of Bai Farma who had died in 1807. He died in 1872, two mamy queens reigning under Lahai Bundu as regent, according to custom.

31 See p 77 below.

32 See p 182 below. The Yonni's indiscriminate attacks on Koya were attempts to get through to the Rokel trading centres. After the 1870s, trade shifted south, following the development of the palm-kernel trade. Now it was the Kpa Mende who blocked the road to Senehun, and the Loko under Sori Kesebe plundered them if they could get through to the Bumpe and Ribbi. The ensuing Temne *v* Loko and Mende hostility led to the British expedition of 1887.

33 Privy Council, *Report of the Lords of the Committee of the Privy Council . . . Concerning the Present State of the Trade to Africa* (1789), part I: 'Slaves'.

34 Quoted in Walter Rodney, *A History of the Upper Guinea Coast* (1970), p 232, qv for reference.

35 *Adam Afzelius*, ed Kup, pp 8, 14, 46, 95, 99ff, 163.

36 Fyfe, op cit, p 148.

37 Quoted from 'The Prospects of the African' (1874) in *Origins of West African Nationalism*, ed Henry S. Wilson (1969), p 239. See also p 229.

38 Leslie Proudfoot, 'Mosque Building and Tribal Separatism in Freetown East', *Africa*, 29, No 4 (Oct 1959), p 414. See also John Peterson, *The Province of Freedom* (1969), pp 219, 238ff.

39 The site was donated by William Henry Savage, a lawyer, to some of his Muslim Yoruba clients, whom he had defended when in 1832 they had helped Thomas Stephen Caulker, of the Plantains, to attack the Temne. The government at the time had feared a general rising of all Muslims in the colony. Savage's clients were all set free since the crimes with which they were charged had occurred outside British jurisdiction. Recaptives were forbidden to wear Muslim gowns.

40 Fyfe, op cit, p 498.

41 Charles Lucas, *A Historical Geography of the British Colonies*, III (Oxford, 1913), 3rd edition, p 305.

42 'A Chapter in the History of Sierra Leone', *Journal of the African Society*, 3 (1903), 83–99.

43 Ijagbemi, op cit, p 192. Fatma Brima was related to the Brima Konkorie, killed in 1816. See p 55 above.

44 Colonial Office, Governors Despatches, Sierra Leone, (267)

(CO) 267/242, Desp Nos 183, 206, Ag Gov Dougan to SoS (Secretary of State); CO 267/232, Desp No 72, 14 April 1853, Kennedy to SoS; CO 267/329, Desp No 59, 13 May 1876, Rowe to SoS; CO 267/330, Desp No 164, 17 Oct 1876, Kortright to SoS; CO 267/277, Desp No 2, 2 Jan 1863, Blackall to SoS. Hansen was consul 1853–61 when the office was abolished.

45   CO 267/208, Desp No 66, 6 Aug 1849, Pine to SoS.

46   *The West African Reporter*, 3 Nov 1883, letter, Caulker to all Muslims resident in Freetown, at the time of his trial.

47   *The Early Dawn* (Bonthe newspaper), 31 Aug 1888.

48   CO 267/376, Desp No 129, 1 March 1889, Hay to SoS; *The Freetown Express*, 19 June 1883, anon letter; *The West African Reporter*, 10 June 1882, editorial, 9 June 1883, editorial.

49   CO Confidential Desp 879/14 No 159, p 12, Rowe to SoS, 28 June 1878; 879/9 No 88, 5 Nov 1885; *The West African Reporter*, 5 Nov 1879, anon letter.

50   *The Early Dawn*, 15 Nov 1887, anon letter.

51   Thomas Winterbottom, *An Account of the Native Africans in the Neighbourhood of Sierra Leone*, I (1803), p 7.

52   Cited in Rodney, op cit, p 236.

53   Ibid, p 236.

54   Ibid, p 237.

55   CO 267/231, Desp No 15, 6 Jan 1853; CO 267/243, Desp No 206, 9 Dec 1854.

56   CO 267/376, Desp No 158, 3 March 1889, Hay to SoS.

57   *The Early Dawn* (Oct 1885).

58   Fyfe, op cit, pp 485, 501.

59   George Garrett, 'Sierra Leone and the Interior, to the Upper Waters of the Niger', *Procs Royal Geog Soc*, NS 14 (1892), pp 442–6. T. J. Alldridge, *A Transformed Colony* (1910), Chaps 31, 32.

60   Fyfe, op cit, pp 517–20.

61   H. G. Warren, 'Notes on the Yalunka Country', *Sierra Leone Studies*, OS 13 (Sept 1928), 25–8.

62   James K. Trotter, *The Niger Sources* (1898), pp 35, 42, 83–4.

63   *Adam Afzelius*, ed Kup, pp 54, 94, 108, 119, 122, 132, 162, 163.

64   Montagu, op cit, Treaty No 22, 8 April 1836.

65   Ibid, Treaty No 24, 11 April 1837.

66   CO 267/231 Desp No 50, 15 March 1853, Kennedy to SoS.

67   CO 267/329 Desp No 133, 4 Sept 1876, Kortright to SoS.

68   *The West African Reporter*, 19 May 1880. See n 30 above.

69 Ijagbemi, op cit, p 261.
70 *The Sierra Leone Weekly News*, 23 March 1889, 'Mandingoes as Government Messengers to Interior Tribes', by 'A Citizen'.

CHAPTER 3

1 Northcote Thomas, 'Who were the Manes?', *Journal of the African Society*, Nos 19, 20 (1919, 1920).
2 Alfred Cowley Lamb, 'An Anthropolitical Survey of the Mende People of Sierra Leone, with special reference to their social structures and material culture; and their relation to the geographical environment', PhD thesis (Leeds, 1946), pp 49–69. Abraham (see n 3 below) also mentions their dual nature.
3 Arthur Abraham, 'Some Suggestions on the Origins of Mende Chiefdoms', *Sierra Leone Studies*, NS 25 (1972), 30–5.
4 See for example the story of the Muslim from Futa who journeyed into Mende country: see Colonial Office, African 332 (1886), p 38.
5 The other three are: Yansane, Dumbuia, Fofana.
6 D. J. Siddle, 'Patterns of Rural Settlement in Sierra Leone', PhD thesis (Durham, 1969), pp 195–200. In East and South Africa similar fissile multiplication occurred when there was plenty of room, eg The Lango (see *The History of East Africa*, I, ed R. Oliver and G. Mathew (1963), pp 177–80), but when land became short and there was population pressure then, as the Zulus found, small-scale fission and political organisation were no good—see J. Omer-Cooper, *The Zulu Aftermath* (1966), Chap 2. Successful warfare implied an increase in wives, which enlarged the population further. See also J. F. A. Ajayi, 'Professional Warriors in 19th century Yoruba Politics', *Tarikh*, I, i (1965), pp 72–81.
7 *The Royal Gazette and Sierra Leone Weekly Advertiser*, 13 March 1824; 25 June 1825; 2 July 1825.
8 Qv p 168 below.
9 Colonial Office, Governors Despatches, Sierra Leone: CO 267/73, No 26, 13 Sept 1826, Campbell to SoS; CO 267/66, No 73, 18 October 1825, Turner to SoS.
10 CO 267/229, No 92, 5 July 1852, Macdonald to SoS; CO 267/232, No 72, 14 April 1853, Kennedy to SoS; CO 267/277, No 2, 2 Jan 1863, Blackall to SoS; CO 879/9, No 88, p 65 (1875). Calipha was replaced by Deriza whose father he had previously dispossessed of the chiefdom—CO 879/24, No 322, p 43. See

P

also, John Davidson, 'Trade and Politics in the Sherbro Hinterland 1849–1890', PhD thesis (Wisconsin, 1969), pp 104, 181–5, 192, and George Thompson, *The Palm Land* (Cincinatti, 1858), pp 24–38, 113, 146, and map, frontispiece where Momando is labelled as a Susu town.

11 C. Fyfe, *A History of Sierra Leone* (1962), pp 156, 185, 193, 210, 298, 311, 316; *The Sierra Leone Weekly News*, 11 Aug 1888, editorial, 2 Jan 1886, editorial; *The Early Dawn* (Bonthe), 30 Jan 1886. See also pp 59ff above.

12 CO 267/377, No 185, 15 April 1889, Ag Governor J. Crooks to SoS.

13 *The West African Reporter*, 1 Dec 1880, anon correspondent.

14 CO 267/329, Desp No 59, 13 May 1876, Rowe to SoS.

15 CO 267/330, unnumbered despatch, 28 Dec 1876, Rowe to SoS.

16 Fyfe, op cit, p 399. Colonial Office, London, Confidential Print, 879/8, p 33.

17 *The West African Reporter*, 5 Feb 1879, anon correspondent.

18 *The Sierra Leone Times*, 14 May 1892.

19 *The Early Dawn*, 15 Nov 1888, 16 Sept 1889; 1888 and 1889 were both bad years for rice.

20 *The Freetown Express*, 8 Nov 1882, editorial; *The West African Reporter*, 9 June 1883; 19 Jan 1884, editorial.

21 CO 879/15, No 175, p 17. It was, of course, Sidney Smith, who said Sierra Leone always had two governors—one just arriving in England, the other just arriving in Sierra Leone. In the 27 years after Governor Sir Charles Macarthy was killed by the Ashante, 1824, Sierra Leone had 28 governors.

22 *The Sierra Leone Weekly News*, 14 April 1888, editorial and anon letter from the Big Bum river. For Makaia etc see p 98 below, and John Davidson, 'Trade and Politics in the Sherbro Hinterland', PhD thesis (Wisconsin, 1969), pp 206–25.

23 *The Independent*, 28 Jan 1875, editorial; 27 May 1875, petition, Sherbro traders to Kortright; *The West African Reporter*, 1 Dec 1880, anon correspondent; 13 Jan 1883; *The Sierra Leone Weekly News*, 11 Oct 1884, editorial; 17 April 1886, anon letter from Sulymah river.

24 CO 879/9, No 88, p 65, S. Rowe, 1876. The difference between the Mende chieftaincy and others is well illustrated in the case of a wealthy slave trader known to the British as Tom Kebbi Smith. The son of a slave, he came to dominate a coastal strip on the mainland opposite Bonthe where trade rivalry seems to

have led him into war with a Muslim, one Lahai Serifu or Salifu, to his east (both imported Mende warriors). For years, and until he died in 1878, he tried to get sovereignty of the country lying between the river Jong and the river Small Bum, but because he was slave born, he could never get the other chiefs to elect him. No such scruples hindered the Mende—see below—CO 267/335, Desp No 182, Rowe to SoS 19 Nov 1878; CO 267/347, Desp No 117, 5 July 1875.

25 See *Sierra Leone Studies*, OS 14 (1929), and A. C. Lamb, 'An Anthropological Survey of the Mende People', PhD thesis (Leeds, 1946), pp 84–7.

26 Thus there were great feuds between the Tikonko Mende under Macavore and the Bumpe Mende ruled by one Bogbuave, though the towns were only 12 miles apart.

27 Cf William Vivian, 'The Mendi Country, and some of the customs and characteristics of its People', *Journal of the Manchester Geographical Soc*, 12 (1896), p 16: 'The Mendies are distinguished by three great family terms of Gallinhas, Gba Mendies and Kaw-Mendies.' He considered the Gallinhas spoke the 'purest' form of the language. What he called the Gba Mendies occupied the 'middle' of the country. Ndawa was born near Segbwema, at Mano. Found seducing the wife of his chief, the latter sold him into slavery with one Selu Tifa. After that, Ndawa swore he would never work on a farm again and he became so quarrelsome, he was sold to Macavore at Tikonko in exchange for a sword. Soon Ndawa became a war-chief. Benya, chief of Blama, was at war with Macavore and Ndawa swore he would defeat Benya. Allying in 1880 with Kailundu, they started a punitive war against him, the *Kpove—qoi*, so called because Ndawa threatened to throw in anyone who ran away, and defeated Benya. As a reward Macavore gave Ndawa his freedom, but his temper getting him into a quarrel, he burnt down, at night, Chief Sarbore's town, Majeihu, across the river Sewa. Chief Sarbore complained to Macavore, saying Ndawa must be surrendered, or the town rebuilt. Macavore promised it would be rebuilt. Ndawa was always reckless. He and his warriors harassed the country as far as Liberia; coming south, he built Wunde and decided on a war of destruction in the Upper Mende country, plundering Kpeje of Manowa, and sweeping south as far as Pendembu. Ndawa threatened Kailundu, and it was now that the other chiefs promised Kailundu,

who was at war with his former ally, that he would be made their principal chief if he defeated Ndawa. Max Gorvie, *Our People of the Sierra Leone Protectorate*, nd, p 48.

28 *The Freetown Express*, 1 Dec 1882; *The West African Reporter*, 26 Nov 1879, 18 April 1883.

29 *The Freetown Express*, 1 Dec 1882; *The West African Reporter*, 26 Nov 1879, and ibid, anon letter, 18 April 1883.

30 G. H. Garrett, 'Sierra Leone and the Interior, to the Upper Waters of the Niger', *Procs Royal Geog Soc*, NS 14 (1892), p 435. Travelling commissioners had first been created by the Act 24 and 25 Victoria cap 31. An Act for the Prevention of Offences in Territories near Sierra Leone, in 1861. Commissioners were not appointed, however, until 1890, though Alldridge began work in 1889. See Colin Newbury, *British Policy Towards W Africa* (1965), p 568; T. J. Alldridge, *The Sherbro and its Hinterland* (1901), pp 166, 250.

31 *The Sierra Leone Weekly News*, 20 Aug 1887; *The Early Dawn* (Bonthe), 31 Dec 1886; *The Independent*, anon letter, 8 March 1877.

32 Gomna, part Mende, part Vai by descent (whom the British idiotically persisted in calling Bokhari Governor), had raided Krim and Kittam countries incessantly from the early 1880s. In 1887 a party of chiefs, led by Fahwundu, met at Gonoru and took a most powerful Poro oath either to kill him or expel him from the Gallinhas. At the end of 1888, invading the Gallinhas again, taking three towns, he was captured and deported to the Gambia—*The West African Reporter*, 29 Sept 1883, 26 Jan 1889. Fanima was the war town of one, Kobah; when Rowe had visited it in 1885, it had four stockades, most of its inhabitants were slaves, and near the gateway stood a pile of one hundred skulls—*The Sierra Leone Weekly News*, 11 July 1885.

33 *The Sierra Leone Weekly News*, 9 Jan, 6 July 1889; *The Early Dawn*, 30 April 1887, 30 April 1889; CO 267/376, Desp No 158, 23 March 1889, Hay to SoS; CO 879/24, No 332, p 28. Edmund Peel to Rowe, June 1886. He was deported to the Gold Coast. Nyagbwa, a war-chief, was the son of Faba, of Dedo, in Upper Mende country—Davidson, op cit, p 179. Arrogant and cruel, at one time he had most of south Kono country under his control, in a state of virtual slavery—T. J. Alldridge, *A Transformed Colony* (1910), p 285.

34 *The Sierra Leone Weekly News*, 9, 26 Jan 1889, editorials. Another frontier road ran from Kambia via Port Loko, Magbele, Roti-

funk, Senehun, Mano Bagru, Bonthe, Pujehun, Bandasuma, Sulima, Mano Salijah, and covering Temne country. See p 177 below and Fyfe, op cit, p 482. Since the British themselves were often in doubt as to the frontier, this was a useful way of marking it.

35 See, for instance, the complaint against the war-chief Shaffra Tom in the Gallinhas—CO 267/335, Desp 182, 9 Nov 1878, Rowe to SoS.

36 *The Sierra Leone Weekly News*, 25 May 1885.

37 CO 267/372, Desp No 9, 8 Jan 1889, enc, letter, Capt Mackay, 8 Jan; and Desp No 10, 9 Jan 1889.

38 *The Sierra Leone Weekly News*, 9 Nov 1889; 8 March, 11 Oct 1890.

39 W. Rodney, *A History of the Upper Guinea Coast* (1970), pp 168–70; Rhodes House Library MS, Africa S 9, 'Remarks on the Coast of Guinea, 1765–1771', anon.

40 A. P. Kup, *A History of Sierra Leone, 1400–1787* (1961), pp 48f, 105f.

41 John Newton, *The Journal of a Slave Trader*, ed B. Martin and M. Spurrell (1962), p 66.

42 *Adam Afzelius' Sierra Leone Journal 1795–6*, ed A. P. Kup (Uppsala, 1967), pp 109, 112.

43 Ibid, p 89.

44 Quoted in Rodney, op cit, pp 200, 201.

45 A Portuguese term meaning those who had 'thrown' themselves among the Africans. Another term was *tanoomoa* meaning a white trader who had adopted African religion, customs and tribal markings; see Rodney, op cit, p 74.

46 See pp 44 and 108.

47 CO 267/367, Desp No 68, 17 Feb 1887, Rowe to SoS. American slave ships were especially numerous at the end of the eighteenth century, trading usually in the northern rivers. Some left offspring there, eg Curtis, Wilkinson. But none achieved the status or power amongst the Fula and Susu, that the Afro-British had in the south.

48 CO 267/367, Desp No 68, 17 Feb 1887, Rowe to SoS.

49 Kup, *A History*, pp 148–50; Rodney, op cit, pp 216–22.

50 A. M. Falconbridge, *Narrative of Two Voyages to Sierra Leone During the Years 1791-2-3* (1794), wrongly calls him his son; some modern writers have been misled.

51 *Adam Afzelius'*, ed A. P. Kup (Uppsala, 1967), pp 79, 80 and refs.

52 Ibid, pp 85, 89.

53　CO 267/350, letter W. T. G. Caulker to SoS, 25 Jan 1882.

54　*Adam Afzelius'*, ed Kup, p 80.

55　CO 267/66, Desp No 70, 20 Sept 1825, Turner to SoS; CO 267/73, Desp No 26, 13 Sept 1826, Campbell to SoS.

56　Canre is a Poro name.

57　CO 267/208, Desp No 60, 11 July 1849, Pine to SoS. T. S. Caulker maintained Canre ba Caulker was not the son of Thomas, another brother of the dead chief, but the son of a slave—a not uncommon accusation amongst claimants of this sort.

58　CO 267/74, Desp No 88, 20 Sept 1826, Campbell to SoS.

59　CO 267/73, Desp No 26, 13 Sept 1826, Campbell to SoS. In old age Harry moved to Sebar, Turner's Peninsula, dying in July 1855—G. Thompson, *The Palm Land* (Cincinatti, 1858), p 352.

60　CO 267/232, Desp No 72, 14 April 1853, A. Kennedy to SoS, and Desp No 76, 20 April 1853, Kennedy to SoS. For Mori Calipha see p 67 above. For the Bum wars, see Davidson, op cit, p 191.

61　CO 879/24, No 322, App 332, p 43; CO 267/367, Desp No 68, 17 Feb 1887, Rowe to SoS.

62　Rowe said in 1879 that, in Bullom, after James Tucker 'the Great', the chiefs in Bullom were: Harry Tucker, 'Baggy John', William E. Tucker—CO 879/15, p 159, Rowe to SoS, 23 April 1879.

63　CO 879/15, No 175, pp 13–15.

64　CO 267/335, Desp No 182, 9 Nov 1878, Rowe to SoS.

65　CO 267/367, Desp No 68, 17 Feb 1887, Rowe to SoS; CO 879/350, p 25, 2 March 1888, Rowe to SoS; *The Early Dawn*, 30 Sept 1888, editorial.

66　S. W. G. Caulker spelt this name Jahrah, the British usually Jaiah. See CO 267/347, letter 15 March 1881, S. W. G. Caulker to SoS; *The Early Dawn*, 30 Sept 1888, editorial; Fyfe, op cit, p 412. The title in 1890 descended to Madam Yata, Prince Manna's sister, when 'recognised' by Britain. CO 267/367, No 68, 17 Feb 1887.

67　Ndawa (Big Mouth) was dead by Aug 1888—*The Early Dawn*, 15 Aug 1888, anon letter. See also Davidson, op cit, p 214.

68　*The Independent*, 13 Jan 1876.

69　CO 267/350, letter, W. T. G. Caulker to SoS 25 Jan 1882; CO 267/370, Desp No 123, 12 May 1888, Rowe to SoS; CO 267/346, Desp No 202, 19 May 1881, Havelock to SoS. *The*

Early Dawn, 31 May, 30 June, 15 July 1887, 31 Dec 1888.

70 For a discussion of this, in a different context, see Robin Horton, 'Stateless Societies in the History of West Africa', *History of West Africa,* eds Ajayi and Crowder (1971), p 89ff.

71 Cf CO 267/329, Desp Nos 57, 59 and minutes; *The Independent,* 24 Dec 1874, anon letter.

72 Cf CO 879/15, Desp No 175, Ag Gov Horatio Huggins to SoS, 1877.

73 CO 267/329, Desp No 89, 20 June 1876, Carnarvon's Minute.

74 Cf Sir Samuel Rowe, CO 267/329, Confidential, 1 April 1876, bound after Desp No 47.

75 CO 267/203, 16 Dec 1848, SoS to Governor Macdonald.

76 CO 267/377, Desp No 299, 19 July 1899, Report from Major Sidney Forster, Sulima; Minute by H. J. Read, Colonial Office.

CHAPTER 4

1 Quoted in Arthur T. Porter, *Creoledom* (1963), p 3.

2 Re Sharp's knowledge of the conditions and customs in Sierra Leone, in seeking help from Pitt to protect the survivors of his Province of Freedom, for example, Sharp correctly told him 'if possession is not speedily regained, the native chiefs will conceive that the rights of the Crown of Great Britain are superseded by evacuation'. Prince Hoare, *Memoirs of Granville Sharp* (1820), pp 338, 343–5. See also John Matthews, *A Voyage to the River Sierra Leone* (1788), p 78: 'present possession is the only tenure they (ie, in Sierra Leone) allow of'.

3 Even so, like nearly all Europeans then, Sharp believed the land had been 'sold' by the Temne, not understanding that such alienation of land was unknown in Temne law.

4 Article 35 of the company's 1791 orders and regulations withdrew the right of popular elections enjoyed by Sharp's settlement. Sierra Leone Company, *Orders and Regulations* (1791).

5 Quoted in L. A. C. Evans, 'An Early Constitution of Sierra Leone', *Sierra Leone Studies,* OS 18, 31.

6 The original name of the Sierra Leone Company, which was changed in the June 1791 Act, 31 Geo III, c 55.

7 Hoare, op cit, p 358. The letter is dated 22 Jan 1791.

8 Sierra Leone Company, *Substance of the Report of the Court of Directors of the Sierra Leone Company to the Court of Proprietors, 19 October 1791* (1792), 50–4.

9   British Museum Additional Manuscripts 41262 (Clarkson Papers) (hereafter BM Add MS 41262), B f 10, Notebook for Speeches.

10 British Museum Additional Manuscripts 41263 (Clarkson Papers) (herafter BM Add MS 41263), f 102, letter 3 Nov 1793. There was also the waterfront question. In Nova Scotia black Loyalists had been excluded from the shorefront, although white Loyalists had not. In Sierra Leone, the company wanted to reserve the waterfront for its quays and warehouses, and the settlers saw this as more racial discrimination. Clarkson sympathised and promised them equal rights to the shore, but the problem was still not settled when he left, and it fell to Macaulay to handle.

11 They also used a coat of arms which they neglected to register with the College of Heralds. Nepean, Dundas' secretary, doubted if Clarkson could recruit volunteers under Governor Parr's nose, or command any fleet Parr might despatch without special powers being given him. CO 267/9, 4 Aug 1791, Nepean to Thornton.

12 BM Add MS 41262 A, f 5, Wilberforce to Clarkson, 8 Aug 1791.

13 BM Add MS 41262 A, ff 164–83, Thornton to Clarkson, 14 Sept 1792.

14 Christopher Fyfe, *A History of Sierra Leone* (1962), pp 24–5, 28–30, 44. Falconbridge arrived Jan 1791, returned to England in June to report to the directors on the treaty he had renegotiated with Naimbana, the Temne regent. He landed in Sierra Leone again in Feb 1792, being superseded by Clarkson, who took the oath as superintendent on 10 March. Falconbridge soon drank himself to death.

15 Quoted from Porter, op cit, p 29.

16 From his *Just Limitation of Slavery* (1776).

17 Quoted in Porter, op cit, p 26.

18 CO 267/9, letter, H. Thornton to Dundas, 17 Aug 1791; Hoare, op cit, pp 355, 357; and, especially, Robin Winks, *The Blacks in Canada* (Yale, 1971), pp 67–70 and refs. Parr, though well-intentioned was not very able; Loyalists disliked him heartily.

19 In the end Settlers had to accept four-acre lots.

20 Anna Maria Falconbridge's *Two Voyages to Sierra Leone During the Years 1791–2–3* (1794), records a Temne saying: 'Read book and learn to be rogue so well as white man.'

21 Thompson negotiated the settlement for Sharp in June 1787. Naimbana, their Temne landlord, had not been there, though he had subsequently 'ratified' it on 12 July 1787. 'Diary of Lt. J. Clarkson, R.N.', ed J. de Hart, *Sierra Leone Studies*, OS 8, 16 (March 1927), 60; Charles Bernhard Wadstrom, *An Essay on Colonisation* (1794), p 221.

22 Falconbridge, op cit, p 33ff.

23 Hart, op cit, 5, 10, 64, 100, 102, 107.

24 There is thus no West African equivalent for the European concept of crown lands. Since all this was un-English, to Thornton it seemed uncivilised. 'You say also,' he wrote loftily to Clarkson, 'that the natives have no idea of their having sold it. This arises I imagine from their being (like all uncivilized nations) as yet unacquainted with the nature of landed property.' BM Add MS 41262 A, ff 164–82, 14 Sept 1792. Moreover, the only kind of white settlement hitherto on the coast, either fort or factory, had bought no land. Up to this time Europeans had rented land, and had been restricted to its environs. There was no question of cultivation, since African headmen made a good living selling local produce, a monopoly they wished to preserve. See Chap 5 below for further discussion.

25 Hart, op cit, 5, 6. Clarkson wrote this in Aug 1792. He was soon threatened with lawsuits by ships' masters and owners.

26 Hart, op cit, 24.

27 Clarkson described them as 'half-pay officers, decayed gentlemen and dissolute adventurers'. They left on 11 Sept. Dalrymple had endeavoured to found a colony of his own some 300 miles north of Sierra Leone, on the island of Bulama. It had been intended entirely as a European settlement, but hardship, the climate, and hostile neighbours had defeated them.

28 Hart, op cit, 3, 7, 12, 22.

29 GB Parlt Sessional Papers, House of Commons 1731–1800 Accounts and Papers, Vol XXIX, No 698 (1790), 173.

30 One captain had refused to recompense the settlers for the nursing and subsequent burial of a sailor.

31 Hoare, op cit, 338n, 343–5.

32 Hart, op cit, 16 Aug 1792. He refers to the anti-slavery clauses in the Act of 1791. Since by British law slave trading was not illegal, Clarkson foresaw his difficulty if any were guilty. An

early example is found at the first council meeting of 17 Feb 1792, where the minutes record a case against one Ashmore for selling a colleague, Smith—both of Granville Town—into slavery. The council resolved that evidence was insufficient, and minuted that for this and for 'other political reasons' he was freed. Public Record Office, Colonial Office (Sessional Papers, Sierra Leone) (hereafter PRO, CO 270), 270/2. When the situation did arise, Clarkson sent the accused to England in irons for the directors to deal with.

33   Public Record Office, Colonial Office (Correspondence from Sierra Leone to the Secretary of State, London) (hereafter PRO, CO 267), 267/9, Thornton to Dundas, 17 Aug 1791, and Hoare, op cit, pp 355, 357. It was his inability as governor to stop the waste of money which worried Clarkson into illness as much as anything.

34   Sierra Leone Company, *Substance of the Report Delivered by the Court of Directors of the Sierra Leone Company to the General Court of Proprietors*, Thursday 27 March (1794). The 1794 report said that the directors 'considered, as they were bound to do, that the British Constitution, as far as it is applicable . . . is transferred thence'.

35   BM Add MS 41262 A, ff 96, 97, Thornton to Clarkson, 3 May 1792.

36   BM Add MS 41263, f 74 v, Clarkson to Hartshorne, 4 Sept 1793; Add MS 41262 A, f 76, Clarkson to Thornton, 18 April 1792. Thornton's advice to Clarkson to 'connive and temporize' cannot have clarified matters.

37   They were *ex officio* JPs.

38   PRO, CO 270/2, Council Minutes, 3 April 1792.

39   Falconbridge, op cit, p 140. The letter is dated 10 April 1792. In July and August 1792 the directors finally dismissed the council, and appointed Clarkson governor; two full-time councillors (Dawes and Macaulay) were to arrive later. Add MS 41262 A, ff 109, 121, 127, 129, 131, 135, 145.

40   At the end of April council considered a letter from William Cass, the storekeeper, which complained he had not enough help to keep his accounts in order. But in the meantime Cass had died and council naïvely swept the awkward question under the carpet, minuting, 'As William Cass was taken sick on writing this letter, and died, of course no notice was taken of this letter.' PRO, CO 270/2.

41 BM Add MS 41262 A, ff 164–82, Thornton to Clarkson, 14 Sept 1792.

42 BM Add MS 41262 A, ff 63–74. The letter also advised him to keep memoranda and if possible get someone to draw local views for him, so that he could write a book. 'Everyone is curious of reading histories of new countries—I will get you £500 for it.' Much of the letter was in the form of a suggested speech to be given council on his arrival, a commentary on the board's instructions.

43 Bars were a movable medium themselves, depending on the type of goods being bartered.

44 It fell to Governor Macaulay to put this right. As he explained: 'Those acquainted with the trade of the Country take the precaution beforehand which I am recommending. No advance whatever is allowed on it. For example 100lbs. of good ivory is offered for which they agree to take goods at the rate of 2s. 6d. per pound according to the invoice price. It is in vain to say, the charges must be added as constituting part of the invoicing price. The custom is otherwise, and glad of a temporary advantage, they oblige us to pay 20 to 30 per cent more than other purchasers.' Huntington Library, Pasadena, California, MS MY418, Z. Macaulay, *Journal 1793–1799*, 16 June 1793, 2.

45 Ibid. Macaulay, father of the more famous Lord Macaulay, was governor of Sierra Leone from 1796 to 1799, after previously being councillor and acting governor. On his return to London he became secretary to the Sierra Leone Company. At one time the directors suggested Freetown should be made a free port. Clarkson was horrified, having already more strangers than they could manage. Hart, op cit, 14–18 Aug 1792. Other wild schemes including 'buying' Gambia Island from the French and Bunce Island from Anderson Bros.

46 On 11 April Clarkson had made the Nova Scotians sign an Instrument promising to obey company laws; local circumstances permitting, these were conformable to those of England. For further discussion, see the author's 'John Clarkson and the Sierra Leone Company', *The International Journal of African Historical Studies*, V, 2 (1972), 203–20.

47 Quoted from E. C. Martin, *The British West Africa Settlements* (1927), p 43.

48 CO 270/2, Minutes of Council, 30 April, 31 Dec 1792.

49 Falconbridge, op cit, p 202.

50 BM Add MS 41262 (Clarkson Papers), f 145, letter, Thomas to John Clarkson, 17 July 1792.

51 BM Add MS 41263, f 19. Extract, letter, J. Gray to Pat Dunkin, 11 Feb 1793.

52 Falconbridge, op cit, p 204.

53 30 July, 1792, eds A. P. Kup and R. Winks (Chicago, 1976).

54 BM Add MS 41263, f 19.

55 Ibid, f 30, letter I, Dubois to J. Clarkson, 7 March 1793.

56 Ibid, f 60, Clarkson to R. Crankpone. Colonial land and finance had recently become more closely related than ever. In 1783 Lord William Grenville had begun to try and get land reserved, as Penn had earlier, and as Dorchester was doing in British North America, the revenues of which would produce a fund the Crown could use for its expenses of defence and civil government (as the Crown in Britain had used its hereditary revenues, exchanged in 1760, for a civil list). Thus the 1789 New South Wales land instructions received some of the best land for Crown use. Such precedents were guiding the Sierra Leone Company. Dawes had served in government at Botany Bay. This and Sierra Leone were the only new settlements attempted so far after the loss of the American colonies. In both HMG saw, above all, a chance of ridding Britain (and Nova Scotia) on the cheap of potentially expensive and explosive problems.

57 See, for example, Philip Woodruff, *The Men who Ruled India*, II (1954), p 38.

58 See Falconbridge, op cit, pp 255–65.

59 See n 44 above.

60 It may have been some consolation to the honest and poor Settlers to see the ill-gotten specie carried off by the French in Oct 1794.

61 CO 270/2, f 53; 270/3, f 18.

62 Macaulay, op cit, 17 Sept 1793. Many were Methodists or Huntingdonians, used to an independence traditional in Methodism. Clarkson had found their preachers had great influence over them.

63 BM Add MS 41263, f 47, letter, Clarkson to Dubois, 1 July 1793.

64 Scipio Channel and Robert Keeling.

65 CO 270/2, Council Minutes, 1 May 1794.

66   CO 270/3, ff 31 vff, 7 March.
67   Ibid, f 85, 6 May.
68   In March 1793 council had imposed a 5s payment on unsuccess-
     ful plaintiffs. CO 270/2, f 37 and CO 270/3, f 84.
69   Ie rioting, bad language, indecént or disorderly conduct. CO
     270/3, f 126.
70   Ibid, f 126, 10 Oct 1795, Minutes.
71   Dawes returned for a second governorship in 1801.
72   London, p 4.
73   Viscountess Knutsford, *Life and Letters of Zachary Macaulay*
     (1901), p 156.
74   Macaulay, op cit, 15, 19, 21 Dec 1796.
75   Knutsford, op cit, pp 175, 176; Macaulay, op cit, 5, 19, 21,
     22 Aug, 30 Sept 1797.
76   See p 164.
77   CO 270/4, f 105, Minutes of Council, 29 Jan 1798.
78   Parliamentary Papers, House of Commons, Sessional Papers
     1806–7, II, p 68, Despatch 29 Oct 1806.
79   CO 270/4, f 131, Council Minutes, 9 Feb 1799.
80   Ibid, f 144 v, Council Minutes, 4 June 1799.
81   Ibid, f 151.
82   CO 270/5, f 22 v. The respective status of colonial and British
     law was a matter which had long confused the West Indian
     and American colonies. See, for example, George Metcalf,
     Royal Government and Political Conflict in Jamaica (1965), p 25.
83   Director's *Report* (1801), p 13.
84   CO 270/5, ff 29, 54.
85   Ibid, f 32; Director's *Report* (1801), p 13.
86   Ibid, ff 59, 64.
87   John Rylands and University of Manchester Library, Man-
     chester, Balcarres Papers, MS 23/10/867, undated (c1795)
     draft letter, Lord Balcarres, to Duke of Portland. Balcarres
     estimated British investment at £70 million.
88   CO Jamaica, Governor's Despatches, 137/95, 1 Sept 1795,
     Balcarres to J. King, and CO 137/95, Council of War,
     Minutes, 31 July 1795. One of their complaints was that the
     1738 treaty had made them free and above slaves. Now slaves
     were above them, having masters to protect them, a slave's
     oath being held above theirs, and the latter swearing false
     evidence against them forced them to live in the woods.

Balcarres Papers 23/11/209, Petition, Maroons to Jamaican Assembly, 11 Dec 1795.

89 Viscount Lindsay, *Lives of the Lindsays*, 3 (1858), pp 98, 99; Walpole to Balcarres, 20 and 25 Dec 1795, private letters.

90 Bryan Edwards. *The Proceedings of the Governor and Assembly in Regard to the Maroon Negroes* (1796), p 27.

91 Ibid, pp 29, 30, 32. On 15 Jan Balcarres spoke of 'the total since the commencement of the present treaty who have surrendered'. It was thus still operative at that date, in his view. However, modern historians have repeatedly stated that surrenders after 31 December were not on the same terms as before that date. Of course B. Edwards, the apologist for the Establishment, began it in *The History, Civil and Commercial, of the British Colonies in the West Indies*, I (Philadelphia, 1806), p 571. Sir Alan Burn's omission of the episode is suspicious in an otherwise standard work (*A History of the British West Indies* (1954), p 555), J. Fage, *A History of West Africa* (Cambridge, 1969), 4th edition, p 120, states blandly the Maroons 'reached an agreement with the Government to transport them out of the island'. It is time these fairy tales were scotched. Likewise, Burns, taking it as face value from Edwards, the 'official' narrator, says (p 554) there was little doubt the Maroons were waiting for the last of the troops being sent from Jamaica to Hispaniola to leave, before rising in revolt.

92 CO 137/96, Balcarres to Walpole, 30 Dec 1795.

93 John Rylands University Library, Balcarres Papers, MS 23/10/92. The despatch has not survived.

94 Ibid, MS 23/10/97, Portland to Balcarres, 12 July 1796; George Bridges, *The Annals of Jamaica*, II (1828), pp 239, 481; William F. Gardner, *History of Jamaica* (1873), p 237; Burns, op cit, p 555; CO 217/67 (Governors' Despatches, Nova Scotia), f 118.

95 CO 217/67, f 108. The despatch has not survived.

96 Public Record Office, War Office, WO 1/92, f 353, Balcarres to Dundas, April 1796. Only 167 were able to bear arms, the rest were children and elderly people. Balcarres papers 23/11/248.

97 Edwards, op cit, pp 65, 68. Edwards, p 571, wrongly says the offers were changed as from 1 Jan. Walpole's correspondence is in CO 137/96 and 97.

98 See R. C. Dallas, *The History of the Maroons*, II (1803), p 177.

99 CO 217/69, f 5; 217/70, ff 210–12. For a fuller account of the 1795 Maroon War, see S. E. Furness, 'The Maroon War of 1795', *Jamaica Historical Review*, 5 (1965), pp 30–49. In fairness to Balcarres it should be noted that Walpole was a grandson of the Duke of Devonshire, the Whig leader, and that his difference with Balcarres was largely a political one, Balcarres supporting Pitt—see A. P. Kup, 'Alexander, 6th Earl of Balcarres, Governor of Jamaica 1794–1801', *John Rylands and University of Manchester Bulletin*, Spring 1975.

100 CO 217/67, ff 108, 122, 124, 126. Portland thought Sierra Leone would have them; if so, he advised Wentworth to send them in ships loaded with spirits, tobacco and lumber, all in short supply. Balcarres Papers 23/10/98, 15 July 1796.

101 CO 217/67, f 136; 217/68, f 99, Wentworth to Portland, 21 April 1797.

102 CO 217/69, ff 231, 237.

103 CO 217/70, f 3, Portland to Wentworth, 20 Jan 1799; CO 217/69, f 85, same to same, 7 June 1798; CO 217/68, f 114, same to same, 12 June 1797; CO 217/68, ff 155, 157; CO 217/69, ff 39, 99, 115; CO 217/69, f 119, B. J. Gray to Wentworth, 18 June 1798; CO 217/68, Wentworth to Portland 2 June 1797. Balcarres estimated the Maroon War alone cost Jamaica £350,000, Lord Lindsay, *Lives of the Lindsays*, III (1858), pp 126, 144n.

104 CO 217/67, f 189, 29 Oct 1796.

105 Transport and victualling for the Nova Scotians had cost about £16,000; in 1789 the entire British vote for the civil establishment in Nova Scotia had been £6,218 17s 6d, as Wentworth reminded them, CO 217/63, ff 198, 286; CO 218/27, f 29.

106 CO 217/69, Draft, Portland to Wentworth, 8 March 1798. CO 217/70, f 1, Draft, same to same, 17 Jan 1799; CO 217/69, f 85, Draft, same to same, 7 June 1798; CO 217/70, f 3, Portland to Wentworth, 20 Jan 1799.

107 CO 217/70, ff 42, 159.

108 Ibid, f 220, J. King (under secretary) to Portland, 24 Feb 1799.

109 Ibid, f 10, Draft, Portland to Directors, Sierra Leone Company, 5 March 1799, and ibid, f 45.

110 Ibid, f 242, Directors to Governor, Sierra Leone Co, 22 March 1799; CO 217/70, f 278, Macaulay to King, 9 Nov 1799;

CO 217/74, p 449, Thornton to King, 12 Feb 1800; WO 1/352, ff 13, 17; CO 217/70, f 220, Thornton to King.

111   CO 217/70, f 200.

112   CO 270/5, ff 59 *et seq.* See also 217/75, p 421, Wentworth to Gray and Ludlam, 5 Aug 1800.

113   CO 270/6, ff 110, 119. The sum was equivalent to about a week's wages as a labourer.

114   Balcarres Papers, 23/11/53, Letter, Quarrell to Balcarres, 8 May 1796.

115   When the Temne lands to the west were distributed. CO 270/5, f 83; 270/6, f 146; 270/8, f 39; 270/9, ff 28, 31, 35. In 1808 a commission was appointed to hear claims, and place on a legal footing land grants in the colony—J. J. Crooks, *A History of the Colony of Sierra Leone* (1903), p 76. But see ibid, p 82, for an annulment of many of Governor Thompson's grants. Only in 1857 was a registry office set up, however.

116   A parliamentary committee (*Report from the Committee on the Petition of the Court of Directors of the Sierra Leone Company*, 25 May 1802, Parliamentary Papers, Commons, Sessional Papers, 1801/2, ii, p 359) had found they 'universally' harboured a desire to return, in the early days. An order in council, 16 March 1808, ordered the collectors of customs to surrender to the naval and military authorities all fit recaptives. But the military were not at that time prepared to enrol them; approval came in 1810 and recruitment began that year—see Porter, op cit, p 37.

117   Porter, op cit, p 38.

118   Quoted in Christopher Fyfe, *Sierra Leone Inheritance* (1964), p 134.

119   Porter, op cit, p 43.

120   Eg as magistrates, supervisors of public works, clearing roads.

121   Quoted in Porter, op cit, p 39. By 1856 there were managers only at Waterloo and in the western district, to watch for slave canoes from the Sherbro. Ostensibly under the Freetown police magistrate, villages were left to their own companies, church classes and the Seventeen Nations. See Fyfe, *A History*, pp 269, 293.

122   See, for example, Sergeant Potts' Benefit Society, founded 1824. Punishment usually meant being sent to 'Coventry' for six months—Fyfe, *Sierra Leone Inheritance*, p 140. I have relied very heavily in this section on John Peterson, *The Province of*

Freedom (1969). See also British Parliamentary Papers 1842, XI, 551, pp 255–76; and XII, pp 249–384.

123 By 1863, when the last shipload of liberated Africans was brought in, about 50,000 had been successfully freed in the colony. For further discussion of the Act, however, see pp 175–8.

124 Local administrators as well as traders had always been anxious to have friendly relations with chiefs and by 1873 there were already at least 73 such treaties round Sierra Leone. See Cherry J. Gertzel, *Imperial Policy Towards the British Settlements in West Africa 1860–75*, BLitt thesis (Oxford, 1953); also: Fyfe, 'European and Creole Influences in the Hinterland of Sierra Leone before 1896', *Sierra Leone Studies*, NS 6 (June 1956), 113–23; John Hargreaves, *A life of Sir Samuel Lewis* (1958); William Grant's proposals, 1874, in Fyfe, *Sierra Leone Inheritance*, p 191.

125 When Alimami Bokhari, exiled chief from French Mellacourie, took refuge at Kambia and his enemies burnt it. In the Upper Rokel and Ribbi, Yonni Temne pressed down upon the unofficial 'protectorate' established in 1879 over Bumpe and Ribi to keep wars out. Near the Liberian border, the succession to the Massaquoi crown was disputed.

126 Porter, op cit, p 53. For Horton see Fyfe, *Africanus Horton* (1972), especially Chap IV.

127 Parliamentary Papers, Commons, Sessional Papers, 1865, V, Evidence, Question 4492.

128 Quoted from Porter, op cit, p 56.

CHAPTER 5

1 See, for instance, Rt Hon Eric Williams, *Britain & the West Indies*, Noel Buxton Lecture, University of Essex (1969), *passim*; A. Mitzman, 'Anti-Progress: A Study in the Romantic Roots of German Sociology', *Social Research*, 33, No 1 (spring 1966), pp 65–85; G. R. Mellor, *British Imperial Trusteeship 1783–1850* (1951), pp 11–14. Some American Assemblies, even before independence, tried to emancipate their slaves (eg Massachusetts 1771) but were overruled by HMG.

2 See *Adam Afzelius' Sierra Leone Journal 1795–6*, ed A. P. Kup (Uppsala, 1967), especially p xii.

3 Baptists 1792, London Missionary Society 1795, Church Missionary Society 1799.

Q

4 Quoted from the *Observer*, 6 Sept 1970, p 38. Cf Chap 4, n 26 above.

5 Until the late nineteenth century Temne settlements did not think of themselves as one people. Small and generally far apart—though the profitable Sierra Leone estuary was an exception—they had little friendly contact and often fought one another. For a fuller discussion see E. Ade Ijagbemi, 'A History of the Temne in the Nineteenth Century', PhD thesis (Edinburgh, 1968).

6 Huntington Library, Pasadena, California, MS MY418, Z. Macaulay, *Journal 1793–1799*, 30 July 1793. This and other facts concealed from the company were well known to all slave traders, and were even in print—see John Matthews, *Voyage to the River Sierra Leone* (1788), p 75.

7 The Directors' *Report* (1791) (pp 6, 9), admitting the title was elective, considered Naimbana's son would succeed him, 'as the chiefs who choose the King generally pay regard to hereditary succession'. This was nonsense. Naimbana was not king, but one of the three counsellors to the Bai Farma, king of Koya. The other two were Pa Kapr and Naimsogo. There were also three mamy queens: Bome Pose, Bome Warah, Bome Rufah. The king ruled with their advice, not despotically as Europeans thought, and when he died was succeeded by each of his counsellors as regent until all were dead (the three queens usually ruling together). Only then was a new Bai Farma elected (and even then not always—see p 167) and a new set of counsellors.

8 Macaulay, *Journal*, pp 92–3.

9 Ibid, pp 87, 168, 27 July, 18 Sept 1793. The Pa Kapr (the Europeans called him Pa Cumbra) died later in 1793.

10 Clarkson's Diary, *Sierra Leone Studies*, OS 8 (March 1927), 60.

11 Anna M. Falconbridge, *Two Voyages to Sierra Leone during the Years 1791–2–3* (1794), pp 33ff.

12 Clarkson, reasonably, agreed to work round their plantations, at a palaver 27 Sept 1792. On Temne land the rights of usufruct are tightly held, much more so than amongst the Mende. Only unfelled mangrove forest is considered communally owned. L. C. Greene, 'The System of Land Tenure in Sierra Leone', MA thesis (Durham, 1966).

13 Over the dismissal of two Nova Scotians, Channel and Keeling,

by Macaulay, for 'answering back' white sailors on a slave ship.

14 By Dawes at a palaver on 7 March 1794—Macaulay, *Journal*, 1 June 1797.

15 Ibid, part V, especially 21, 22 Oct 1794. Macaulay finally settled things at a palaver on Boxing Day 1797.

16 Ibid, 1 June 1797. King Tom was installed Dec 1796. Like all others, he was looking for a special payment on his accession.

17 Ibid, 30 June 1797. It is worth noting that in 1804, testifying before the House of Commons Committee to examine the company's petition for finance, Macaulay said before the Temne attack of 1801, no differences existed between them, and the attack was chiefly for plunder, though partly, he admitted, in fear of the settlement's growing power. A few moments later, asked if the Temne showed a 'favourable disposition', he said in his time there were no palavers in the neighbourhood which did not mostly arise from petty disputes between Settlers and Temne visiting Freetown. As a modern French premier has remarked: 'people who work in Government lose contact with reality'—Jacques Chaban Delmas. Parliamentary Papers, Commons, Sessional Papers 1803/4, V, pp 132, 137. He conveniently forgot that Bai Farma had seized two company boats in Sept 1794 in exasperation at not having his rights recognised —Macaulay, *Journal*, 4, 18, 26 Sept, 18 Oct 1794

18 Macaulay, *Journal*, 30 Dec 1797; Huntington Library MS MY636, letter Macaulay to Thornton, 1 Dec 1796. J. H. Kopytoff, *A Preface to Modern Nigeria* (1965), p 181; David F. Apter, *Ghana in Transition* (Princeton, 1959), pp 24ff.

19 CO 270/4, ff 88, 103.

20 Viscountess Knutsford, *Life & Letters of Zachary Macaulay* (1901), pp 206–7, 214; CO 270/4, ff 131, 144, 146; CO 270/5, f 20.

21 Pa London, a brother of Naimbana's successor as regent, and Signor Domingo.

22 Macaulay, op cit, 27 Nov 1793, 23 April 1798.

23 CO 270/8, f 39; Director's *Report*, 1804, p 40.

24 Public Record Office, War Office 1/352, ff 173, 193, 201, 241. In 1801 HMG granted £11,000 for fortifications, and in 1801 and 1802 other grants of £4,000 and £10,000 respectively. In 1803 Commodore Hallowell's critical report on the settlement meant no grant that year; a commission of enquiry being set up.

From 1803 the company began to suggest handing over to HMG. The government temporised, being no more anxious to foot the bill than with the Maroons. Nova Scotians, Black Poor and Maroons had been shunted about, unconsulted in the interest of parsimony; perhaps this could be done again and they could be moved cheaply elsewhere. Asked about this, Day said it would be expensive and once the plan was known, would need 'great force' to prevent rebellion. As the least expensive solution, Britain in 1804 granted £4,000 for fortifications and £10,000 for running expenses for 1803. In Feb 1805 a further £14,000 was voted for 1804 and in Aug £14,000 more for the current year. By 1806 they grossed £67,000; by 1808 the total from HMG was £96,518 8s. There was also a bill to the treasury for settling the Maroons and for troops, in which the company claimed £24,474 2s 5d. By 1815 they had received £18,000 of this. The Temne wars cost £8,700, and there had been an annual excess of expenditure over the grants of £12,000. Both these had to come out of company funds. The shareholders never got a dividend, the board having spent some £45,000 more than the subscribed £230,000. *African Institute Report* (1807), pp 41–54; *Special Report, African Institute* (1815), p 8; *Letter to HRH the Duke of Gloucester from Z. Macaulay* (1815), p 58. The parliamentary committee of 1803–4 recommended eventual transfer to HMG, but the director's insistence on Abolition naturally held up the transfer until that became law in all British colonies.

25   Ijagbemi, op cit, p 127. See pp 58, 250 and n 7.
26   CO 270/5, f 65v.
27   The directors expressed: 'considerable doubt whether under all the circumstances . . . the company will be entitled to support the British claim . . .', WO 1/352, ff 13, 209, 213, 217.
28   British Sessional Papers, Commons 1803–4, V, p 164.
29   CO 267/24, 11 April 1808. Macaulay made £100,000 out of Sierra Leone trade, then went bankrupt.
30   CO 267/24, enc Macaulay to Edward Cooke, 16 Sept 1808, and Macaulay to Castlereagh, 8 May 1807, misc section.
31   In particular:
     6 July 1818, chiefs of Bago, ceding Iles de Los.
     25 May 1819, Pa London, when Waterloo and Hastings were founded.
     21 July 1820, Pa London, and T. Caulker and Koya Temne.

20 Oct 1820, T. and G. S. Caulker. These last two ceded the Banana Islands.

2 July 1824, with Bai Mauro of Loko Masama, ceding islands along the north shore of the river Sierra Leone.

24 Sept 1825, king of Sherbro and Caulkers, ceding coast from river Kamaranka to Kamalay at the end of Turner's Peninsula—not ratified by HMG.

12 Dec 1825, chiefs of Bacca Loco. Sovereignty was proclaimed, under these terms, over Port Loko in 1893.

18 April 1826, chiefs of Sumbia Susu, ceding northern coastline opposite the colony—not ratified.

8–10 March 1827, with Kafu Bullom.

24 June 1827, king of the Biafras, ceding Bulama Island. Other treaties referred to certain small islands, and to territory subsequently agreed as being French, by the convention of 10 May 1889.

32 Macaulay said of Bathurst's letter to Turner refusing to ratify: 'By a single line he has unconsciously done more to retard the progress and aggravate the miseries of the countries in question, than can well be even imagined by one who has not seen . . . the slave trade in unrestrained act and operation.' Quoted in G. R. Mellor, 'British Policy in Relation to Sierra Leone 1808–52', MA thesis (London, 1935), Chap 9.

33 Ibid.

34 By the treaty of 13 Feb 1841.

35 That of 4 July 1849, with the Sherbro chiefs.

36 The Bullom Shore chiefs, already 'protected' in that the Susu and Kala Modu, had been made to 'recognise' them, now asked Britain to take over their country. The governor knew HMG would not agree and refused, though a nominal sovereignty along a quarter-mile-wide strip of the Bullom Shore, was accepted. These two treaties with Loko Masama and Kafu Bullom, both in 1847, were the only two concerned with sovereignty.

37 Goderich.

38 See C. Fyfe, *A History of Sierra Leone* (1962), pp 308–10. Retroceding it in 1872, Britain reserved the right to resume sovereignty at any time—J. J. Crooks, *A History of the Colony of Sierra Leone* (1903), p 229.

39 Parliamentary Papers, Commons, Sessional Papers, 1865, V, p 3. However, since the 1890 Foreign Jurisdictions Act, and the

1895 Order in Council declared the Crown had acquired jurisdiction in adjacent territories, the matter is at best an academic one. See also Dundas Campbell below, and PP 1842 (xi), Questions 8764–7.

40 As Fyfe has pointed out in 'European and Creole Influence in the Hinterland of Sierra Leone before 1896', *Sierra Leone Studies*, NS 6 (June 1956), 117ff, despite treaties with chiefs in the northern rivers area, these were lost to France by 1882.

41 There was one very notable exception: the 1854 expedition to Maligiah where the chief, Bamba Mina Lahai, siding with Nathaniel Isaacs, an Englishman suspected of slave-trading, ordered all Europeans to leave the Mellacourie. Acting Governor Robert Dougan, without even summoning his council, called in the navy and army on two occasions in 1854 and 1855. Thoroughly mismanaged, they attacked the second time during the Ramadan ceremonies when the town was full of visitors. They met a murderous fire from ten to twelve yards, were cut off from their boats, which they had beached where the tide, ebbing, left them a large muddy expanse to negotiate. Many, throwing themselves into the mud, were never seen again; one boat was so riddled it sank. A last stand was made on an island; in a few seconds 17 men fell, the rest plunging into the river to swim downstream. Some 2,000 on the banks shot at them, HMS *Teazer* watching helplessly, having run out of ammunition; 95 were killed or wounded out of a total of 135. Alfred B. Ellis, *The History of the First West India Regiment* (1885), pp 236ff.

42 By the 1843 Act, 6 Victoria cap 13.

43 Of course, in the Gold Coast, chiefs were ready to submit themselves to the British courts, in Sierra Leone they were trying to *make* British subjects submit themselves.

44 16 and 17 Victoria cap 86.

45 24 and 25 Victoria cap 31.

46 Parliament paid Sierra Leone's debts in 1877 with a grant of £38,000. In 1876 Britain acquired the right of collecting customs on the seaboard of the Ribbi, Bumpe and Cockboro countries; in 1883, at Sulima, Mano Salija and Kittam Point.

47 See Chap 3 above.

48 CO 267/328, Desp No 111 and minute by A. W. L. Hemming, principal clerk. CO 267/329, Desp Nos 17 and 57–9.

49 Dividing the Mellacourie and Scarcies—as in 1882—the settlement continued inland along the Gt Scarcies to the 10° N lati-

tude. The boundary commission began work on the ground in 1891. The 1895 Agreement extended this to run south-east along the Niger Watershed, to the Franco-Liberian frontier agreed on, 1891. The delimitation was almost purely geographical, and took no account of political boundaries. For a resumé of treaties concluded see Crooks, op cit, pp 294–301.

50   CO 267/328, Desp No 178, 1 Dec 1875.

51   Colonial Office, Confidential Print, CO 879/15, No 175.

52   Quoted from C. Fyfe, *Africanus Horton* (1972), p 61. Cf H. Hume, *Life of Edward John Eyre* (1867), writing of Governor Eyre and the 1865 Jamaican rebellion: 'What the negro was in 1795 so he is now. Emancipation has only made him more lazy, more cunning, more sensual, more profligate, more prone to mischief, and more dangerous.' Quoted in Eric Williams, *British Historians and the West Indies* (New York, 1966), p 123.

53   See especially J. Hargreaves, 'The Education of the Native Affairs Department', *Sierra Leone Studies*, NS 3 (1954), 168–84; C. Fyfe, 'European and Creole Influence in the Hinterland of Sierra Leone before 1896', *Sierra Leone Studies*, NS 6 (June 1956), 113–23; J. Hargreaves, 'The French Occupation of the Mellacourie 1865–7', *Sierra Leone Studies*, NS 9 (Dec 1957), 3–15.

54   Such as it was. Creoles were deeply disappointed in its limited powers. They had hoped it would extend the area of colony rule.

55   Fyfe, *A History*, especially p 517.

56   This was later repealed because, by empowering the government to dispose of 'waste lands', it seemed to imply land was vested in the Crown. In 1897 a second ordinance set up three courts, presided over respectively by: chiefs alone, chiefs and the DC, the DC alone. Some chiefs in treaty with HMG, like the earlier Bai Farma and the Sierra Leone Company, not understanding Britain's concept of sovereignty, wanted to return their stipends and so annul the treaty. The recent 1893 treaty with Bey Inga, chief of the small Scarcies, had promised the customs of the country would not be interfered with beyond anything necessary to keep peace and stop slaving. The repeal of the first ordinance was never properly explained to chiefs, and their lands appeared therefore expropriated.

57   Ronietta, Bandajuma, Karene. The five police districts did not coincide with the protectorate ones—see Crooks, op cit, p 308.

58 Quoted in M. Crowder and L. Denzer, 'Bai Bureh' in *Protest and Power in Black Africa*, eds R. T. Rotberg and A. A. Mazrui (1970), pp 169–212.

59 Elected by the elders in 1887 in the absence of any hereditary claimant. The British, wrong as usual, with vague notions of royal lineage, disputed his election, but it was quite customary in such cases. It is not certain he was even a Temne; possibly he was a Loko. He first comes to notice in the 1860s, fighting for the Muslim Chief Bokhari against the French in the Mellacourie. Bokhari was trying to impose Islam on his people. His sphere of action was hinterland and coastal stretch from Freetown to Conakry, an area where Islam had become a major force, attracting hinterland trade through new ports and hence immigration of Susu from Mellacourie and Fourecariah to the Scarcies and Upper Limba chiefdoms. Bai Bureh, who used Muslim clerks and sent messages to the British by Muslim traders, never became a Muslim. After being crowned, he soon fell out with Britain because an 1871 treaty obliged Kasseh to accept government mediation. When a Susu party, led by Karimu, a chief in Upper Limba, entered the British Limba sphere, chiefs appointed Bai Bureh their war leader and he headed a Limba-Loko-Temne coalition against the Susu; ignoring repeated British requests to stay peaceful, the Frontier Police in 1891 were told to arrest him, but then he was found useful as an ally and so not arrested!

60 Later, Chamberlain confided that it was a tax that should never have been imposed. Though he had supported Cardew, he felt he had been hard on Africans, taking no pains either to ascertain their views, or to remove their suspicions. In Dec 1897 the Ag DC, Ronietta, reported chiefs were making no effort to pay the tax, and that the Mabanta and Bagru districts were in a very disturbed state. Cardew's reaction was to replace the Ag DC with an inspector of Frontier Police. Almost his first act was to sentence an important chief to thirty-six lashes. Chiefs were arrested almost wholesale. The Chalmers' Commission of Enquiry held arrests and imprisonment of chiefs illegal under the Protectorate Ordinance, or under any other law under which DCs acted—see Crooks, op cit, p 341.

61 Memo, Blyden to Colonial Office, 28 July 1898, quoted in Samson C. Ukpabi. 'The West Africa Frontier Force (an Instrument of Imperial Policy 1897–1914)', MA thesis (Birm-

ingham, 1964). Under Sorie Burki, the people fired their houses and ran away rather than be ruled by him.

62 *Telegraph*, 4 April 1898, and especially *The Last Military Expedition in Sierra Leone*, by 'an Africanised Englishman', 1898 (Sawyer).

63 With one exception, when the Rev W. J. Humphrey, Principal of Fourah Bay College, was murdered.

64 In 1892 Creoles held 18 of some 40 senior government posts; in 1912 they held only 15 (5 of which were abolished as their holders retired) out of a total of 92. Fyfe, *A History*, p 615.

65 In 1929 the slump saw prices drop from £13 to £5 a ton. By 1937 production had reached 60,000 tons a year and was worth £1½ million. Most economic activity until the opening of Marampa, and, to a lesser extent, the discovery of gold in Tonkolili in the 1930s, was in the south, where agricultural activity was centred—encouraged by the railway and the navigable creeks. See Rhodes House, Oxford, MS Br Empire S280, Lt-Col P. F. White, topographical survey, 8 vi 1929.

66 See especially John R. Cartwright, *Politics in Sierra Leone 1947–67* (Toronto, 1970), Chap I.

CHAPTER 6

1 Paul Hair. Review article on C. Fyfe's 'History of Sierra Leone' in *Sierra Leone Studies*, NS 17 (June 1963), 29. The new executives were looked down on by the administrators, even though it was technology above all that the country needed. In the 1960s there was still a feeling that the executive class was reserved for 'nitwits', see *Studies in Nigerian Administration*, ed David Murray (University of Ife, Nigeria, 1970), p 168. At independence, though they subscribed to the same pension ordinances as expatriate administrators, the Colonial Office refused to give them the same benefits. As a result many, especially widows, live in virtual penury today.

2 Martin Kilson, *Political Change in a West African State* (Harvard, 1966), p 11.

3 Ibid, p 13. That attitude still persists in places. In 1973 some British firms, after agitation in British newspapers, were giving black South Africans pay increases of up to 40 per cent. There can be no friendship in that kind of exploitation.

4 Rhodes House, Oxford, MS Afr S1203, Letter, Paul Shuffrey, to Prof Hale Bellot, 24 April 1913, and same to same, 23 April

R

1918. Shuffrey later acted as Provincial Commissioner, South-East Province, retiring in the 1920s to run his family's wrought-iron works. He was exceptional. Too many colonial officers having little money and few prospects to fall back on, dared not criticise, and were well conscious of the fact that those who did not read and practise their Lugard were apt to be considered unsound for promotion.

5 The lack of the charter before 1800 embarrassed the company. Thus the Nova Scotian rebels surrendered by Bai Farma, were reserved for the first quarter sessions after the charter arrived. Even so, the charter did not permit the company to try cases of treason, whilst a lesser charge might not have permitted deportation which, in the case of the ringleaders, they felt safety demanded. So they were tried and convicted 'for capital felonies'. For lesser rebels a court of enquiry was set up, because, here again, quarter sessions could not have deported on these lesser charges, but a court of enquiry had no such disability. Thus the Council had asked the two army and one navy lieutenants who had accompanied the Maroons to Freetown to act as a court, whilst the Council played the part of attorney-general and brought the charges. From 1808–11, there were not enough white people, without using the officials, to operate the legal system: quarter sessions, mayor's court, court of requests, police court (all of which save the first sat once a week), and the appeal court to the governor and Council. Officials therefore had to be used, much against the principles of British justice, devoting as much as two days a week to this business. The judge sat as judge of the admiralty, at quarter sessions, and presided over the mayor's court. The office of mayor included no municipal right or authority. There was no one to take on the office of JP and officials took it in turns. No professional judge, or barrister to give advice, had ever been to the colony. (Parliamentary Papers 1816, Vol vii, pp 125–34).

6 The Gold Coast's Executive Council and Legislative Council were established in 1850.

7 Quoted from Arthur T. Porter, 'The Social Background of Political Decision Makers in Sierra Leone', *Sierra Leone Studies*, NS 13 (June 1960), 4. See also Gershon Collier, *Sierra Leone, Experiment in Democracy* (New York, 1970), pp 5–6. The first unofficial member was Kenneth Macaulay, second cousin of Governor Zachary Macaulay, and a trader.

8 See John Hargreaves, *A Life of Sir Samuel Lewis* (1958), p 30.

9 Legislative Council now had 4 *ex-officio* members and 3 or 4 unofficial members, nominated by the governor, though 2 of the 4 were in fact officials, but chosen by name rather than office.

10 Quoted from Porter, op cit, p 7. On 1 March 1882, when Lewis took the unofficial seat which he was to hold for 21 years, we begin to pass from the era of the merchant to that of the professional man in Legislative Council. After 1882 unofficial members were drawn increasingly from the professions. This lasted until 1924. As early as 1811, as the Report of the Select Committee on Papers Relating to the African Forts (PP 1816, Vol VII, 8, pp 125–34), noted, there was an unwelcome tendency in the colony to feel that a right to a seat on the governor's Council meant freedom to discuss anything, and the governor should take care to have a majority. They were relieved to have counsel's opinion that the governor alone was still constitutionally the governor and Council.

11 Quoted from John Hargreaves, 'Colonial Office Opinions on the Constitution of 1863', *Sierra Leone Studies*, NS 5 (Dec 1955), 5.

12 However, see C. Fyfe, *A History of Sierra Leone* (1962), p 147: in 1818 Thomas Carew, an Afro-Barbadian, was appointed mayor; in 1824 James Wise, government printer and a Nova Scotian, and Stephen Gabbidon, a Maroon, were appointed aldermen. In 1825 Wise became mayor.

13 Ibid, p 513. The House and Land Tax, imposed 1851, was first collected 1852. A minimum of 5s, it tended to oppress the poor. Abolished in 1872 along with all direct taxes by Governor James Pope-Hennessey, Governor Rowe proposed reviving them in 1888, but such an outcry was raised, the Bill was withdrawn. A house tax was imposed on the colony, outside Freetown, in 1900. Direct taxation was anathema, a legacy of the quit-rent troubles. The possibility of an imperial loan in 1885, proposed by Lewis and the Sierra Leone Association to finance the peaceful occupation of the hinterland, was opposed because loans implied repayment, and repayment meant a municipal council to collect taxes to pay interest. Ordinances of 1908, 1927, 1945, 1964, replaced that of 1893; the first two reducing, and the last two widening democratic government in the city.

14 John Hargreaves, *A Life of Sir Samuel Lewis*, p 96. Cf Martin

Kilson, *Political Change*, pp 132–4 and n 23. The relevant Order in Council was that of 7 March 1913.

15 See Kilson, op cit, p 18. The Northern and Central Provinces had four districts each, the Southern five. Political officers' duties were administrative, judicial and departmental. Each DC was assisted by a body of court messengers, by African clerks, and by a senior African staff officer. In 1954 the SL Police Force was introduced into the protectorate, and court messengers disbanded.

16 See, for example, *The Principles of Native Administration in Nigeria*, ed Anthony M. Kirk-Greene (1965).

17 The Protectorate Ordinance of 1896 had originally laid a 10s tax on houses of more than 4 rooms, 5s for smaller ones, to begin 1 January 1898. In fact only the lower rate was demanded and in 1901 the whole ordinance was re-enacted, and the 5s tax retained. The 1937 Ordinance then changed the direct tax to 9s and the house tax to a poll tax. In 1955 district councils (below) were authorised to levy a 'precept' on their chiefdoms, this added some 9s to 15s. In 1956 another 5s was added, which meant legal local taxes had just about tripled in 3 years, and was partly the cause of the Northern Province riots of 1955–6.

18 Prior to 1937 a paramount chief's income included the product from farms worked for him, and tribute in kind as well as money. The relevant ordinances of 1937 are: The Chiefdom Treasury Ordinance, 1937, No 11; The Tribal Authorities Ordinance, 1937, No 8; The Chiefdom Tax Ordinance, 1937, No 10. The new taxes were those in the Local Tax Ordinance, 1954. The term Native Administration had no legal sanction.

19 See Kilson, op cit, pp 101–10, 144. The NCBWA, founded 1919, asked for the introduction of the franchise, equal opportunities for white and black in the civil service, opportunities for higher education and a clearer separation of the judiciary from the colonial administration. It is doubtful if any artisan would have seen political advance in those assimilatory terms, even if he had understood them.

20 For the phrase, see John Hargreaves, *Sir Samuel Lewis*, p 34. Likewise the Creoles boycotted that stormy petrel I. T. A. Wallace-Johnson who, studying in Moscow in the 1930s, returned to Freetown in 1938, founding the West African Youth League. Its radical appeals and Wallace-Johnson's Marxism turned the Creole élite against it. Thus the first political

organisation bridging the gap between colony and protectorate failed. Wallace-Johnson and all but one of his executives were interned in 1940 for the duration of the war.

21 B. M. Jusu, 'The Haidara Rebellion of 1931', *Sierra Leone Studies*, NS (Dec 1954), 147–9; Kilson, op cit, pp 113–17.

22 Lugard held that imperial powers had a mandate to exploit the natural resources of the colonies and to train 'natives' in 'civilisation'.

23 See the Petition, 19 Oct 1920, printed in C. Fyfe, *Sierra Leone Inheritance* (1964), p 316; and Slater's speech to Legislative Council, 25 Nov 1924, ibid, p 319.

24 Chiefly power was actually strengthened in some ways under British rule, since, being part of the administration, they tended to get official support against traditional (and other) checks from below, ringleaders often finding themselves deported from the chiefdom. The Poro and other societies became less powerful, traditional fission and creation of new chiefdoms by dissidents was prevented by the British who wanted to preserve as far as possible the picture in 1896, seemingly not realising that the nineteenth-century wars had thrown up innumerable new chiefdoms, and new chiefs. Bo school from its founding in 1905 until 1941 admitted only the sons and nominees of paramount chiefs. In 1947 only 18 per cent of PCs were literate in English; by the mid 1950s this had risen to about 50 per cent.

25 One DC, who later became a governor, remarked in 1953 about the development and change encouraged from within amongst local authorities that these had always been built on some indigenous unit or authority, geographic, social or economic: 'as a result local government in Sierra Leone is vigorous and effective and has excited the envy of authorities in other parts of Africa . . .' Rhodes House, Oxford, MS Af S957, 'Notes on the Future Developments in Local Government in Sierra Leone'. John Watson, Bo, March 1953. (It should be noted that this was written only two years before the 1955–6 riots, when the ensuing commission of enquiry said that District Councils had failed utterly to be either representative or effective.)

The Native Administrations were, in fact, a genuine unit of local government and provided such services long before the emphasis on local government was stressed by Creech-Jones. A main fault, apart from being a preserve of the elders, was their unwieldy size. Another, of course, was that the paramount chief, as chief, was the executive officer, as well as the judicial officer, and president of the Native Court. It was rare, especially in the north, for a member to express any view contrary to the chief. It was traditionally ingrained that there must be 'one word' (ie agreement) with the chief, and chiefs tended to see independent opinions in the Authority as a complaint. M. Kilson, op cit, p 182.

In 1946 in the colony area, a committee—apart from the chairman, all unofficial members—were appointed to review Ord 26/1936. It reported in 1948 and subsequently this formed the basis of Ord 11/1949. It set up a pyramid with three tiers of authorities, each subordinate to the other, with the village at the base, then the Rural District Council, and then the Rural Area Council. Here again some colonial officers looked askance at the two latter units as 'artificially simulated'—ie not indigenous.

The fundamental difference between colony and protectorate systems of local government in the late 1940s and 1950s was that in the colony they formed a pyramid of authority; in the protectorate they followed the pattern in England, with horizontal autonomous units each responsible directly to the centre. In the colony their powers were very specifically defined by law, as was Bo's, the only Urban Area in the protectorate. District councils and NAs, on the other hand, were not specifically restricted in powers and it was assumed they could perform all functions not specifically forbidden by law. The District Council Ordinance 17/1950 says only: 'to promote the development of the District. . . . with the funds at its disposal.' It was purposefully non-restrictive.

26   Quoted in C. Fyfe, *The Sierra Leone Inheritance*, p 325.
27   Quoted by John R. Cartwright, *Politics in Sierra Leone* (Toronto, 1970), p 70. See especially his chapters 2 and 3 on this period.
28   Member of Legislative Council, he had supported the railway strike that year—see Kilson, op cit, p 121. The Creole maverick party was that of Lamina Sankoh, born E. N. Jones, he changed his name as a gesture of solidarity with the protectorate, later joining the SLPP. The National Council of Sierra Leone, as it came to be called, was founded by merging Dr Bankole-Bright's Sierra Leone Democratic Party with various other colony movements, especially Wallace-Johnson's West

Africa Youth League. See *Five Elections in Africa*, eds W. J. M. MacKenzie and R. Robinson (1960), pp 187–92, from D. J. R. Scott's chapter: 'The Sierra Leone Election, 1957'.

29 Of the 17 who appeared before it, 5 favoured a universal franchise, 6 a taxpayer franchise, and only 6 the *status quo*; see Cartwright, op cit, p 91.

30 Parties contesting the election were the United Progressive Party, backed by Creoles led by Cyril Rogers-Wright and formed in 1955 during the riots, it had some backing at least in the north (it won 5 seats, 3 in the colony); the Kono Progressive Movement (the only other party besides the SLPP and the UPP to contest seats outside the colony. Founded 1952–4, as a result of the diamond boom, it was the first ordinary man's party, followed by many farmers who, in theory should have got part of the profits when their land was leased to diamond diggers, but in practice found the chiefs getting it, and so were dissatisfied with the ruling SLPP for allowing it.) The KPM won 1 seat. The SLPP candidates won 25, including 9 seats in the colony. The remaining 8 were Independents who all declared for the SLPP. The 11 PCs also declared for the SLPP. The Labour Party, which emerged from the Freetown industrial strike, 1955, led by Marcus Grant, an active union leader, won no seats. Edward Blyden in 1956 founded the Sierra Leone Independence Movement. It too failed to secure a seat.

31 See Cartwright, op cit, p 97.

32 Later the Viscount Boyd of Merton.

33 In fact 3, but only 3 out of 16 were given places in the ministry. This was because of the weakness of the UPP and PNP, neither of which was radical in any sense, neither holding any ideology which differentiated them much, if at all, from the SLPP. The UPP was handicapped by being known as Creole based.

34 Cartwright, op cit, p 69. There were also the Verandah Boys (by the late 1950s some 6,000 boys a year either finished, or dropped out of primary school, few returning to their family farms) and minority groups like the Yalunka, Koranko and Kono.

35 Quoted from Cartwright, op cit, p 132.

36 There is evidence that some chiefs in the north supported it too, albeit surreptitiously, fearing government (ie SLPP) reprisals.

37 After the election the APC to broaden its Freetown base,

merged with what was left of the United Sierra Leone Progressive Party (UPP).

38 This is not to say the governor-general's decision was incorrect, even in the northern province the SLPP had managed to win a quarter of the total votes in every district. Several independents were known SLPP sympathisers and would have stood as SLPP if they could have got the nomination, some having been excluded because of inter-party rivalry or because the local chief preferred another. Central party organisation played only a limited role in the election. See Cartwright, op cit.

39 A common practice in new African states, see Humphrey Fisher, 'Election & Coups in Sierra Leone', *Journal of Modern African Studies*, VII, 4 (Dec 1969), 611–36, and especially 612.

40 Sir Milton Margai died 28 April 1964.

41 I have relied heavily on Cartwright, op cit, Chaps 11, 12 for this paragraph. See also his article, 'Shifting Forces in Sierra Leone', *Africa Report*, 13, No 9 (Dec 1968), 26–30.

42 Dr Karefa-Smart, a Temne, had held ministerial office, and had had a distinguished academic careers. Mr Jusu-Sheriff, a Mende, was another intellectual. Y. D. Sesay another northerner had been one of Albert Margai's foremost supporters and formerly vice-principal of Bo School, whose old boys' association was an extremely powerful and active unit in protectorate politics. He had been minister of works, but was now dismissed despite an abject public apology. Another northern dissident of importance, Amadu Wurie, a minister, was forgiven. Cartwright suggests this was because the PM could not afford to remove all northerners from the cabinet. It also shows, however, that many thought it was time a Temne became prime minister. Sir Albert's arrangement with President Sekou Turé of Guinea, for support, alienated many, especially the Temne where hostility towards the Fula became very tense after the Sierra Leone/Guinea anti-subversion pact.

43 He was knighted. The three northerners in the cabinet were: Wurie, Kande Bureh, Chief Yumkella.

44 Meanwhile the twelve paramount chiefs declared for the SLPP. Seven of them were from the south, though not all of those were Mende, some being Bullom, Vai or from Gallinhas. SLPP government patronage played its part. For discussion of this, and for an anti-Creole, pro SLPP point of view see Gershon Collier, *Sierra Leone, Experiment in Democracy* (New

York, 1970), pp 88–92. The author attributes Sir Albert's unpopularity (p 114) to the fact that during nearly twenty years of public life, he 'had violated many political taboos and ruffled many conservative spirits on his way to supreme office'. In 1948 he had challenged Creole dominance in Sierra Leone politics, rallying the protectorate round the SLPP, led the avant-garde of the young educated élite in the protectorate in the 1950s to challenge the traditional hierarchy; tried to wrest power from Dr Margai in 1957, and failing, formed the PNP. See also: Christopher Allen, 'Sierra Leone Politics Since Independence', *African Affairs*, 67, No 269 (Oct 1968), 305–29. There was also the question of the army where officer-opponents were forced to resign or were sent abroad to get them out of Sir Albert's way. The counter coup leaders, Majors Blake, Jumu and Kai-Samba were in fact all Mende, but Lansana and Margai had by now become liabilities for the Mende hierarchy.

45 Major Charles Blake's radio speech, 23 March 1967. H. Fisher, 'Election and Coups in Sierra Leone', *Journal of Modern African Studies*, VII, 4 (Dec 1969), has suggested the NRC coup was carried out to resolve tensions within the army itself, rather than to reform national politics. The Mende-dominated NRC was given a Creole façade by the appointment of Juxon-Smith as chairman, and Commissioner Leigh, chief of police, as deputy chairman. The NRC had 4 Mendes, 2 Creoles and 2 Temne members.

46 Total exports for 1968, 1969, 1970 were respectively in Leones (2 Leones = £1) 75·6 million, 84·8 million, 84·7 million. Diamonds accounted for respectively, 45·6 million, 58·5 million, 52·8 million; iron ore: 10·2 million, 10·3 million, 10·2 million; palm kernels: 8·6 million, 4·6 million, 7·0 million. Cocoa exports rose from Le 1·9 million in 1968 to Le 3·3 million in 1970. Total imports for these years were: Le 75·5 million, Le 93·0 million, Le 96·9 million. There is therefore a trade deficit. New tax measures include a business registration fee payable by companies, an annual pay-roll tax on expatriate staff, increases in various licenses and registration fees. See *Africa Contemporary Record*, especially Vol 4 (1972), pp B688, 689.

47 The entrenched clauses were got round by reintroducing Sir Albert's bill, which his parliament had already passed. The president did not like it very much, but was prepared to put up with it, provided another constitution was passed before the

end of Parliament's current term in 1973. For discussion of the 1966 bill see Fisher, op cit, p 616.

48 In 1964–5, 19 per cent of children of school age attended school in the western area, 4 per cent in the southern province, but only 1 per cent in the north and east. Allen, op cit, p 306, n 4.

49 There were eighty-five elective seats, and twelve for chiefs.

Select Bibliography

CHAPTER 1
Sierra Leone's archaeology has scarcely been studied. Information can be found in the following:

Clark, J. D. 'The Spread of Food Production in Sub-Saharan Africa', *Journal of African History*, III, 2 (1962), 211–28.
———. *The Prehistory of Africa* (1970).
Davies, O. *West Africa before the Europeans* (1967).
Murdock, G. P. *Africa, Its People and Their Cultural History* (1959).
Pedler, F. J. *Economic Geography of West Africa* (1955).

Particular studies are rare. The most valuable are:

Atherton, J. H. 'The Later Stone Age of Sierra Leone', PhD thesis (University of Oregon, 1969).
Ozanne, P. 'A Preliminary Archaeological Survey of Sierra Leone', *The West African Archaeological Newsletter*, 5 (Institute of African Studies, Ibadan, W. Nigeria, 1966), 31–6.

For the later period see:

Ajayi, J. F. A. and Crowder, M. (eds). *History of West Africa* (1971), Chaps 1–2.
Atherton, J. and Kalous, M. 'Nomoli', *Journal of African History*, XI, 3 (1970), 303–17.
Clarke, J. I. (ed). *Sierra Leone in Maps* (1966).
Hair, P. 'Ethnolinguistic Continuity on the Guinea Coast', *Journal of African History*, VIII, 2 (1967).
Kup, A. P. *A History of Sierra Leone, 1400–1787* (1961).
Kup, A. P. (ed). *Adam Afzelius' Sierra Leone Journal, 1795–6* (Uppsala, 1967).
Rodney, W. *A History of the Upper Guinea Coast, 1545–1800* (1970).
Winterbottom, T. *An Account of the Native Africans in the Neighbourhood of Sierra Leone*, 2 vols (1803; repr 1969).

CHAPTER 2

The Sierra Leone Studies, Old Series and New Series contain useful information on most aspects of the country's past. Especially relevant here is the long article by E. F. Sayers, 'Notes on the Clan or Family Names Common in the Area Inhabited by Temne-speaking People', OS 10 (Dec 1927), 14–122.

Finnegan, R. H. *Survey of the Limba People of Northern Sierra Leone* (1965).

Ijagbemi, E. Ade. 'A History of the Temne in the Nineteenth Century', PhD thesis (Edinburgh, 1968).

Laing, A. G. *Travels in the Timmannee, Kooranko and Soolima Countries* (1825).

Person, Y. 'Samory and Resistance to the French', in *Protest and Power*, eds R. Rotberg and A. Mazrui (1970).

Siddle, D. J. 'Patterns of Rural Development in Sierra Leone', PhD thesis (Durham, 1968).

CHAPTER 3

Alldridge, T. J. *The Sherbro and Its Hinterland* (1901).

——. *A Transformed Colony* (1910).

Lamb, A. C. 'An Anthropological Survey of the Mende People', PhD thesis (Leeds, 1946).

Newton, J. *The Journal of a Slave Trader*, eds B. Martin and M. Spurrell (1962).

Rodney, W. *A History of the Upper Guinea Coast* (1970).

Thompson, G. *The Palm Land* (Cincinatti, 1858).

Vivian, W. 'The Mende Country', *Journal of the Manchester Geographical Society*, 12 (1896).

CHAPTER 4

Banton, M. *West African City* (1970).

Cox-George, N. A. *Finance and Development in West Africa* (1961).

Falconbridge, A. M. *Narrative of Two Voyages to Sierra Leone in the Years 1791-2-3* (1794; repr 1967).

Fyfe, C. *A History of Sierra Leone* (1962).

——. *Africanus Horton* (1972).

Hargreaves, J. *A Life of Sir Samuel Lewis* (1958).

Knutsford, Viscountess. *Life and Letters of Z. Macaulay* (1901).

Kup, A. P. 'Alexander Lindsay, 6th Earl of Balcarres, Governor of Jamaica 1794–1801', *John Rylands and University of Manchester Bulletin* (Spring 1975).

Peterson, J. *The Province of Freedom* (1969).

Porter, A. T. *Creoledom: A Study of the Development of Freetown Society* (1963).

Winks, R. and Kup, A. P. (eds). *John Clarkson's Diary* (Chicago, 1976).

CHAPTER 5

Crooks, J. J. *A History of the Colony of Sierra Leone* (1903).

Denzer, La R. 'Bai Bureh' in *West African Resistance*, ed M. Crowder (1971).

Fyfe, C. *A History of Sierra Leone* (1962).

——. 'European and Creole Influences in the Hinterland of Sierra Leone before 1896', *Sierra Leone Studies*, NS 6 (June 1956), 113–23.

Hargreaves, J. 'The French Occupation of the Mellacourie', *Sierra Leone Studies*, NS 9 (Dec 1957), 3–15.

Mellor, G. R. 'British Policy in Relation to Sierra Leone, 1808–1852', MA thesis (London, 1935).

Report and Correspondence on the Insurrection in the Sierra Leone Protectorate 1898 (The Chalmers Report) (1899).

CHAPTER 6

Cartwright, J. R. *Politics in Sierra Leone 1947–67* (Toronto, 1970).

Collier, G. *Sierra Leone, Experiment in Democracy* (1972).

Fisher, H. 'Election and Coups in Sierra Leone', *Journal of Modern African Studies*, VII, 4 (Dec 1969), 611–36.

Fyfe, C. *The Sierra Leone Inheritance* (1964).

Kilson, M. *Political Change in a West African State* (Cambridge, Mass, 1967).

Lucan, T. A. *Primary Civics for Sierra Leone*, 2 vols (1970) (a text for local schools).

Mackenzie, W. J. M. and Robinson, K. (eds). *Five Elections in Africa* (1960), pp 169–280.

Sierra Leone Report of Commission of Inquiry into Disturbances in the Provinces, 1955–6 (Cox Report) (1956).

Index

Abolition, 54, 66, 71, 114–26, 150, 161, 252 n 24
African Institution, 167
Afro-Europeans, 100ff
Agriculture, 19f, 28, 32, 39, 66, 81, 102ff, 117, 127, 130, 146, 149, 154ff, 172, 188ff, 191, 218
All Peoples Congress (APC), 210ff
Animism, 23, 28, 54
Archaeology, 20, 22, 26
Assimilation, 32, 63, 114, 139, 145ff, 150–1, 163, 190, 201, 206, 211, 260 n 19

Bai Bureh, 59, 183ff
British West Africa, administration, 153, 194
Bulama expedition, 124
Bullom, early history, 24ff, 30, 32, 37, 39
Bulom, 32
Bunduka, 45, 55–6, 61, 78

Chiefdom treasuries, 199
Chiefs, role in Legislative Council, 203, 208, 209; in House of Representatives, 216; *see also* Warrior chiefs, Women chiefs
Chiefs' conferences, 203
Clans, 11, 36, 42ff, 81, 192
Clarkson, John, 119–32
Climate, 16ff
Colonial policy, 65, 74ff, 91ff, 112, 158, 167ff, 173ff, 191ff, 202, 205ff
Colony, concepts of, 116, 125ff, 138ff, 167ff
Colony villages, 151ff
Cotton, 22, 29, 40, 154
Coups d'état, 215–18
Crown Colony government, 150ff, 167ff, 194ff
Currency, 128, 133, 135, 152

Diamonds, 189, 211, 218–19
District Commissioners, 11, 15, 26, 181, 193, 197ff
District Councils, 204–9, 214–15
Diyula, 26, 42, 44, 71ff, 81, 226 n 17, 233

Education, 63ff, 111, 132, 139, 147, 151ff, 207, 209, 221
Europeans, attitude to Africa, Africans, 12–15, 74, 77, 81, 112ff, 121, 161ff, 241 n 24

Fina, 44
France, 55, 58, 74, 79, 134ff, 157ff, 167, 170, 172ff, 175ff, 190
Freetown Municipal Council, 196, 211
Frontier, the, 44, 61, 77ff, 83, 91ff, 107, 110, 112, 158, 165ff, 174ff, 180, 236 n 34
Frontier Police, 99, 111, 113, 180–1, 185ff, 188

Gambia, the, 155

Historiography, 13ff
House of Representatives, 209, 216

Imperialism, 15, 171ff, 174ff
Iron Age, 21
Iron ore, 190, 218ff
Islam, Ch 2 *passim*, 84, 93, 95, 106, 109, 157, 190, 208, 256 n 59
Ivory carving, 39

Jamaica, 141ff, 150, 157

Kissi, early history, 24ff, 37, 46
Kono, early history, 25ff, 30, 35ff, 48
Koranko, early history, 25ff, 44ff
Krim, early history, 24ff
Krio, 156
Kru, early history, 30, 35ff

Land allotments, 116, 119, 123, 130ff, 135, 146, 148–9
Languages, 24ff, 36, 225 n 17
Lawson, T. G., 58, 179ff
'Lebanese', 179
Legal systems, 65, 128ff, 136, 139, 155, 174, 181, 193ff
Legislatures, 126, 128, 135ff, 138ff, 159, Ch 6 *passim*
Legitimate trade, 89; *see also* Trade
Lewis, Sir Samuel, 158, 181, 183, 191, 197ff
Liberated Africans, *see* Recaptives

Liberia, 19, 79, 177, 188
Limba, early history, 24, 48ff
Loko, early history, 26ff, 37
Luawa chiefdom, 94ff

Macaulay, Zachary, 128, 132–9, 167
'Mandingo', 46, 61ff, 68ff, 78, 226 n 17
Mani, 28ff, 37–40, 48
Margai, Sir Albert, 207–17
——, Sir Milton, 203–14
Maroons, 141–51
Massaquoi, 28, 44, 108ff
Medical services, 198, 218
Mende, early history, 37, 80–4
Mercenaries, 14, 79, 82, 84–5, 89–90, 108ff, 219
Military enlistment, 121, 150, 152, 156
Ministers of State, creation of, 208
Missionaries, 63, 137, 153, 162, 183, 186, 191, 201

National Reformation Council, 217
Native Affairs Department, 179ff
Neolithic Age, 19ff
Niger river, 27, 76
Nonconformity, 134, 137, 164
Nova Scotia, 120, 122, 144ff

Orthography, 11ff

Peters, Thomas, 121, 129, 146
Petitions, 119, 121, 132ff, 146ff, 183, 195, 261 n 23
Politics, 155, 159, Ch 6 passim
Population, 16, 21–5, 27, 81, 89–90, 97, 190
Pottery, 20, 22, 39
President, the, 208ff
Proper names, 12, 24
Protectorate, 97, 158ff, 168ff, 171ff, 174ff, 180ff, 197ff
Protectorate Assembly, 204–5, 209

Railway, 180, 188, 200, 218, Map 9
Recaptives, 151ff
Regents, Temne, 31, 58–9, 77, 163, 167
Republic, the, 215, 217, 218ff
Resistance, to Europe, African, 117, 138, 149, 163ff, 174, 181ff; Settler, 129, 134–41, 149ff, 164
Rice, 20, 32, 35, 103, 218
Riots, 67, 138ff, 206, 211, 220
Royal African Company, 102ff

Salt, 32, 37, 41, 84, 89

Sapi confederation, 24, 30, 32, 37
Settler, 114
Seventeen Nations, the, 155
Sierra Leone Company, 30, 50, 58, 61ff, 103ff, 117ff, 193
Sierra Leone Peoples Party (SLPP), 207ff
Slave Trade, 41, 48, 54, 57, 65ff, 77, 84, 90, 97, 102, 104, 107, 154, 161, 173, 180–1
Sofa, 71ff, 82ff, 157
Sovereignty, concepts of, 23, 26, 32, 112, 123, 141, 163ff, 170, 178, 241 n 24
Stevens, Siaka, 207–23
Stone Ages, 16ff
Strikes, 132, 200, 262 n 28
Susu, early history, 24, 37; jihad, 45ff

Taxation, 14, 118, 122, 135ff, 148ff, 158, 175, 181ff, 188ff, 195, 197ff, 201, 260 n 17
Temne, early history, 24ff, 37, 41
Timber, 55, 58, 85, 104, 157, 172
Towns, 25, 36, 41, 46, 61ff, 81ff, 94, 97, 100, 102
Trade, 22, 26, 37, 41ff, 47, 49, 53ff, 61ff, 65ff, 71ff, 74ff, 79, 83, 89ff, 102ff, 133, 156ff, 170ff, 176, 179, 188, 218ff
Trade Unions, 200, 203, 206ff
Travelling Commissioners, 15, 95, 97, 177, 180
Treasury grants, 153, 175, 251 n 24, 254 n 46
Treaties, 82, 91–4, 96, 98, 106, 108ff, 116ff 120, 123, 141, 163ff, 166, 168ff, 178
Tribal headmen, 63, 155, 185
Tribute, 23, 164ff

Vai, early history, 25ff, 30, 35ff

Wages, 89, 135, 149, 154, 157
Warrior chiefs, 59, 85, 91, 94ff, 108, 110, 184, 192
War towns, 82–3, 97, 110, 192
West Africa Frontier Force, 188
West African Regiment, 185, 188
West India Regiment, 150, 185, 187
Women chiefs, 91, 94

Yelli, 44
Yoruba, 63ff, 155–7

DATE DUE

GAYLORD			PRINTED IN U.S.A.